D1271728

The Aesthetics of Imagination in Design

Design Thinking, Design Theory
Ken Friedman and Erik Stolterman, editors

Design Things, A. Telier (Thomas Binder, Pelle Ehn, Giorgio De Michelis, Giulio Jacucci, Per Linde, and Ina Wagner), 2011

China's Design Revolution, Lorraine Justice, 2012

Adversarial Design, Carl DiSalvo, 2012

The Aesthetics of Imagination in Design, Mads Nygaard Folkmann, 2013

The Aesthetics of Imagination in Design

Mads Nygaard Folkmann

The MIT Press
Cambridge, Massachusetts
London, England

MIT Press books may be purchased at special quantity discounts for business or sales promotional use. For information, please email special_sales@mitpress.mit.edu or write to Special Sales Department, The MIT Press, 55 Hayward Street, Cambridge, MA 02142.

This book was set in Stone Serif and Stone Sans by the MIT Press. Printed and bound in the United States of America.

Library of Congress Cataloging-in-Publication Data

Folkmann, Mads Nygaard, 1972–
The aesthetics of imagination in design / Mads Nygaard Folkmann.
  pages   cm. — (Design thinking, design theory)
Includes bibliographical references and index.
ISBN 978-0-262-01906-4 (hardcover : alk. paper)
1. Design—Philosophy. 2. Aesthetics. I. Title.
NK1505.F65   2013
745.401—dc23
2012036811

10 9 8 7 6 5 4 3 2 1

Dedicated to my family—Lone, Ane, and Lea

Contents

Series Foreword   ix
Preface   xv

1   Introduction   1

2   Design and Possibility   13

3   Aesthetics   25

4   Imagination   67

5   A Phenomenology of Imagination in Design   81

6   Imagination and Design Epistemology   95

7   Schematization   105

8   The Imaginary in Design   139

9   Symbolism   153

10   Transfiguration   185

Conclusion   217

Notes   223
References   249
Index   265

Series Foreword

As professions go, design is relatively young. The practice of design predates professions. In fact, the practice of design—making things to serve a useful goal, making tools—predates the human race. Making tools is one of the attributes that made us human in the first place.

Design, in the most generic sense of the word, began over 2.5 million years ago when *Homo habilis* manufactured the first tools. We were designing well before we began to walk upright. Four hundred thousand years ago, we began to manufacture spears. By forty thousand years ago, we had moved up to specialized tools.

Urban design and architecture came along ten thousand years ago in Mesopotamia. Interior architecture and furniture design probably emerged with them. It was another five thousand years before graphic design and typography got their start in Sumeria with the development of cuneiform. After that, things picked up speed.

All goods and services are designed. The urge to design—to consider a situation, imagine a better situation, and act to create that improved situation—goes back to our prehuman ancestors. Making tools helped us to become what we are; design helped to make us human.

Today the word *design* means many things. The common factor linking them is service: designers are engaged in a service profession in which the results of their work meet human needs.

Design is first of all a process. The word *design* entered the English language in the 1500s as a verb, with the first written citation of the verb dated to 1548. *Merriam-Webster's Collegiate Dictionary* defines the verb *design* as "to conceive and plan out in the mind; to have as a specific purpose; to devise for a specific function or end." Related to these is the act of drawing, with an emphasis on the nature of the drawing as a plan or map, as well as "to draw plans for; to create, fashion, execute or construct according to plan."

Half a century later, the word began to be used as a noun, with the first cited use of the noun *design* occurring in 1588. *Merriam-Webster's* defines the noun as "a particular purpose held in view by an individual or group; deliberate, purposive planning; a mental project or scheme in which means to an end are laid down." Here, too, purpose and planning toward desired outcomes are central. Among these are "a preliminary sketch or outline showing the main features of something to be executed; an underlying scheme that governs functioning, developing or unfolding; a plan or protocol for carrying out or accomplishing something; the arrangement of elements or details in a product or work of art." Today we design large, complex processes, systems, and services, and we design organizations and structures to produce them. Design has changed considerably since our remote ancestors made the first stone tools.

At a highly abstract level, Herbert Simon's definition covers nearly all imaginable instances of design. To design, Simon writes, is to "[devise] courses of action aimed at changing existing situations into preferred ones" (Simon 1996, 111). Design, properly defined, is the entire process across the full range of domains required for any given outcome.

The design process is always more than a general, abstract way of working. It takes concrete form in the work of the service professions that meet human needs, a broad range of making and planning disciplines. These include industrial design, graphic design, textile design, furniture design, information design, process design, product design, interaction design, transportation design, educational design, systems design, urban design, design leadership, and design management, as well as architecture, engineering, information technology, and computer science.

These fields focus on different subjects and objects. They have distinct traditions, methods, and vocabularies, used and put into practice by distinct and often dissimilar professional groups. Although the traditions dividing these groups are distinct, common boundaries sometimes form a border. Where this happens, they serve as meeting points where common concerns build bridges. Today, ten challenges uniting the design professions form such a set of common concerns.

Three performance challenges, four substantive challenges, and three contextual challenges bind the design disciplines and professions together as a common field. The performance challenges arise because all design professions:

1. Act on the physical world

2. Address human needs

3. Generate the built environment

In the past, these common attributes were not sufficient to transcend the boundaries of tradition. Today, objective changes in the larger world give rise to four substantive challenges that are driving convergence in design practice and research:

1. Increasingly ambiguous boundaries between artifacts, structure, and process

2. Increasingly large-scale social, economic, and industrial frames

3. An increasingly complex environment of needs, requirements, and constraints

4. Information content that often exceeds the value of physical substance

These challenges require new frameworks of theory and research to address contemporary problem areas while solving specific cases and problems. In professional design practice, we often find that solving design problems requires interdisciplinary teams with a transdisciplinary focus. Fifty years ago, a sole practitioner and an assistant or two might have solved most design problems; today we need groups of people with skills across several disciplines, and the additional skills that enable professionals to work with, listen to, and learn from each other as they solve problems.

Three contextual challenges define the nature of many design problems today. While many design problems function at a simpler level, these issues affect a number of the major design problems that challenge us, and these challenges also affect simple design problems linked to complex social, mechanical, or technical systems. These issues are:

1. a complex environment in which many projects or products cross the boundaries of several organization, stakeholder, producer, and user groups;

2. projects or products that must meet the expectations of many organizations, stakeholders, producers, and users; and

3. demands at every level of production, distribution, reception, and control.

These ten challenges require a qualitatively different approach to professional design practice than was the case in earlier times. Past environments were simpler and made simpler demands. Individual experience and personal development were sufficient for depth and substance in professional practice. Experience and development are still necessary but no longer sufficient. Most of today's design challenges require analytical and synthetic planning skills that cannot be developed through practice alone.

Professional design practice today requires advanced knowledge. This knowledge is not solely a higher level of professional practice. It is also a qualitatively different form of professional practice that emerges in response to the demands of the information society and the knowledge economy to which it gives rise.

In a recent essay "Why Design Education Must Change" (2010), Donald Norman challenges the premises and practices of the design profession. In the past, designers operated on the belief that talent and a willingness to jump into problems with both feet gives them an edge in solving problems. Norman writes:

In the early days of industrial design, the work was primarily focused upon physical products. Today, however, designers work on organizational structure and social problems, on interaction, service, and experience design. Many problems involve complex social and political issues. As a result, designers have become applied behavioral scientists, but they are woefully undereducated for the task. Designers often fail to understand the complexity of the issues and the depth of knowledge already known. They claim that fresh eyes can produce novel solutions, but then they wonder why these solutions are seldom implemented, or if implemented, why they fail. Fresh eyes can indeed produce insightful results, but the eyes must also be educated and knowledgeable. Designers often lack the requisite understanding. Design schools do not train students about these complex issues, about the interlocking complexities of human and social behavior, about the behavioral sciences, technology, and business. There is little or no training in science, the scientific method, and experimental design.

This is not industrial design in the sense of designing products, but industry-related design, design as thought and action for solving problems and imagining new futures. This new MIT Press series of books emphasizes strategic design to create value through innovative products and services, and it emphasizes design as service through rigorous creativity, critical inquiry, and an ethics of respectful design. This rests on a sense of understanding, empathy, and appreciation for people, for nature, and for the world we shape through design. Our goal as editors is to develop a series of vital conversations that help designers and researchers to serve business, industry, and the public sector for positive social and economic outcomes.

We will present books that bring a new sense of inquiry to design, helping to shape a more reflective and stable design discipline able to support a stronger profession grounded in empirical research, generative concepts, and the solid theory that gives rise to what W. Edwards Deming (1993) described as profound knowledge. For Deming, a physicist, engineer, and designer, profound knowledge meant systems thinking and the understanding of processes embedded in systems; an understanding of variation and the tools we need to understand variation; a theory of knowledge; and a foundation in human psychology. This is the beginning of "deep design": the union of deep practice with robust intellectual inquiry.

A series on design thinking and theory faces the same challenges that we face as a profession. On one level, design is a general human process that we use to understand and shape our world. Nevertheless, we cannot address this process or the world in its general, abstract form. Rather, we meet the challenges of design in specific challenges, addressing problems or ideas in a situated context. The challenges we face as designers today are as diverse as the problems clients bring to us. We are involved in design for economic anchors, economic continuity, and economic growth. We design for urban needs and rural needs, for social development and creative communities. We are involved with environmental sustainability and economic policy, agriculture competitive crafts for export, competitive products and brands for microenterprises, developing new products for bottom-of-pyramid markets and redeveloping old products for mature or wealthy markets. Within the framework of design, we are also challenged to design for extreme situations, for biotech, nanotech, and new materials, and design for social business, as well as conceptual challenges for worlds that do not yet exist, such as the world beyond the Kurzweil singularity—and for new visions of the world that does exist.

The Design Thinking, Design Theory series from the MIT Press will explore these issues and more—meeting them, examining them, and helping designers to address them.

Join us in this journey.

Ken Friedman and Erik Stolterman
Editors, Design Thinking, Design Theory Series

Preface

This book investigates design as a dual phenomenon of the material and immaterial, the sensual and conceptual, and the actual and possible. My claim is that design objects always will be both at the same time. In this way, the possible is not something to exist before or after the becoming of a new object; rather, it is contained as a structure of meaning within the objects of design that act as part of our interface with the world and as a stimulation of cultural potentiality.

The book deals with three conditions in design: the possible, the aesthetic, and the imagination. Thus, the title of this book, *The Aesthetics of Imagination in Design,* highlights two of the key concepts: imagination, as it constitutes a central formative power behind not only the creation but also the life of design objects, and aesthetics, as it describes the sensual as well as the conceptual and contextual codes through which design objects communicate. Thus, this contributes knowledge about the role of aesthetics and imagination in design. Behind these concepts lies the concept of the possible because much design deals with envisioning or enabling something new through the imagination and in aesthetically communicating media. In exploring these topics in relation to design, this book relates the question of aesthetics to imagination and other issues related to creativity in the design process and to the mutual communication of designed objects within culture.

Design can be seen as the material expression of a mental process. Thus, in its material structure, design can be regarded as concrete imagination and is related to the topic of possibilities and limitations of human imagination. Seen in the context of its Latin root, *designare,* to draw, project, or plan, design is indeed about imagining the appearance, structure, and texture of our surroundings as a concrete, material expression. Thus, the book is carried by two profound interests: an interest in human imagination, which is at the heart of all design as it engages and evokes possibilities, and an interest in the ontology of the material object that is basically open in its structure and in the stimulation and promotion of possibilities.

In my opinion the field of design knowledge, or design science, often fails to ask certain fundamental questions about what design is and how it works; how design objects, through their specific expressions, construct, transmit, and transform meaning and culture and how design comes into being at the intersection of immaterial structures of designing and the material being and tactility of most design objects. This division of material and immaterial is challenged by new immaterial types of design, as in design generated by digital technology—for example, in pervasive or ubiquitous computing, where the design is not so much manifested in the outer casing as through the inner operation of the object or in conceptual types of design, as in the case of service design. In any case, all design takes place at the intersection of the material and the immaterial.

In essence, this book is a contribution to the philosophy of design. It is theoretically informed within the areas of aesthetics and the phenomenology of imagination. *Philosophy* literally means "love of wisdom," and the aim of this book is to contribute to the ongoing discussion about what design is, how it is created, and how it operates within the many contexts where it is applied. As a design scholar, I was motivated to write this book by *philodesign*, a love of design. I mean not only a passion for design objects (I am not a collector, and my home is not stylish) but also for the ways, impacts, and consequences of design as it assists us in seeing, perceiving, and understanding contemporary culture. In its many manifestations as products, graphics, Web sites, concepts, service structures, and principles of organization, among many other expressions, design is an essential medium for the articulation and transformation of our late modern culture, constantly on the verge of developing new perspectives on and responses to the cultural, societal, and environmental challenges of the future.

The scope of this book reflects the many different entries into the field of design. I hope to make a contribution to the understanding of design itself and the kinds of practical and theoretical discourse that can be employed in relation to it. Consequently the ideas I use are diverse and range from practice-focused perspectives on design methodology to cultural studies on design and ideas inspired by philosophy on design epistemology, design ontology, and design phenomenology. Although the book operates primarily within a phenomenological perspective, which is highly reflective of continental European thinking, I apply a problem-oriented stance, drawing on relevant sources from other traditions of knowledge. American pragmatist philosophy is at its heart closely associated with phenomenology, and it is important in informing issues of experience, creativity, and imagination. I draw on a number of sources outside the English-speaking world, and unless I explicitly note it in the text, all translations from German, French, Swedish, and Danish are mine. I mostly refer to the sources in their original language, even when translations exist (e.g., the texts on design by Otl Aicher and the philosophical texts by Kant and Sartre), but I also include translations (e.g., Rancière). Occasionally, and especially in lengthy quotes, I provide the original text in the notes. I have used the texts in their language of origin in part to introduce them to a wider audience, in part because they are important for the discussion.

My arguments in this book have been developed in the process of making proposals for journal articles and conference papers and receiving invaluable feedback from the reviewers and at conferences. Central sections of some of the chapters have previously been published in the journals *Design Issues* (chapter 3), *The Design Journal* (chapter 5), and *Design and Culture* (chapter 9), and presented at conferences. I am grateful to the journals for permission to expand the material in this new context where the elements that I have been working with until now have been contained within an overall framework of possibility, aesthetics, and imagination. And I am most grateful to the many anonymous reviewers who have commented and, often with great enthusiasm, offered valuable suggestions for improvement.

I thank the reviewers for their suggestions for refining and sharpening the arguments and the staff of the MIT Press—in particular, Katie Helke Dokshina and Deborah Cantor-Adams, for their constant engagement with the text—among others. A special thanks to acquisitions editor Doug Sery for the productive dialogue on the scope and aim of the book.

I am indebted to the Danish Centre for Design Research, the Danish Ministry of Culture, and the Centre for Design, Culture and Management in Kolding for funding the research grant that ultimately made the writing of this book possible. The initial English copyediting was undertaken by Dorte H. Silver, who offered useful comments on issues of language and content. I am indebted to the providers of the illustrations, who kindly allowed me to reprint their images.

Most of all, I thank colleagues and friends in the Danish design research community and at my home university, the University of Southern Denmark Kolding. A great many people have contributed more to this work than they know. In addition to Per Galle, who offered important comments on the philosophical concepts of the book, one other person deserves to be singled out: Ida Engholm, who got me started in the design "business" and has continually encouraged my work in the area of design and meaning, and whose invaluable comments I could not have done without.

1 Introduction

What makes a design possible? This sentence can be interpreted in more than one way. It can mean, What factors make the design possible? That is, what conditions enable the possibility of the design? Or, if we rephrase the question and see the design as the subject of the sentence—A design makes *what* possible?—it can mean, What *does* the design make possible? That is, what possibilities are created or achieved by the design? To illustrate, the famous Panton chair (1960, figure 1.1), made as a single form of injection-molded plastic by Verner Panton, is both the result of a struggle to make the chair possible and, when completed and marketed as a piece of design, an enabler of possible new ways of using, conceiving, and experiencing design. So on the one hand, the chair is the result of a design process that took about ten years from the initial idea of a one-structure chair in modern materials to the final realization. In its final iconic presence, which balances modernist ambitions and swooping organic curves, the chair changed the space of cultural possibilities for chairs. As a design object without precedent, the Panton chair set new standards for what design is and what a chair can look like.

The possible in design can be elusive. It is, by and large, defined by the individual design case; thus, there are as many versions and scopes of possibilities in design as there are design objects. Each design object has its own story of becoming in the design process and in its specific impact. Hence, in its material constitution, each design object has a specific potential within the range of possibilities. As a type of design, for example, a tangible, manifest piece of design such as a chair with a detectable outer design undergoes a process of being designed and entering the cultural arena that is different from, say, industrial products or design objects with a high degree of inner design, as in objects that employ digital technology in the form of ubiquitous computing, where most of the design in terms of the potential operations of the object is hidden from the eye of the user. As a term, *ubiquitous computing* designates

Figure 1.1
Panton chair. *Design:* Verner Panton. *Photo:* Panton Design.

the incorporation of digital technology and information processing in all kinds of products—for example, in communication devices such as personal digital assistants (PDAs) and smart phones and also in seemingly low-tech products such as toasters and coffee machines. Still, as a key aspect of the formative dynamics of design, whether in its phase of becoming or being a design object, it is relevant to move from the level of concrete stories to a general level of the possible in design: analyzing the role of the possible as a primary factor in initiating, structuring, and enabling design processes and processes of attributing meaning to design objects.

Possibility, Imagination, Aesthetics

Design is a passage to the new. *Design* is not only a term for describing certain categories of objects or solutions; it is also a process and a medium for envisioning something new. This process takes place in the intersection of material and immaterial properties, sensual and conceptual meaning, actuality, and possibility.

Design deals with the possible. To sharpen this thesis, the ability to address, mediate, and evoke new possibilities, thereby creatively exploring new territories of use, meaning, and impact, is a defining feature of design. It is capable of transforming the possible into actual, tangible, useful objects that can have a huge impact on human life and behavior (with widely distributed products) or on widespread notions of what objects are or mean (in experimental design). By *objects,* I mean not only physical objects or products but design solutions in a broader sense, for example, including service design. In service design, the conception of a systemic solution and its context are in focus—for example, in the organization of postal services from sender to receiver or in the planning of infrastructure for bicycle traffic with bicycle lanes, and so on. Crucial for service design is the connection of the conception of the overall context of the service and the various concrete components that make the service come into being. The point is that all kinds of design solutions necessarily have some physical extension (e.g., mailboxes for a postal service or interfaces on a screen in interaction with the user); pure immaterially in design does not exist.

Thus, the overall aim of this book is to conceptualize the possible in design. In order to address the elusive concept of the possible, it takes the design object as its focus. A design process may take its point of departure in an idea, that is, before the object, while it is the cultural context after the object that ultimately determines the meaning of the design object. However, it is the object that gives the idea its tangible expression. Most design processes are directed toward developing a concrete design, and it is through the object that the context is affected and perhaps transformed. Thus, when we look at the possible in the development of a design object, we first note that the possible exists in the becoming of design objects; next, the design objects give rise to new possibilities and experiences. In the phase of becoming, that is, in the design process, design converts and transforms the possible into forms and appearances. Accordingly, as final objects, some aspects of the possible remain as a structure of meaning afforded by the objects. Thus, another central thesis of the book is that the possible is found not only before and after the realization of the design object but is also contained within it.

The argument of the book is that the concept of imagination is tightly related to the possible and the potential that it engages. Thus, the overall argument may have the possible in design as its key premise, but the central entry point to the discussion is the role and workings of the imagination. To be able to imagine is a central human capacity for all of us. Indeed, the idea that imagination is a part of designing is so obvious that it is almost redundant to speak of imagination in design because it lies at the heart of design. But as a concept, imagination is not obvious. In a historical perspective, imagination has been regarded ontologically as a faculty, almost a physical entity located in the human brain, or functionally as an ability to perform the task of imagining and creating imaginary meaning. Regardless of definition, the point about imagination in design is that imagination performs an operation of abstraction, negation, transfiguration, and envisioning of something new, and this is an important condition for conceiving possibilities in design. For my use of the concept of imagination in relation to design, it is important that it operates as a vehicle in connecting sensual and conceptual meaning, a process that can be labeled *schematization*, and that design is a medium where this process is enabled and made detectable.

In the design process, imagination leaves its mark on the coding of the resulting design objects and solutions. Design objects are in this way permeated by imaginary meaning. This means that imagination is not only a mental capacity that provides epistemic access to the possible. Imagination in design may also be viewed as a structure that operates as a formative power in the process of designing and subsequently follows the design object. In this sense, the imaginary can inform the established knowledge of what happens in the cultural production of meaning in design products and solutions; it can reveal how design, with its structures of realized and imaginary meanings, engages with culture and creates symbolic meaning.

In this context, the concept of the imaginary is crucial as it deals with dimensions of meaning in design, while an excessive emphasis on the role of imagination may lead to an outdated celebration of the creative genius of the (individual) designer.[1] My claim is that the implication of imagination, at least on a conceptual level, should be loosened from the traditional notion of the creative subject as the origin of all meaning. By focusing on the imaginary as a structure of meaning that can be centered in objects but points back to subjectivity, I seek to deliver an entry to understanding design that overcomes the classic and often static dichotomy of subject and object. Both subject and object are, of course, present in the actual process of designing (and they rely on imagination and imaginary meaning), and the conceptual framework should situate the role and status of the dichotomy with an emphasis on the act of meaning process between and across these poles.

What ultimately interests me, however, is not so much the ideological level concerning the nature of creativity in a line that runs from romanticism to contemporary guidebooks on managing creativity or the issue of gaining control over the modern flux of mediated images by being more conscious of the power of imagination and its ability to create models of reality (Wettig 2009). My focus is on how imagination is reflected in a medium and how the imaginary is evident in actual design objects. By extension, design sets the stage for imagination in particular ways, both during the design process, that is, before the actualization of the design objects, and in the design objects themselves. Thus, imagination may be engaged as "the designer's trump card" (Jones 1980, 10) in design processes as a means of opening up possibilities and interpreting them, as Stolterman and Nelson (2003), one of the few sources to connect design explicitly to processes of imagination, have noted:

Imagination is not only needed as a way to create the unexpected, but also in the process of interpreting the present—the client's needs and desires, as well as future demands and possibilities. Imagination is the reflective skill we use to explore and analyze the overwhelming number of ideas that are possible in every design situation. By imagination, we can visualize future compositions and explore the consequences of bringing a particular into existence. (179)

Moreover, it is crucial to my argument that imagination is not only an internal matter of consciousness actively operating in the phase of creative production; it is also mediated and, as imaginary meaning, made tangible by and detectable in design objects. In a strict sense, this can be said about all human, aesthetic creations: they all give actual existence and presence to the space of possibility that unfolds in imagination. What is particular about design in this context is two aspects: on the level of design methods, some of the structural mechanism of imagination is laid open, and on the level of the objects, there is an attempt at influencing human action and behavior directly. Even if not all design objects are strictly oriented toward solving a problem or fulfilling a goal, they normally do relate to basic organizing principles of human life. Even experimental design and art design, mostly conceived for circulation in galleries, contain a component of use and function, even if it is in the form of a challenge. By this I mean that most design objects or design solutions aim at affecting the world they are a part of rather than at being objects of disinterested, artistic perception. Although this kind of perception also has an indirect function on an epistemological level in proposing models of how the world is to be experienced and approached,[2] design objects are generally aimed more directly at becoming active agents or actants in people's everyday life.[3]

An exploration of the roles of the imagination and the imaginary offers an entry point that allows us to discuss the possible in design. While the overall argument of the book is that design is capable of opening a space for possibility and, by giving form and structure to the possible, can itself be a medium of the possible (or, rather, a possibility that derives from the verge of actuality), exploring the concepts of imagination and the imaginary can reveal how the possible operates in design.

Tightly related to a conceptualization of imagination and the imaginary in design is the concept of aesthetics in design. This may seem surprising because aesthetics is normally associated with the beauty of the outer appearance of a work of art (or design), just as theories on aesthetics traditionally have been a "playground for the True, the Beautiful, and the Good" (Adorno 1970, 99) or, dating back to eighteenth-century German classicism, has been connected to the project of educating people to taste and into freedom (cf. Schiller 1910), a project that later became attached to the arts. Aesthetics is not, however, only about beauty, the arts, or artistic creation and experience; it is also about our sensual relation with the world. It is, however, not just a question of surface and appearance but also of epistemology and of organizing our relationship with the world through design and the formation of design through imagination.

In general, I regard aesthetics as an overall matrix for conceptualizing and understanding design as the creation and communication of meaning. The idea is not to exclude parameters of function, user concerns, materials, or technology but to propose aesthetics as an avenue for understanding and investigating design as a medium of meaning construction at the intersection of a concrete-sensual as well as a conceptual relationship with the world. The concept of aesthetics gives tools to describe the connection of the sensual and the conceptual, the material and the immaterial, which is fundamental for my understanding of the operation of imagination in design.

Several concepts of aesthetics can be used to give structure to the unfolding of the imagination and the imaginary in design. To speak of the aesthetics of imagination is to combine different models of aesthetics with the imagination. This produces three models of aesthetics in relation to imagination.

First, modern theories of aesthetics have explored the notion of the old Greek *aisthetá*, "that which can be sensed," and searched for the sensual qualities of the perceived or sensed. This sensual-phenomenological dimension of aesthetics informs us about the workings of design as sensually appealing and leads to reflection on the sensual-bodily matters of the imagination when it operates in the individual consciousness as part of the process of cognition. At the same time, this dimension of aesthetic theory tries to challenge the dominant Western dichotomy of a perceiving subject and a perceived object and seeks to combine them in concepts of "ambience" (Böhme) or "experience" (Moore) seen to encompass the relation of subject and object.

Second, there is a strong and long conceptual-hermeneutical tradition in aesthetic theory from Kant to Adorno that has mostly been attached to the debate on works of art but can be actualized in relation to design.[4] In a dialogue with this tradition, urgent and contemporary questions asked about the nature of aesthetic coding in design can relate to a general discussion of meaning construction in design. Within the context of imagination, I will point to the role of the imaginary and the symbolic in design.

Finally, a discursive-contextual dimension of aesthetic theory goes into the debate on how design functions as an organizer and distributor of sensual material and thus contributes to the formative logic of a social imaginary, that is, shared structures of meaning that form a dynamics on the level of societal institutions. This level can be hard to grasp but is nevertheless important because its focus lies in the societal and cultural context and the transsubjective dimension of aesthetics. It can open to analysis the generative dynamics of the interdependence of subject and collective, of design objects and context, and demonstrate how these are intertwined and mutually shape and influence each other. Any individual act of imaginative creation is always part of a collectively staged context that circumscribes and conditions the act of the individual; and the context is always altered, just a bit perhaps, by the influence of the individual act.

Methodological Approach

In terms of methodology, the book is a contribution to the philosophy of design from a phenomenological perspective. Since the beginning of the 2000s, different approaches have contributed to the discussion of fundamental aspects of what design is, what its constituents are, and what it is for. Whereas the philosophical discussion about design has been raised through perspectives of analytical philosophy (Galle 2008, 2011), the philosophy of technology (Verbeek 2005; Vermaas et al. 2009), or philosophical investigations of use and action in relation to design and material culture (Dorschel 2003; Preston 2012), my approach is phenomenological: it deals with experience and focuses on design as a vehicle for enabling, creating, and mediating the possible in relation to experience.

The term *phenomenology* was coined by the German philosopher Edmund Husserl based on the Old Greek etymology of the theory, *logos*, or that which shows itself, *phainomenon*. Thus, phenomenology is relatively new, even if it does build on previous disciplines, including epistemology. It asks the questions a little differently, however, its main focus being not primarily how we know in epistemology but what is experienced. Essentially based on a dichotomy of subject and object, phenomenology asks about the phenomena as they appear to the human subject. According to Husserl, our way to phenomena goes through our experience of them; interestingly, his search for the being of the phenomena, the world of objects, leads him back to an investigation of the formation of the mental structures that perform the conditions for meaning to come into being.[5] Our consciousness always intentionally directs itself toward something and thus determines the appearance of this something; things may, for example, be intentionally viewed as imaginary, a fundamental aspect of Sartre's subsequent phenomenology. Basically the prevalent paradox of phenomenology lies in the fact that it strives to get to the objects and the core of things, *zu den Sachen*, but continually refers back to the formation of the conditions of experience in consciousness. In this sense, phenomenology is a philosophical discipline that investigates possible appearances of objects and, in connection with this, reflectively searches for the "structures of understanding that let the objects appear as they are"; what is of interest is not so much the specific objects but their way of appearing (Zahavi 2007, 127).

Even if phenomenology is based fundamentally on a problematic dichotomy of subject and object with a perhaps too narrow focus on humans and human intentionality at the expense of the objects (Latour 2005), my aim is to apply it as a framework for discussing the formation of experience in the dynamic intersection of subject and design object: not only through the subject and its formative powers, as in notions of creative subjectivity, or with too much privileging of the agency of object as in actor-network theory and recent notions of material aesthetics of a postphenomenology (Verbeek 2005), but in a dynamic exchange between poles. Within phenomenology, Maurice Merleau-Ponty seeks a concept of experience that comprises both poles, and even if he does not take the full step of reversing their position in relation to experience so that subject and object are seen as the product of the structure of experience rather than its origin, as Gernot Böhme later suggested (see chapter 3), it can be seen as an inherent element of phenomenology to try to challenge or even transgress the pure dichotomy of subject and object. Having said that, my investigation often narrows its focus on design objects, their ontology (cf. chapter 8), and their role in the constitution of experience (chapter 10); however, the overall framework is phenomenological in its acknowledgment of the importance of experience and the framing of experience by design.

Research in design, a multidisciplinary field, invites a variety of ideas to inform the discussion. This book is thus informed by and discusses many different ideas in relation to design (e.g., studies in design methods, aesthetic theory, critical theory, pragmatism, hermeneutics, cognitive theory, and cultural studies) and seeks to traverse and comprehend several perspectives. Nevertheless, its overall structure is based on the framework of phenomenology.

Due to the complex and multidisciplinary nature of design, I believe that research in this area should be broad and comprehensive in theoretical scope and address theories dealing with the development of design, analysis of the objects of design, and the wider implications and effects of design and at the same time propose a central framework in order to focus the discussion. Hence, I offer my ideas about design using many theories and positions, navigating through them and describing positions of design epistemology, design ontology, and a phenomenology specific to design. The purpose is to offer a philosophical statement about design as produced and traversed by possibility as analyzed through the concepts of aesthetics and the imagination/imaginary and seen through how humans engage with meaning through design and how design is a means to produce structures of experience.

Throughout the book, the examples I discuss illustrate my theoretical points, and they also show how the theoretical insights can be grounded. An exception is chapter 7 on schematization, where I have interviewed several designers about their methods. My dialogue with the designers has informed the conceptual framework of the chapter, even though I have chosen a synthetic argumentation where I present the concepts and then illustrate them. I introduce two of the designers I have worked with: the design consultancy 3PART and the designer Ditte Hammerstrøm.

Structure

This book starts by describing the possible in relation to design (chapter 2), then introduces the founding framework of aesthetics (chapter 3), unfolds reflections on imagination (chapter 4–7) and the imaginary in design (chapter 8–9), and concludes with a discussion of the effect of design on experience (chapter 10).

The theoretical discussion about design, possibility, and imagination has three conceptual dimensions, which correspond to the division of different platforms for describing aesthetics in design: a sensual, a conceptual, and a contextual paradigm of design (see table 1.1). The sensual paradigm not only describes the sensual impact of design objects; in relation to imagination, the sensual anchors design processes inside consciousness. In contrast, the conceptual paradigm deals with the construction of meaning in and through design objects; here, imagination operates through the imaginary as a principle of creating symbolic meaning. And the contextual paradigm designates the effect and impact of design on how it can project new modes of experience.

In chapters 2, 3, and 4, the three paradigms are represented in different ways. In chapter 2, the possible is related to phases before, in, and through the design objects. In chapter 3, the central framework of aesthetics as sensual-phenomenological, conceptual-hermeneutical, and discursive-contextual entries into the conceptualizing and understanding of design as the creation and communication of meaning are introduced and discussed. In chapter 4, the historical, especially the romantic, concept of

Table 1.1
Conceptual structure of the book

	Sensual paradigm	Conceptual paradigm	Contextual paradigm
Phase of design(ing)	Design processes	Objects of design	Effect of design
Phase of possibility (chapter 2)	Possibility before the design: The not-yet-existing	Possibility in the design: Inner potentiality of design objects	Possibility through the design: Evoking experience by means of objects
Dimension of aesthetics (chapter 3)	Sensual-phenomenological	Conceptual-hermeneutical	Discursive-contextual
Concepts of imagination (chapter 4)	Internalization-externalization Fullness-emptiness	Enthusiasm-reflection	Immanence-transcendence
Moment in the process of imagination (chapter 5)	Internalization	Unrealization	Transfiguration
Discourse	Design epistemology: The role of imagination in developing design (chapter 6)	Design ontology: The role of the imaginary (chapter 8)	Design phenomenology: Effect and meaning (chapter 10)
Operative function in design	Schematization (chapter 7)	Symbolism (chapter 9)	Direction and scaling of new meaning and experiences (chapter 10)

imagination is introduced through a series of meaning-generating dichotomies,[6] which can be related to the three platforms, even if this division is not part of the discourse in the chapter.

In chapter 5, I propose a phenomenology of imagination in design that in its internalization, unrealization, and transfiguration lays the foundation for understanding the scope, impact, and implications of the possible in design and provides a structure for the remain of the book:

Thus, in connection with the internalizing imagination—where meaning develops within imagination—the concept of schematization is described in chapter 7 as an operative function in design of making meaning through the use of imagination. As background for this discussion, I introduce the concept of design epistemology in chapter 6. *Design epistemology,* often used as a technical term in practice-based design theory, refers to the specific ways and forms of knowing or experiencing that designers employ to see the world as they do and their way of using this epistemological base as a platform for the design process.

Chapters 8 and 9 describe design through the process of unrealization. Here, the meaning produced by imagination is seen as both a negation of the actual, as it is imagined and not real, and as a productive asset for the production of new meaning as the negated, imaginary meaning provides new possible ways to relate to the actual. On the basis of design ontology—the question of the nature of being of design objects—and, in relation to this, the role of the imaginary in design, I discuss the coding of symbolic meaning in design. Through the unrealizing function of the imaginary, I view objects not as closed entities but as objects that are permeated by traces of possibility. I propose a concept of design that takes into account that being is always permeated by structures of imaginary nonbeing that are difficult to grasp but nevertheless leave traces and are involved in structuring the symbolic coding of design objects, the topic of chapter 8. Here I propose a model of the cultural potential of the imaginary in design that can be analyzed according to product versus system and materiality versus immateriality. As a mediator of material as well as immaterial dimensions of cultural meaning, design can essentially be conceived as a medium that mediates culture. Design objects are embedded in culture; culture also works through design via the imaginary. By virtue of their constitution, design objects are objects of cultural potentiality.

Finally, in chapter 10, imagination is seen as a force for transfiguration in design. Based on a reflection of design phenomenology, I investigate the notion of transfiguration and how design in its various manifestations can affect major paradigm shifts in our ways of seeing, perceiving, and understanding the world. In mediating experience, design is capable of having a transfigurative effect on experience; it may even offer a radical transfiguration of the structure of experience. With its double quality of material and immaterial, of physical-visual presence and imaginary meaning, design can contain and perform "matrices of ideas" that can be altered and thus impose "coherent deformations" (Merleau-Ponty 1960) on the appearance of the world. Thus, the final chapter addresses how the direction and scaling of transformative processes of design can be conceptualized, that is, in what way and on what level design can be conceived as a medium for structuring and conditioning experience.

In this sense, the discussion of ethics in design gains in importance. As a medium of experience, all design has ethical implications in terms of designating ways and modes of living, and hence, all design choices have consequences that reach beyond the design object. No outer shape or appearance is ever innocent but contributes to framing the conditions of human existence.

2 Design and Possibility

To conceive design as a medium that enables and contains the possible touches on our understanding of design, how it is conceived as a discipline, and what we understand design to mean. It focuses on design as a dually constituted phenomenon of material extension and immaterial meaning, sensuous appeal and conceptual structure, and a here-and-now presence of the given and actual that at the same time is open to the new and the possible. As an introduction to this understanding of design, this chapter describes my understanding of possibility in relation to design. As I see it, possibility is not only something that stands outside, before or after, the given design object through the imaginary; it also permeates it in its structure of meaning. I first describe my notion of design and then how it relates to possibility.

Design

As a means of envisioning and creating the new, design is both an old and a new discipline. It is a new discipline in the sense that only within the past 250 years has it established itself as a professional discipline that operates in relation to industry and modern mass production as a deliberate effort to affect our physical surroundings.[1] As a scientific discipline, design is even younger: research has contributed to our knowledge about design for approximately fifty years, and efforts to create a research discipline remain ongoing (Michel 2007; Mareis, Joost, and Kimpel 2010). Conversely, there is an intense focus on design and design methodologies within many disciplines. According to Wolfgang Schäffner, a comprehensive "design turn" is taking place within the humanities, engineering, and the natural sciences, where design as a discipline connecting theory and practice in objects of synthesis is at the center of the production of knowledge (Schäffner 2010). At the same time, the concept of design has expanded from being associated with products and graphics to being associated as well with areas such as communication, environments, identities, systems, contexts, and futures (Heskett 2002). Furthermore, technology is now a more integral part of design than ever before as it shapes the concrete objects of design from within. Design has been associated with a culture of the artificial (Simon 1996) and viewed as an art of technology (Buchanan 1995), but at the concrete level of design objects too, technology plays a growing role in both the material and immaterial culture of today's design objects through the use of miniaturized microchips and computing.

Design as a medium for envisioning the new is always changing in terms of both the culture of objects and professional disciplines. Recently the term *design thinking* has been used to describe the ability to use design tools and design methods in relation to business strategies with processes oscillating between problem formulation and solution generation, and with the formulation and generation of abstract concepts in the materiality of actual design solutions (Borja de Mozota 2003; Stolterman 2007; Brown 2008, 2009; Rylander 2009). In sum, the connection of design and thinking has been used in describing the specific cognitive style of designers as a heading for a general theory of design oriented toward complex problem solution and as an "organizational resource" (Kimbell 2011) Often the claim of the importance of "individual cognition" or the "organizational innovation" (300), or both, has been led by a strategic motivation to state the central role of design tools in developing new solutions. Design thinking is an example of a discursive mechanism where ever (more or less) newer paradigms and frameworks attempt to comprehend design in its increasing complexity as a reflection of developments in society and new requirements by culturally demanding consumers. Consequently, design within this kind of paradigm is situated at the frontier of the new.

Design is also one of the oldest human capacities. The very concept of design thinking, which in its strategic approach to designing might use new and refined tools, defines a basic competence in design: the connection of the conceptual explored in the design process (What do we want from the design?) and concrete materiality (How does this come into being?). In this sense, design thinking is nothing new. At a fundamental level, design can be seen as the general ability to conceive and carry out plans as well as designating and giving meaning to these plans (implied in the Latin root *designare*). As a consequence, design operates as a transformative process in the span of the mental and the material. It applies mental capacities for conceptualization, aims at turning conceptualization into concrete mental images of new objects, and strives to transform these mental images of given objects into material manifestations. Through this process, design is a way for people to interact with their surroundings with a conscious intention and through material objects. In this sense, we can speak of a world that is created, constructed, and structured by design. Thus, John Heskett (2002) can state that "the forms or structures of the immediate world we inhabit are overwhelmingly the outcome of human design" (8).

Human creation is always situated within a historical context, and what specifically defines design in contrast to, say, craft, is its close connection to industry, where it has the potential to be widely distributed as a means of giving form, structure, and meaning to products. Design is a central part of our interface with the modern world; we see, perceive, and understand contemporary culture through its design and its various material (visual, haptic, auditory, olfactory, and even gustatory impressions and impulses) and immaterial (conceptual, critical, systems-oriented) representations. Design can be said to be a *Leitmedium* of modernity, in the sense that it creates meaning in an intersubjectively binding way (Hörisch 2009), which means that design is the unavoidable access point for our perception and understanding of the world in its cultural formations. We can even, as the French philosopher Stéphane Vial (2010) suggested, regard design as a production of effects rather than objects; objects of design are objects that have been submitted to a process of design, which consists of conceiving and producing effects that point to "experiences to be lived by means of forms" (115). The effects of design operate on the level of form, social meaning, and experience; thus, Vial sees design primarily as a "generator of human existence that proposes possible experiences" (65). In his view, design deals not so much with the being as with events; not so much with the existing as with the new that will emerge (56).

In this way, I view design as a way of imaginatively envisioning the new, conceiving of and grasping possibilities of living in and engaging with the world. Thus, I define *design* as a means for human beings to envision and realize new possibilities of creating meaning and experience and for giving shape and structure to the world through material forms and immaterial effects. As a medium with wide distribution, that is, as a part of modern mass culture, design potentially has a massive impact. In its many forms, it designates the specific appearances of the world of objects. As we sense and perceive the modern world through its tactile and visual surfaces, it becomes clear that they affect and structure our experience in particular ways. For example, there are huge differences between experiencing the world through the formal, strict geometrical structures of functionalistic design and architecture and through Verner Panton's experimental, psychedelic roomscapes (see figures 3.2, 3.3, and 3.4).

Furthermore, when conceptualizing design as a medium, it is important to reflect on how design itself acts as a medium. In general, a medium does not operate as an innocent or transparent conveyor of a given content to be transmitted as simple data but affects the meaning of the content. From communication theory, we have learned that meaning is something that is exchanged or even produced in the process of mediation (Barnard 2006), that the medium plays an active role in the construction and communication of meaning, and that, conversely, the medium carries and conveys meaning in a way that also is fundamentally determined by what is conveyed (Krämer

2008). The medium affects its content, and the content affects the medium. In this way, design objects are important as media expressing and affecting, for example, cultural meaning, while at the same time they are not static entities in this process but dynamically being influenced by what they are expressing. To illustrate, a chair not only expresses and influences cultural meaning (as the Panton chair in figure 1.1 both reflects the culture of the 1960s and attempts to define it) but is also a medium marked by its cultural meaning as an object meant for use. Most design objects are conceived to adapt to their surroundings and enter a dialogue with the user; as media, they are affected by their role in relation to a context of use.

In sum, design objects are both expressive media reflecting and affecting a meaning that may exceed their material extension (e.g., their possible impact on experience and their potential cultural meaning) *and* being marked by their context of meaning. Next, design objects have modalities that make them specific media for this process. They operate on levels of sensual, conceptual, and contextual impact of meaning, as I describe in the next chapter in relation to aesthetics.

The Possible

Possibility evolves at the threshold of actuality. It is a dimension of the actual that both transcends the actual and is inherent in it. Through this double constitution, possibility can push the actual (and hence is bound to it) in new directions or break free new dimensions of meaning (and hence transcend it). I introduce what the possible is in design in broad terms and in relation to design.

In one of the most powerful cultural expressions of the possible, the seminal 1930s novel *Der Mann ohne Eigenschaften* (1978; *The Man without Qualities*, 1995), the Austrian author Robert Musil states how one's sense of the actual, *Wirklichkeitssinn*, must be complemented by a sense of the possible, *Möglichkeitssinn* (Musil 1978, 1:16). The important point in Musil's reflection is the simultaneously utopian and reality-bound nature of the possible. A person capable of conceiving the possible always thinks that "things might be different": "So the sense of the possible could be defined as the ability to think of everything that also could be and, conversely, not to regard the given as more important than the nongiven" (1:16).[2]

In the context of Musil's novel, the sense of the possible leads the protagonist on a search for new possibilities. The utopian horizon is wide open, as the sense of the possible also leads in the radical direction of the "as yet un-awakened intentions of God" (Musil 1978, 1:16). At the same time, the possible is connected to the actual, as it is always the actual that provides the foundation for the possible. Thus, the possible in this conception is marked by immanence as well as transcendence. The sense of the possible is given and must be awakened. This requires a specific mental setting in a paradoxical attachment to/detachment from reality.

This mental setting in relation to the possible actual is the setting that characterizes design and designer. Musil speaks of having the "will to build and a conscious ambition to the utopian that does not abandon reality but treats it as task and invention" (Musil 1978, 1:16).[3] To conceive of the possible and utopian in a reinvention of reality is at the heart of design. At the same time, this is also an experimental task: Musil speaks poetically of dragging a line through the water without knowing whether it is baited (17). In most design, searching is hardly this open-ended, but the key point here is that the means of searching for the possible can be hard to define. Working actively with design and design processes is, however, an attempt to specify the bait.

In a design context, the possible can be seen as Musil's open space of the new and nonexisting or, rather, the not-yet-existing. My claim is that the possible should not be seen only as something that comes into being before the actualization of the final design or that has an effect after the realization of the object; it is also an inherent structure of design. In this way, we may ask a double question to the constitution of the possible in design objects: the extension and limitation of the possible and its phases in the life of design objects.

The Extension and Limitation of the Possible

Addressing the possible in design opens the discussion about what design on a general level is for and asking how it can be used as a medium of meaning that shows new directions. To conceive of design as a medium and a driver for the possible makes it an activity of far-reaching impact. This underlies Herbert Simon's famous 1969 dictum that "everyone designs who devises courses of action aimed at changing existing situations into preferred ones" (1996, 111). Simon's statement is loaded with modernity's optimistic ideology of using design to create a better world, but even seen apart from its historical context, which relates, for example, to the discussion in the 1960s about the role of artificial intelligence, the statement still has something important to say: that design can be a flexible tool, capable of taking a wide variety of shapes and expressions (encouraging "action") and that it can be an active means of engaging with the surroundings (accomplishing "change").[4] Thus, design is potentially unlimited in its scope.

However, when possibility is mediated in the use-oriented medium of design, it is never unlimited. Possibility in design should not be understood as counterprojections of reality, that is, in asking what would be possible beyond reality. Instead, possibility in design has to do with making possibilities of this world relevant and tangible. Design is bound to reality and does not start from scratch. In design, there is, in the words of Bruno Latour, "nothing foundational," and in fact, it is quite the opposite: design changes and remediates what exists, which also enables it to enter the "inner definitions of things" and make them open to improvement and change (Latour 2008). For Latour, design gives shape to human existence through environments and artificiality in "everything from chairs to climates"; he boldly states that *Dasein ist design*, that is, "being is design." At the same time, design is less a "matter of fact" than a "matter of concern" where the objects of design are open to interpretation and open in meaning, and hence, open to possible new directions of meaning. In this way, Latour points to a central duality and apparent paradox in design with regard to the possible: design is a medium for immanent transcendence in the sense that it can be a medium of and search for change and the possible, hence the transcending element, but that it does not leave the sphere of reality, hence the immanence.

When we focus on design objects as concrete material entities, it would seem that they convert abstract possibilities into specific potentialities of use and application. Indeed, design objects often gain their concrete relevance in contexts of use by pointing to specific potentials, for example, when a cup, due to its shape (it can contain liquids) and material (thermal insulation), can be used for drinking coffee. Thus, there are ways for objects to afford possibilities, that is, to constrain the possibility of specific actions that may be inherent in an object (Gibson 1977; Norman 2002). At the same time, my claim is that design objects carry with them an open-ended constitution of possible meanings; they may condense and limit the space of possible ways of their engaging with the world, but they also carry with them this whole space of possibility that they condense. Focusing only on the object, a cup may be limited in use and specify potentiality, but taking its ability to actively organize our interaction with the world, it implicitly points to a whole range of possible ways of doing so: Design objects are both limited in being anchored in a specific potentiality due to material extension and use and unlimited in their engagement with principles of organizing meaning.

In its extension, the possible is both entirely open-ended and bound by limitation. On the one hand, design can seek out the "not-yet-being," even as the exploration of unknown ground: "in all professional doing and regularity to take the risk of moving into zones of the inconceivable" (Welsch 1996, 215, 217).[5] On the other hand, the possible has its limitation in the impossible, that is, the radical other side of the border of what can be enabled. Or, rather, seen as a dialectic, the possible and the impossible co-condition each other, and the impossible can even be a driver of the possible, as Barry M. Kātz has articulated it in relation to Branco Lukić's experimental and often disruptive proposals for designs that are made of nonexisting materials or could not possibly be produced or made to work (Kātz 2011). Lukić's designs, featured in the 2011 book *Nonobject* (carrying the same name as his firm), showcase the power and importance of integrating the experimental and explorative perspective into the design process (Lukić 2011): The designation of "impossible objects," for example, the CUn5 "superpractical" mobile phone, made exclusively of buttons, views design seen not only as practical objects for the benefit of human life and progress but also as a means of questioning and an "epistemological probe" of the order of things and the "space between the user and the object" (Kātz 2011, xxv–vi). Thus, in the space that intersects the possible and the impossible in design, we can ask the fundamental questions of what things are, what they are for, and why we engage with them. Thus, to quote Kātz: "By better understanding the infinite possibilities that inhere in our object world we can better understand ourselves" (xxix).

Phases of the Possible

In the temporal development of a design object, the possible can be attached to three phases: before, in, and after the object. My claim is that the possible is not only to be found before and after the realization of the design object but is also contained within it. Within field design theory, the first and the last phase have been discussed, that is, the dimension of possibility in the design process, before the finalized design, and the generation of possibilities after or by effect of the design object.

The possible plays a prominent role within design epistemology, as the starting point of a design process is often a search for a solution that has to come into being. Here, the possible is a part of the early formation of the design object before it is finalized as a solution with a physical aspect. In design epistemology, the debate has revolved around such issues as generating ideas, enhancing creativity in the process of seeking new proposals, and promoting the creative leap in design when design is used as a device for creative processes of anticipating and grasping for something new and not yet existing. Furthermore, it is exactly due to its ability to devise concrete proposals and solutions for something yet unknown—thus bridging the gap between unknown and known, possibility and actuality—that design is often seen as having a prerogative in comparison with disciplines that only describe characteristics of the world (e.g., sociology and humanities) without necessarily projecting anything new. From this perspective, the design discipline is more synthetic than analytical; it has a progressive, future-oriented, and openly interpretive orientation: when we initiate a design process, we never know what the ultimate outcome will be.

With regard to the methodology and process of creating concrete design objects, the possible can play a central role. Daniel Fällman (2008) has discussed the dimension of design exploration in the design process, as design is used critically to question what design is for. In this context, "design becomes a statement of what is possible, what would be desirable or ideal, or just to show alternatives and examples" (7). Thus, design exploration can be used "to show what is possible," that is, to explore "a possible future by transcending (i.e., breaking down and going beyond) the boundaries of an existing design paradigm" (15).[6]

In an extension of this kind of reflection, Per Galle (2008), with inspiration from the conceptual precision requested by analytical philosophy, raises a series of fundamental questions regarding the act of reaching into the future with design. He asks what design predictions refer to, since design at this stage has not yet manifested itself in the form of objects. Therefore, the questions facing designers may be ontological in nature, asking what the "subject area of design" may be, "given that it cannot be the actual artifacts themselves." This leads to a central epistemological question: "How can the designer *know* the truth of his predictions (or at least justify his faith in them)?" (279–280). Galle examines various theoretical or philosophical models, or worldviews, that might help us understand the design process and its relationship with an object that does not yet exist, and he makes the general statement that designers need to be aware that all approaches to the design process (as described in design theory) have a conceptual foundation: "What threatens to disintegrate our body of design theory is not the world views *per se* but our lack of awareness of them" (298). This is true, and as a consequence, we also need to be aware of the preconceptions implied in the notion of possibility on the level of the design process. This kind of design thinking implies that designers might think and act within a field of possibilities, but also that these possibilities are often thought to exist in the form of a large reservoir of latent design choices that disappear as the design process is condensed into a final product. The sphere of possibilities is often conceived as transient and eventually transformed into the actual of the design object. Thus, it is when mediated through the medium of the design object that the open space of the possible can be connected to specific potentialities of the object in its affordance of a limited set of meanings and use. Seen from the perspective of the design process, then, the possible is active as a force behind the process but loses its relevance when actualized in an object.

Within design ontology and design phenomenology, the notion of the possible is engaged on another level, as the possibilities are created by and around the design object. Thus, the design object can generate new possibilities as design is regarded as a catalyst for generating cultural possibilities. Design can be a means of opening up a space of cultural meaning. In this vein, John Heskett (2002) states that "cultural identity is not fixed, like a fly in amber, but is constantly evolving and mutating, and design is a primary element in stimulating the awareness of possibilities" (133). Heskett's statement contains an element of a one-way model, where the design object has a stable and secure ontology and points to an ever-changing and unstable culture; however, it does indicate an understanding of the dynamic relationship between design and culture with the design object as the starting point. Thus, Heskett views design as integrated in a general anthropology; in his perspective, design is a natural extension of man, which responds dynamically to human nature and culture.

In a statement on the same level of abstraction and ambition as Herbert Simon's dictum, Heskett (2002) says that "design, stripped to its essence, can be defined as the human capacity to shape and make our environment in ways without precedent in nature, to serve our needs and give meaning to our lives" (7). Furthermore, the notion of the generation of new possibilities through the design object is close to the bias of experimental design—for example, the critical design movement and its proposal that design critically could, and should, project productive counterimages of a given reality, thus functioning as a critique of everyday habits and practices of creating and using design (Dunne 1999; Dunne and Raby 2001). Since, on a fundamental level, design operates as "orientation" and communication between individuals and collectives (Schneider 2009, 197), it has the potential to indicate new directions. This approach may also be future-oriented in nature; design can be used "as a methodology to create examples of how the future *should* be" (Hjelm 2007, 120). Also, the use of design as a means of exploring the possible casts a reflective light back on design. Shana Agid states that the "engagement with possible worlds and futures is also a reimagining of design as a language for exploring the multiple shapes and ramifications of these possibilities" (Agid 2012, 47). Hence, to investigate the possible in design is not only to investigate the possible itself but, perhaps even more, to challenge and question the role of design as an operating and dynamic factor in this game. Seen in this light, the purpose of this book is to seek ways for reimagining design as an aesthetic medium for creating new meaning through the process of imagination.

In a philosophical context, Peter Sloterdijk (2010) tightens the argument of opening up possibilities through design. He speaks of design in the paradoxical phrase of "the capacity of incapacity," "Können des Nichtkönnens" (12). On the level of a phenomenology of use, design, according to Sloterdijk, has a ritual quality in simulating the kind of sovereignty that emerges when we are able to conceive of otherwise incomprehensible objects. When this occurs, users are fundamentally enabled and empowered. For example, in interface design, the hermetic black box of an otherwise incomprehensible product can become "useful" and develop an "unlocked exterior" through design devices; design can be seen to be serve the "need of competence for structurally incompetent users" (15–16).[7] On the level of design ontology, however, Sloterdijk is more radical. He speaks of design as a reshaping of things, "Neuzeichnung von Dingen" (17), which, by transcending the existing, places design in an open space where it designates the new on the basis of the unstable condition of the exception:

> A designer can never understand himself as simply a curator of the existing. All design arises from anti-reverence; it begins with the decision to put the questions of form and function of things in a new way. Sovereign is the one who can decide over the permanent state of exception in questions of form. And design is the permanent state of exception in issues concerning the forms of things. (19)[8]

Furthermore, Sloterdijk speaks of design as a strategy of renewing things whereby design objects become comparative objects; they are always dependent on previous objects and are "results of a forward-looking story of optimization" (20). As a consequence, in Sloterdijk's perspective, design objects can emerge at the intersection of actuality and possibility in two ways. In a synchronic perspective, design objects can be media of new possibilities that are based on the paradoxical process of making capable what is not capable and on the openness characterizing the permanent state of exception. In a diachronic perspective, this structure unfolds in the temporal process where new products realize possibilities that older products did not have and in the enabling of new possibilities in the design process.

Thus, on the level of the design object, the possible can be present as the stimulation of cultural possibilities (Heskett) or as the not-yet-given possibility of becoming capable (to rephrase Sloterdijk).

My point is, further, that the possible can also be seen as an inherent structure in virtually all design objects. This stems from the role of the imaginary in design objects. Beyond specific potentials of objects, the imaginary offers an understanding of the flexibility of meaning in design objects that stems from their constitution in an act of meaning creation in the design process and lives on in the design objects in their stimulation of possibility. Thus, the imaginary in design may point to the inner dynamics of expanding the space of possibility in design. The imaginary refers back to the designer's use of design as a medium for imagining something new and thus transforming creativity into innovation, that is, creativity put into a practical and concrete context of use. This connection should not, however, be seen as an attempt at finding the true intention in the designer's mind (which would be a fallacy). Rather, by using the concept of the imaginary to conceptualize the complex relationship between a mental process of immaterial imagining on the one hand and the realization in a physical, concrete, and material medium on the other, we are able to discuss how meaning, through the vehicle of the imaginary, can be transferred in a way that detaches it from the designer.

My aim in the following chapters is to specify the medium of design through its aesthetics, describe a phenomenology of imagination, and examine the implications of this for the constitution and ontology of the object. This reflection can be productive on a cultural level in an examination of the potential of design objects to enable and create culturally circumscribed meaning. The concepts of possibility and the imaginary reveal that objects are always more than mere materiality, that they are permeated by structures of meaning that are given in an interplay of negation and positioning, of absence and presence, and that this opens up the possibility that lies hidden in the object, a latent aspect of its structure.

3   Aesthetics

Aesthetics is a fundamental issue for design. In this chapter, I focus on the operations of aesthetics in design and the formative structures of meaning in design. The chapter can be read independently as an introduction to the little-described field of design and aesthetics,[1] but in a wider context, a discussion of aesthetics in design can also lay the foundation for conceptualizing the element of imagination in design.

Central to my argument regarding design as a medium of meaning and imagination as a means of producing and enabling meaning is the connection between the sensual and the conceptual. This can be described within a framework of aesthetics. Importantly, then, aesthetics is not just a question of appearance but also of epistemology and of organizing our relation to the world and using design for this purpose. This requires an explication and elaboration of this framework, as the discussion of aesthetics in design is often founded on a series of paradoxes. The concept of aesthetics is integrated in the common discourse on design and often set in relation to design, while at the same time, what is meant by the concept is rarely clarified; furthermore, there is a strong philosophical tradition for the discussion of aesthetics, especially in relation to art, while this is rarely related to design.

In my discussion of aesthetics in design, I use three platforms to approach the concept:

- Sensual-phenomenological
- Conceptual-hermeneutical
- Contextual-discursive

Each platform describes a specific entry into the investigation of aesthetics in design, which applies to discussions on two levels: in relation to design perceived as objects with a certain aesthetic appeal and impact, very much in line with the classic conception of aesthetics, and in relation to the mode of operation of the imagination.

Thus, to speak of the aesthetics of imagination in design is to see different types of aesthetics in relation to the mode of operation of imagination in design.

In this sense, the sensual-phenomenological dimension, which concerns the sensual communication of design, applies to the sensual aspects of the engagement of imagination in design and the creation of solutions that connect sensual appearance with conceptual meaning (so the focus of chapter 7). The conceptual-hermeneutical dimension, which in terms of aesthetic theory has to do with comprehending the manner and structure of aesthetic coding in design, connects to the constructive-critical role of the imaginary in evoking possibility through the means of symbolic coding in design (see chapters 8 and 9). Thus, aesthetic and symbolic coding can be seen as analog operations on different layers in the process of constructing meaning in design. Aesthetic coding deals with the matter of how design objects stage meaning and relate to their content of meaning, that is, aesthetic coding focuses closely on the relationship between design object and the construction of meaning, whereas symbolic coding supplements this reflection by considering how this construction of meaning can be made open and, through the object, relate to the sphere of the possible.

Finally, the contextual-discursive dimension of aesthetics in design concerns the double movement of organizing and distributing the sensual material and employing design in a discursive context of organizing meaning. This relates to the phenomenon of everyday aestheticization, which not only has ethical implications for our ways of accessing the world. In this way, aesthetics in design is not merely centered around superficial styling; it also points to the way that design can be involved imaginatively and on a large scale in creating new schemata for perceiving and understanding our surroundings and, ultimately, in changing, altering, and transfiguring given schemata (see chapter 10). Thus, through the schemata, design can have a transformative effect on experience, that is, it may point to a radical transfiguration of the structure of experience.

In this chapter, I describe these three platforms with regard to their role of serving as foundations for aesthetics in design. I address the relation to imagination only briefly here; the various aspects of imagination in design are the topic of the remainder of the book. In line with my overall approach, my perspective here is phenomenological: I regard aesthetics as a central entry point for understanding how design mediates and conditions experience and our basic access to experience. Sensually, conceptually, and contextually, design structures our experience; in its formation of meaning, design connects sensual material with concepts and frames our experience through this relationship. First, though, I outline some of the existing perspectives on aesthetics in design as a starting point for my positioning in the field of aesthetics.

The Field of Aesthetics and Design

Discussing aesthetics as an aspect of design touches on one of the most vital matters of how design functions as a means of communication. Especially in nonprofessional contexts oriented toward lifestyle, when design artifacts are noticed and appreciated, it is more often for their aesthetic surface qualities than their practical or functional ability to solve more or less complex or well-defined problems. Regarded as a phenomenon of the visual-sensual surface of design objects, aesthetics has often been considered a means of differentiating products on the market, which is equally reflected in the literature on marketing and design management (Borja de Mozota 2003) and the interest in the symbolic-communicative aspects of the exchange economy of commodities (see the seminal work by Haug 1986 and, recently, Drügh, Metz & Weyand 2011). Furthermore, working with aesthetics is often regarded as a core competence in design; in fact, the pervasive attention paid to aesthetics can even be annoying to designers because it implies that their work solely concerns issues of surface, appearance, and styling as opposed to, for example, functionality.

Although aesthetics in design has been a neglected area of research, attempts have been made to conceptualize the specific field of design aesthetics.[2] Roughly speaking, these attempts take their starting point in either design, often in issues of design practice, or the philosophical understanding of aesthetics.

In relation to design, a dominant concern has been to understand the aesthetic qualities of the nonfunctional, emotionally appealing factors in design and how they affect the process of designing. With a number of approaches seeking to make the often psychologically biased field of emotions applicable in design practice (Jordan 2000; Norman 2004; Desmet and Hekkert 2007; Desmet 2010), the interest in emotions has contributed to setting the agenda for research into the sensual-cognitive aesthetic impact of design; this is reflected in the success of the recurring Design and Emotions Conferences organized by the Design and Emotion Society.[3] In a paradigmatic expression, Sabine Döring (2010) states how the aesthetic is connected to the emotional, as "to experience something aesthetically is to give it emotional value" (67). Here she also points to a key element in the discussion of aesthetics, namely, where it should be located: in a specific perception or apprehension in the subject, who then attributes aesthetic value to the given design object, or as an inherent aspect of the object. As I discuss later in this chapter, the aesthetic is to be regarded as a relationship between subject and object rather than an essence that can be physically grasped, determined, and circumscribed. Döring thus states that emotional experiences, where the object is seen by virtue of its intrinsic value, beyond aspects of function, "by means of itself"

(67), can be enhanced by types of objects that encourage this perception of emotional properties; thus, the objects themselves can contain and promote this quality. However, the question that Döring does not answer is how design objects specifically (as opposed to art, for example) can incorporate this quality and how they can operate as specific media for this relationship since they also contain functional qualities.

In relation to the philosophical interest in aesthetics, the field has expanded from an interest in art and taste toward an interest in design. This is reflected by the anthology *Ästhetische Werte und Design* (2010), with a number of essays written by philosophers. In the context of philosophy, it makes good sense to deal with design because a certain branch of philosophical aesthetics deals with the role of sensual appeal for cognition and with the prevalent aestheticization of ordinary, everyday life as the world of late modern capitalism has been dominated by an overwhelming visualization and search for sensual appeal through all types of products and dreamscapes. Aesthetics is no longer the exclusive domain of art but is also applied to our immediate, sensuous experience of the world.

The purpose of pointing back to the philosophical concept of aesthetics is not to employ a philosophical, conceptual discourse to establish the "true" meaning of the word *aesthetic* to define it once and for all, an impossible task given the heterogeneity of the concept. Importantly, the history of the concept has moved in many directions, which may serve as starting points for a discussion about aesthetics.

The concept was developed by the German philosopher Alexander Baumgarten in the work *Aesthetica* (1750–1758, written in Latin) to describe a philosophical discipline that investigates the "lower" sensual aspects of human experience as opposed to the higher realm of logic. This led to the debate on taste and value judgment of beauty and the sublime in Kant's seminal *Kritik der Urtheilskraft* (1790), which preceded the close link between the work of art and the philosophy of aesthetics from Schelling's romantic-idealistic celebration of the work of art in *Philosophie der Kunst* (1802) to Adorno's modernist *Ästhetische Theorie* (1970).[4]

Following the philosophical line of reflection, I pursue the directions that a contemporary design aesthetics may take if it is serious about being an aesthetics specific to design and not to art, the classic topic of romantic and modern aesthetic theory. Hence, my path to a new understanding of aesthetics in design will not go through the traditional discussions of art as a medium of aesthetic appreciation and communication, as this risks reducing design to a matter and medium of artistic aspiration. Of course, a design object may be the result of purely artistic and autonomous self-expression, but it always relates to wider contexts. In terms of design methodology, it will be more justified to speak of design as a meeting point of multiple interests (those of a client, a designer, a manufacturer, and the user) and as a complex negotiation between problem formulation and solution generation. From the point of view of cultural analysis, design is a practice of innovation and change that creates symbolic meaning, inseparable from the culturally circumscribed patterns of consumption. Furthermore, an appropriation of design by the aesthetics of art, implying a view of design as art, might hamper an understanding of the unique complexity of almost any design object or solution: that design is not the expression of a lone artist but rather the result of complex commercial and societal processes.[5]

The Aesthetic Relationship

One of the dominant discussions in aesthetic theory has been about the location of the aesthetic, its site in the act of aesthetic appreciation. Kant's *Kritik der Urtheilskraft* is symptomatic of this discussion: On the one hand, he speaks of value judgment and taste, that is, of matters of subjective concern. On the other hand, the purpose of his thorough philosophical investigation of the field of aesthetics is to search for trans-subjective criteria for aesthetic evaluation in a *sensus communis* and to employ aesthetics in a wider epistemological ambition of being able to reflect concepts in a way that they relate to metaphysical entities that we do not have concepts for (i.e., ideas of morality or freedom). That is, the judgment of taste is also bound to a series of more objective conditions; it is not only submitted to arbitrary subjective evaluation and taste.

We may state that aesthetic qualities must by necessity be arbitrary because they depend on the viewing position (e.g., I might appreciate the aesthetics of garden gnomes, for instance, in Philippe Starck's design, while my neighbor does not). Taste is individual and often given within the frame of certain cultural values and social groupings. This also erodes the classic and often elitist notion of "good taste" (Boradkar 2010), the idea of the Good, the Beautiful, and Truth as guidelines for aesthetics,[6] and the distinction between a high culture of *les beaux arts* from the eighteenth century onward and the popular mass culture that began to form around the middle of the nineteenth century, even if a key concern of the history of aesthetics has been to separate the domain of the aesthetic from that of the nonaesthetic or the mundane. Instead, there can only be variations in taste that are different but in principle have equal value. In many respects, design can be seen as an aspect of the rise of popular culture, and it can be conceptually described by the aestheticization of everyday life. Thus, all sorts of objects (refrigerators, tables, garden gnomes, movies, works of art, books) may serve as vehicles of aesthetic appreciation according to some specific taste. The field is open, and virtually anything can be regarded as aesthetic if we choose to view it with an aesthetic perception.[7]

Some objects, however, encourage aesthetic appreciation more than others. They seem to promote and motivate an aesthetic appreciation of certain qualities.[8] From the history of the arts, we may notice that objects within the domain of the arts seem to have the effect of encouraging this, and thus one of the key tasks of art-oriented aesthetic theory has been to describe these characteristics in works of art. Correspondingly, another key task is to embrace this angle of the discussion on behalf of design: What feature of design makes it "aesthetic"? What is, then, aesthetics in design? How are design objects aesthetically coded?

For now, we must state that aesthetics evolves as a relation and in a relation between a subject with an intention to see and perceive something as aesthetic and an object with certain aesthetically coded features (Genette 1999). This prohibits any assumption of aesthetics as an inherent essence of certain privileged objects (e.g., high art or of ancient Greek or classical provenance). The philosopher Morten Kyndrup (2008b) has described the relational aspect of aesthetics quite precisely:

"Aesthetic objects" (that is, objects "we" attribute aesthetic value to) only exist in so far that something is actually made the object of subjective perceptions as "aesthetic", that is, as an empirical category, they only exist in the sense of a given testimony of a fulfilled, actual aesthetic attribution of value. . . . [In addition,] a series of artifacts of meaning are construed *with the intention* of partaking in aesthetic relations. (101)

Furthermore, in loosening the bond between aesthetics and art, Kyndrup speaks of surroundings that can be seen as "aesthetically calculated," where the artifacts in question are conceived with a high degree of implicit "aestheticity," using aspects of art's ambition to be perceived "aesthetically" (102). It is clear, then, that every process of aesthetic "appreciation" implies a perceiving and aesthetically focused subject; nevertheless, at the same time, categories of aesthetically appealing objects—objects wanting to be perceived *as* aesthetic—can be separated from other objects.

Thus, to define aesthetics is to describe a functional relation that combines the subject's intentional viewing and desire to perceive aesthetically and an aesthetic coding of the objects, their "intentional aesthetic function" (Genette 1999, 2), and thus constructs the aesthetic at the precise intersection of these two aspects.[9] In addition, Wolfgang Iser (2003) speaks of the aesthetic as a functional movement of play between polarities (subject-object; actuality-possibility), where the aesthetic should not be confounded with the final product of this movement. To speak of aesthetics in design, then, is a matter of analyzing how design objects partake in this process; this is the topic I pursue here in the description of the three platforms of the engagement of aesthetics with design.

Besides being functional, the aesthetic relationship is contextual and informational. The aesthetic relationship is informational in the sense that it takes place within an act of communication; the aesthetic message is sent off with some sort of artistic intention (to employ Genette's terminology) in order to be perceived by a receiving subject in a certain way.[10] That is, aesthetics evolves within the framework and the factors of an act of communication; what is aesthetic is, so to speak, agreed within the chain of aesthetic intention → coded message → aesthetic perception. Thus, this act acquires its value and importance in certain contexts that ultimately define what is perceived and appreciated as aesthetic. In this sense, a large part of the history of aesthetics has been about normatively defining the right framework of appreciation, from Schiller's ambition in *Über die ästhetische Erziehung des Menschen* (1795) of letting the creation of the new, ideal nation go through the aesthetic education of man, learning the value of beauty, to the later development of a canonical discourse on the value of art, the establishment of art museums as temples of artistic appreciation, and the education of "good taste."[11]

Even if we attempt to detach the contextual determination of aesthetics from normative parameters, it is still important to reflect on the role of the context in defining aesthetics. In this way, Jakob Steinbrenner leads a discussion of functional definition of design in the anthology *Ästhetische Werte und Design* (2010), where he abandons his initial question of *what* design is in favor of exploring *when* design is, and when *good* design is, as he sees the decisive moment for defining what design is in the interpretation of a specific artifact within a specific aesthetic system of signs: "An aesthetic system of signs is to be understood as a system that defines which characteristics of an object are aesthetically relevant" (16). Although Steinbrenner tends to define aesthetics with references to the domain of art, that is, as being in opposition to objects of purpose and function (thus employing a prevalent method of segregating function from aesthetics) he does attempt to relate the two domains to each other.[12] His point is that design objects are not seen as works of art, even if the aesthetic systems of works of art are in play and that instead we see the functional aspects within an aesthetic reference system. In his view, design is design when its "functional features . . . gain value within an aesthetic sign system" (20). This means that an object can "have design" only when "certain features of the object are ascribed certain meanings" (26), which again points back to the role of context in determining these meanings. As important contextual frames of reference, Steinbrenner points to artistic movements that design can relate to (e.g., the relationship of Bauhaus and post-Bauhaus design to, for example, the experiments of space and color in the avant-garde movements of the first third of the twentieth century, for example, the De Stijl movement), or design history, as design does not develop in a vacuum but always exists in a "continuation of historical design culture" (20).[13]

In summary, we cannot presuppose any defining essence of aesthetics; we can go back into the history of aesthetic theory and note a series of attempts to find such an essence or employ of aesthetics for the sake of some higher purpose, for example, education. Due to the functional, informational, and contextual determination of aesthetics as relational, such essences prove impossible. That does not mean, however, that *anything goes* (to repeat a postmodern phrase) and that we are left within a field of entirely undifferentiated meanings. It simply means that we have to move, unprejudiced, into the field of aesthetics and, more specifically, into the field of aesthetics in design, because investigating design in this context is different from exploring the domain of art, precisely because design involves objects or means of use and function that often appeal to the market and to society.

In the sections that follow, I claim that design is important by virtue of its sensual effects (the sensual-phenomenological platform), its ability to challenge our understanding (the conceptual-hermeneutical platform), and its capacity for creating and construing meaning on the level of society (the discursive-contextual platform). The last dimension of aesthetics proves the field to be anything but superficial, although the everyday use of the word *aesthetic* often relates to superficial form or styling. In fact, by staging meaning on a large scale, design also has profound ethical implications. Because both ethics and aesthetics deal with value (Findeli 1994), aesthetics is a serious issue.

The Sensual-Phenomenological Platform: Form and Sensuous Experience

A first level of conceptualizing aesthetics in design is grasping its sensuous qualities or, rather, the distinctive appeal of design to the senses. That does not mean that aesthetics can be conceived solely as a matter of outward appearance, as in stylistic strategies, for example, but it does emphasize the function of design objects as sensually appealing artifacts and draws attention to issues concerning form and surface. Regardless of the reservations against entering the field of the superficial aspects of design, the sensual appeal of physically given, material design objects is a defining factor of design: we engage with design objects through their physical form, and the first impression is often mediated through visual appreciation.[14] My goal here is to explore how form and appearance can be qualified as means of a type of aesthetic communication that challenges experience and discuss the role of form as a challenge to our understanding of things.

These issues of form, experience, and understanding in design can be situated within two powerful frameworks: contemporary aesthetic theory and phenomenology.

First, in recent years there has been a tendency to loosen the connection between art and aesthetic theory and to revisit, from various perspectives, Baumgarten's original idea of applying aesthetics to sensual matter (in Old Greek, *aisthetá*, that which can be sensed); in terminology there has been a similar tendency toward a shift from aesthetics to *aisthesis* (Engholm 2010b). This movement from works of art to general sensuous experience and, further, to questions concerning how reality is arranged and perceived aesthetically, is the topic of a new era of aesthetic theory that has been unfolding since the 1990s, especially in works by the philosophers Richard Shusterman (1992/2000), Martin Seel (2000, 2007), and Gernot Böhme (1995, 2001). Tellingly, the title of one of Böhme's recent works, *Lectures on Aesthetics as a Common Doctrine of Perception* (2001), features the Greek root of the word *aesthetics*: *Aisthetik*.

In a German-speaking context, the new approach to aesthetics as a matter of sensual experience has developed in close dialogue with the tradition of philosophical aesthetics, whereas Shusterman points back to American pragmatist philosophy, especially John Dewey's 1934 book, *Art as Experience*. The title of Shusterman's book, *Pragmatist Aesthetics: Living Beauty, Rethinking Art*, is direct testimony to Dewey. The core idea of this pragmatist approach to aesthetics is to focus on aesthetic experiences as something that evolves in context and is not necessarily bound to art. Aesthetic experiences derive their quality not from a relationship with specific objects (e.g., works of art) but instead as a particular aspect of the experience itself, indeed of the whole field of experience, which can emerge in any situation. This includes the element of an aesthetic experience where "the experience is an integrated complete experience on its own account" (Dewey 2005, 57). Here, Dewey also points to qualities such as coherence, balance, equilibrium, harmony, and unity as constitutive for this specific type of experience.[15]

Experience is at the heart of Dewey's theory of aesthetics, and because "every experience is constituted by interaction between 'subject' and 'object,' between a self and its world, it is not itself either merely physical nor merely mental" (Dewey 2005, 256); further, "esthetic experience" combines and unifies both desire and thought, the practical and the intellectual, as well as (sensuous) sense and meaning (266, 270). To Dewey, "aesthetic expression *means* experience and enables inner participation" (Balmer 2009, 139). To conceive the aesthetic experience as a potential, immanent, but nevertheless particular aspect of all experience is not far from Seel's position and stresses the importance of focusing on the conditions and contexts of experience, on the one hand, and the means and artifacts that encourage aesthetic experiences, on the other. Dewey states directly that what the work of art (he too speaks mostly of works of art)[16] does "is to concentrate and enlarge an immediate experience" and to present a "pure experience" freed "from factors that subordinate an experience as it is directly had to something beyond itself" (Dewey 2005, 285–286), while 'ordinary experience' is often "infected with apathy, lassitude and stereotype" (270). That brings us back to the framework of the aesthetic relationship. Then, the aesthetic relationship as an open structure for investigating aesthetics is an inherent part of the pragmatist approach to aesthetics. Thus, subject and experience co-affect each other (i.e., the relation is not static), and the "aesthetic experience is not narrowly associated with the domain of art but may occur in any domain of human existence" (Engholm 2010b, 145).[17]

Shusterman brings central elements of Dewey's philosophy (the general focus on experience) into the present, while leaving other parts behind (e.g., Dewey's postromantic ideology of coherence). On the one hand, he opposes Dewey in stating the relevance of an experience-oriented pragmatist aesthetics for the understanding of popular culture that emerges along with mass media in late modernism. On the other hand, he enhances the reflection on the role of the body in the aesthetic experience through the concept of "somaesthetics" as a way of studying "the experience and use of one's body as a locus of sensory-aesthetic appreciation (*aisthesis*) and creative self-fashioning" (Shusterman 2000, 267).[18] Shusterman does not, however, deal directly with design but instead with popular culture in the form of music and film. In general, Shusterman acknowledges the importance of the contextual, diachronic-historical frame of the aesthetic experiences, while Dewey remains more synchronic-conceptual in his philosophical approach to the general topic of art and poetry (thus conceiving of aesthetics as an element within the larger framework of pragmatist philosophy).[19]

Next, this experiential bias of recent aesthetic theory is evident in the contextualization of phenomenology as a philosophy that addresses the fundamental premise of the importance of experience and the basic conditions of experience. The point is that phenomenology, as a theory of experience, is capable of addressing certain aspects of aesthetics related to sensuous appearance and experience. I will use the theory of the French phenomenologist Maurice Merleau-Ponty to discuss and address various modes of sensual qualities in design and thus also approach an understanding not only of the effect on the subject but also of the power of the object to raise this effect (which, in the end, is my interest). In an important essay, "L'entrelacs—Le chiasme," Merleau-Ponty (1964) introduces two kinds of interlaced structures in experience (Merleau-Ponty 1964), which I refer to in the following discussion of two important aspects of aesthetics in design. The first aspect deals with the sensual relationship and address in this section, while the other deals with the relationship between ideas or concepts and material manifestation, but still within the framework of phenomenology, and will be addressed in the next section within the framework of a conceptual-hermeneutical approach to aesthetics in design.

Aesthetics and the Sensual Relationship

Merleau-Ponty's first structure takes its point of departure in immediate and concrete experience. Here he follows a basic assumption in phenomenology: that experience is a matter for a concrete and specific subject whose consciousness is incarnated in a body that is located in a concrete world of things and intersubjective relations. Consequently, the "world" is only ever a matter for a bodily incarnated subject.

For Merleau-Ponty, the implications are radical in the sense that it becomes impossible to separate the experiencing subject from the experienced world; subject and object are reciprocally intertwined. The sensing subject cannot be separated from the sensed material, and the viewer cannot be separated from the viewed but participates in it and is influenced by it. Likewise, the sensing or viewing subject can herself be sensed or viewed and thus become an object. In this way, Merleau-Ponty criticizes the traditional dichotomy of subject and object. Furthermore, in a sort of deconstructive gesture, he attempts to reverse the dichotomy in order to show that it has a common foundation in a figure of continuity that he calls the flesh *la chair*. He speaks of density of the flesh (*l'epaisseur de chair*) as a means of communication between the viewer and the object. Similarly, the body is located in a chiastic structure within the world: "The body participates in the order of things, and likewise the world is universal flesh"[20] (Merleau-Ponty 1964). Experience, in Merleau-Ponty's phenomenology, is an ongoing exchange between subject and object that takes place in the common material of *chair*.

Almost as an explication of Merleau-Ponty's notion of *chair*, Gernot Böhme has developed the powerful concept of ambience, *Atmosphäre*, to analyze how things, situations, and surroundings appeal to us. Or, rather, Böhme similarly deconstructs the dichotomy of subject and object, defining ambience as a kind of relationship between subject and object. The point is that ambience can emerge only if there is an experiencing subject. However, it is not an inherent part of the subject[21] but rather objective, the result of an effect evoked by a specific constellation of things (Böhme 1995, 33). Thus, to Böhme, the concept of ambience becomes the main designator for the conditions of perception, the "primary object of perception" (48):

Obviously, ambiences are neither conditions of the subject nor characteristics of the object. Still, however, they are only experienced in the actual perception of a subject and are co-constituted in their being, their character, through the subjectivity of the perceiver. And even though they are not characteristics of the objects, they are obviously produced through the characteristics and interplay of objects. That is, ambiences are something *between* subject and object. They are not something relational, they are the relation itself. . . . For us, the ambience is the first reality of perception [*Wahrnehmungswirklichkeit*], out of which subject and object can be separated. (Böhme 2001, 54–56)

In this context, three aspects of Böhme's theory are particularly important. First, as a theory of sensuous experience and relations, the main concern of aesthetics for

Böhme (2001) is how ambience works and constitutes a specific relationship between subject and object: "For aesthetics, the ambiences are therefore the first and essential reality. They are the perceptible co-existence of subject and object" (57). In Böhme's perspective, there may be a "real reality" behind the operations of ambience, but what is important to aesthetics is the "reality of appearance," which emphasizes how (perception of) "reality" is mediated through ambience, the effect of surface and form, and the value of staging meaning (121, 159–164).[22]

Second, ambience is experienced and expressed as a coherent whole. Instead of separating the various aspects of sensuous experience (sight, hearing, scent) and asking how one sense might evoke effects in another, ambience serves as the perceptual background against which things and surroundings present themselves and where one may look for sensuous differentiation. In this context, Böhme discusses the traditional aesthetic concept of synaesthesia and especially the effects of color, among other aspects, the conception of color in Goethe's *Theory of Colors*, which was developed in the first decades of the nineteenth century.[23]

And third, ambience is not only something to be experienced but also something to be made or manipulated. Böhme speaks of "aesthetic work," the intention of giving things, surroundings, and people certain qualities that let them appear as something special with a power of appeal to be perceived in a certain (controlled) way (Böhme 1995). In this context, he mentions creative areas such as stage work, commercials, art, architecture, and design as examples. This notion of aesthetic work is clearly linked to today's prevalent concept of the experience economy and to the pervasive strategies of aestheticizing all aspects and elements of our surroundings, a key concern in late modern societies.[24]

Design as a Structure of Appearance

The strength of Merleau-Ponty's phenomenological and Böhme's aesthetic-philosophical frameworks is that they conceptualize the relationship of sensual experience between subjective apprehension and objective appearance. However, the fundamental shortcoming of Merleau-Ponty's theory is that he does not address the meaning and importance of how the world appears to us with its concrete things, surroundings, and people. Merleau-Ponty thus follows the phenomenological dogma of reducing the world of phenomena to abstracta in order to investigate the basic structure of experience in itself. Böhme, through the notion of ambience, seeks to conceptualize the importance of the specific world we encounter, but in the end, he too remains in the realm of abstract speculation by virtue of his prevailing philosophical interest in, for example, the issue of perception.[25] To deal with an increasingly designed and aesthetically staged world, we need more precise concepts for discussing the structure of appearance.

One promising contribution was made by Prasad Boradkar with the proposal of the "skin" as a sensually given and materially present mediating factor between an experiencing subject and an object aiming to appeal (Boradkar 2010). Without explicit reference to phenomenology, Boradkar uses the metaphor of the skin to contract the dichotomy of subject and object into a specific property of the object: the surface of the skin, which is then seen as an interface that constitutes "boundaries between the insides of things and the outside world" (151) and as the location "where the aesthetic experience originates" (158).[26] Thus, through their surfaces, design objects can communicate matters of form, symbolic values, and function, which may even be projective in the construction of its recipients:

Designers tinker with the surface characteristics of form, contour, materials, color and texture to create the aesthetic experiences that users seek and desire. These physical features of things are by no means the sole preoccupations of designers who strive to create aesthetic experiences and consumers who seek them. Price, performance, packaging, advertising, warranties and other factors play a role as well. Many of these attributes of the products are "written" on the surfaces. And just as the human skin operates as a protective, communicative, aesthetic layer of the human body so does the object skin. (151)

As a next step, then, Boradkar tries to differentiate various types of skin: protective, informational, technological/intelligent, and mythical/fetishistic. The strength of this approach is that it seeks to combine and connect concrete matters of form with cultural analysis, that is, how the surfaces or skins of objects operate within and appeal to cultural logic.[27] The problem is that the analysis of the function of the skin, its mode of operation, is only touched on and barely elaborated.

Boradkar (2010) proposes an interesting framework that offers an instrumental typology for designers and initiates a dialogue with a variety of cultural questions, for example, when the concealing skin of the iPod constructs a product of mystery and fetishism (156). In this way, he makes a serious contribution to cracking the design enigma of (people's desire for) the Apple product: By making the product interiors inaccessible (or visible only in the seductive translucent and semitransparent cabinet design of the iMacs of the late 1990s), Apple effectively and successfully creates not only a product that is functionally sealed off in relation to the intervention of creative users (to the annoyance of people who want to work open source) but also a myth of how the design can be magical in offering pure, effective operation without displaying how. Due to this magical effect, the iPod leads to a "subordination of use-value by brand-value and fetish-value" (156).

In my opinion, the problem with Boradkar's approach is that it fails to address the important epistemological questions of how surfaces contribute to the constitution of experience. Thus, the iPod is not only an object of fetish value; it also inaugurates new conditions for the sensual mode of experiencing technology. Its surface—in all its material and sensually appealing texture as "skin"—is not only an interface of transmission and communication between inside technology and outside world. On a fundamental level it also structures the way we organize, engage, and interact with meaning, in this case music; it is a locus for mediating meaning that can be related to us.[28] That is the important aspect of Boradkar's notion of skin: that it attributes the meaning of sensual and cognitive comprehension of the world exactly at the intersection of subjective interest and object appeal through the specific structure and appearance of the design object.

Thus, in a philosophical, cultural, and material context, design is important as a major means of structuring the appearance and the surface that signify "world" in our perception and cognition. An example of an important design that also goes beyond being a surface for intimate, tactile interaction is the Swiss engineer-designer Hans Hilfiker's famous 1944 railway clock, which, by emphasizing the importance of the minute as a "signum" for the regularity of time, sets the stage for a functional experience of time (figure 3.1). The minute hand moves only when a minute has passed. In general, clocks communicate the structure of time; this particular clock will persuade us to see the minute as the structuring unit of experiencing time. Furthermore, it reflects time as having a structure in opposition to being in a flow. The question, then, is how the world of (designed) objects in general influences the modality of the experiencing subject (i.e., the conditions of experience and how the objects' contribution to experience can be analyzed).[29]

As an example of a kind of design that creates an ambience and thus stages a certain kind of relationship between subject and object, I point to the interior design created by the Danish designer Verner Panton (1926–1998). Interior design often evokes a high aesthetic effect of ambience because it is capable of creating an encapsulating and highly calculated environment.[30] This is certainly the case in Panton's interior design for Spiegel in Hamburg (1969, the basement swimming pool, figure 3.2), his home in Basel, Switzerland (the dining room, figure 3.3), and the exhibition project *Visiona II* (1970, figure 3.4). With the ambition of being a sort of surrealist—or rather psychedelic—Gesamtkunstwerk[31] and seeking to suspend the normal coordinates of space, Panton's projects show design at its extreme, rethinking and reshaping our conception and perception of the environment.[32]

Here, *Visiona II* is of particular interest. Created in collaboration with the German chemical company Bayer to demonstrate the use of Dralon, an acrylic fiber material, the project is an early example of advertising and branding a product by staging events (Engholm 2006). *Visiona II* was a complex of spaces that used, for example, red or green colors, displayed surfaces in hard plastic bubbles or organic, fuzzy carpets, and employed plastic lamps in the shape of mushrooms or as suspended silvery, glittering

Figure 3.1
Railway clock, 1944. *Design:* Hans Hilfiker. *Photo:* MOBATime.

Figure 3.2
Interior design for the basement swimming pool in the Hamburg headquarters of the German magazine *Der Spiegel*, 1969. *Design:* Verner Panton. *Photo:* Panton Design.

Figure 3.3
Dining room in the Panton home in Basel, Switzerland, 1985. *Design:* Verner Panton. *Photo:* Panton Design.

metallic elements with a fluctuating, almost hypnotic effect.[33] Of special interest is the 48 square meter interior space with organically shaped modules in brightly colored textile (figure 3.4). Each (upholstered) module forms an unbroken, organic line that curves along the floor, walls, and ceiling without any angles; in combination, they create a space full of variety, where users can sit or lie down in a variety of positions. As an exhibition project, *Visiona II* is difficult to get to experience today, although it is occasionally presented in retrospective exhibitions of Panton's design. Usually, however, these displays do not include the sound effects and intoxicating odors that were part of the original concept. Thus, the original project was meant to have a massive appeal to all the senses.

Panton's interior designs explicitly and powerfully employ basic constituents of ambience such as intense color, the textures and fabrics of materials (especially materials that were novel in Panton's time), and elements of form as variations of geometry. In this way, Panton not only creates a certain ambient space that suspends the tradi-

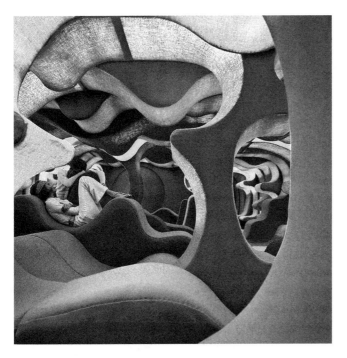

Figure 3.4
Visiona II, exhibition project, 1970. *Design:* Verner Panton. *Photo:* Panton Design.

tional organization of space; he intensifies this ambience. In the words of Martin Seel (2007), Panton's spaces enable a kind of "aesthetic perception," *ästhetische Wahrnehmung,* that not only invests itself in the immediate appearance—a key word for Seel—of the world, in the sense that the world is given to us as "a momentary and simultaneous abundance of appearance," but also intensifies the appearance of the pure present that is otherwise inaccessible to ordinary perception (13). Thus, to Seel, aesthetic perception is a matter of looking in a certain intent way that involves "attention to the play of appearances." The focus is still on the given objects, which are simply seen in another way, that is, with an enhanced sense of the presence of the situation (14).[34] The point in this context is that Panton's design points reflectively to itself and urges a kind of "aesthetic perception," apparently "wanting" to be perceived with an enhanced sense of presence, of being specifically in this room, right here and right now, and achieving this through "designerly" and sensuous means such as color, materials, and form. Combining these means into a whole creates not only ambience but a reflective space that challenges our perception of space. As a consequence, design with this kind of intensified ambience seeks to attract attention and thus both engages the users or the audience in the process of creating ambience and reflectively points to itself as a place of meaning making.[35]

The Conceptual-Hermeneutical Platform: Challenging Concepts

Next, apart from the sensual aspect, aesthetics deals with issues of meaning and understanding. The layers of meaning encapsulated in design may, for example, appeal to a linear process of understanding where meaning is immediately apprehended, or it may demonstrate a resistance to understanding. Thus, interior designs such as Panton's may present themselves as riddles or with a content of riddles or features (in the form of sensually communicating details, such as fur on the walls, or abstract idea content) that almost defy comprehension.

As a discipline, hermeneutics frames processes of understanding (*hermeneuein* in Old Greek means interpretation) based on the assumption that we can never complete the process of attributing and constructing new meaning in our quest for understanding. Thus, acts of interpretation and understanding are always dynamic processes; parts always relate to an ongoing construction of a whole (Gadamer 1960), and every process of understanding implies the flip side of nonunderstanding, whereby a plurality of meanings is acknowledged (Hörisch 1998). In this context, hermeneutical devices deal with our access to understanding (and with the denial of understanding) as well as with the aesthetic coding of this access or denial in design objects. This is indeed a question regarding the relationship of the design to its content of meaning. In addition, this level of aesthetic coding not only deals with the specific content (*what* the intended meaning of a specific design might be on a conceptual level, its idea) but also with the question of its rhetoric: how the meaning is staged and how the design reflects this meaning through its actual presence and unfolding in a physical setting by means of sensual aspects of form, materials, and color, for example. Thus, what is the "meaning" (if it can be stated), how is it conveyed, and by what means? How does the design present itself to our understanding? As something that is easily comprehended or as something that resists comprehension? That is, how does the object relate to meaning?

The Sensual Incarnation of Meaning

In his second interlaced structure of meaning, Merleau-Ponty deals with the physical incorporation of meaning in sensually given objects. The relationship of sense and meaning is also central to Dewey's aesthetic theory and to the Kantian concept of schematization where imagination engages in the construction of new meaning in combining the sensuous and the conceptual (see chapter 7). To anticipate this discussion as well as the general concept of imagination (see chapter 4), one of the central capacities of the imagination seen within the context of aesthetic artifacts is to create new modes and models of relating the sensuous-material and the ideational-conceptual. Hence, Merleau-Ponty addresses the way in which physical objects relate to their content of meaning—how every concrete, visible manifestation carries with it an invisible idea or meaning. Thus, I combine the frameworks of phenomenology, with its focus on the conditions of sensual experience, and hermeneutics, with its grasp on the conditions for understanding. My argument is that meaning in design, as a basic condition, is given only within a material (i.e., a sensually given) presence that appeals to experience and is capable, within this "aesthetic" frame, of challenging the boundaries of understanding. This leads the discussion into the realm of classical art-oriented philosophical aesthetics, which, roughly put, deals with the mediation of meaning in aesthetic objects and our understanding of them.

Merleau-Ponty (1964) speaks of a bond "of the flesh and the idea, of the visible and the inner brace [*l'armature intérieure*] that the visible makes manifest and hides," meaning that the idea is not the opposite of the sensual but rather its double and its depth (193). An additional point is that the idea, although it is always a part of the sensual, cannot reach the surface of direct manifestation; instead it operates as "transparence behind the sensible" (194). This idea paradoxically hides and displaces itself as it reaches manifestation. The radicalism in this dialectic of the sensual and the idea lies in the fact that Merleau-Ponty breaks with the metaphysic, post-Platonic notion of the idea as something otherworldly or transcendent. According to Merleau-Ponty, the idea may be difficult to grasp, but it is always inherent in the sensual as a structure of immanent transcendence.

It is this structure that I consider productive to investigate in the context of aesthetics and design. In the same way that the sensuous relationship between an appealing object and a sensitive subject can be called aesthetic, I wish to shed light on the relationship between sensuous surface and incarnated idea and the challenge to understanding inherent in this more or less complex incarnated idea; the purpose of this analysis will be to further our understanding of why some objects are regarded as aesthetic.

That Merleau-Ponty's notion of incarnated ideas can be applied to design is obvious. Any design item contains an idea, a dimension of immateriality, and design is conceivable only as something that is concretely manifest. In relation to immaterial design, Merleau-Ponty's structure of interlaced meaning indicates that it is nothing without a physical manifestation. The structure must, however, be elaborated if it is to contribute to the field of aesthetic knowledge. I consider this to be a matter of communication, that is, how the relationship between manifestation and idea displays itself in design. While the question has been how design establishes a sensuous relationship with a perceiving and experiencing subject, it now relates to the object itself, asking how the object in its sensual being points to a level of idea content or meaning that it simultaneously contains and conceals in a complex process of displacement.[36]

I consider this operation aesthetic in two respects. First, it unfolds through the sensual being of an object, which links it to the aesthetics of the sensual relation. Second, the relationship between physical manifestation and idea, which can be more or less direct and more or less problematic, has also been a topic of modern, art-based aesthetic theory. The question has been how the work of art is constituted through a specific "form" that (un)reveals its meaning or resists or challenges understanding.[37] I focus on this aspect under the heading of *aesthetic coding*, which examines how an object can attract attention and appeal to the senses (as in the sensual relationship) and be constituted in a way where it demands or even commands a specific order of alignment or mode of understanding by establishing a specific relationship between physical manifestation and idea. It is clear, however, that any process of aesthetic "appreciation" implies a perceiving and aesthetically focused subject; nevertheless, categories of aesthetically appealing objects—objects wanting to be perceived *as* aesthetic, as discussed above in the context of the aesthetic relationship—can still be separated from other objects. The Russian linguist Roman Jakobson (1960) speaks of a self-reflective "poetic function," which, in focusing on the act of communication itself, may be more or less activated within language, thus proposing "poetic language" as having a dominance of poetic function. Thus, we can follow the line of objects with a high degree of "aestheticity," that is, in Kyndrup's conception, with an implicit, communicative construction that points in this direction.[38] This question about the communication of aesthetic objects can be raised historically, as the process of conceiving aesthetic qualities varies throughout history and especially throughout the historical process of augmenting aestheticization. However, my focus in this section will be on some of the general constituents of aesthetically coded communication.

The Concept of Added Quality in Aesthetic Objects

How aesthetic objects contain something "more" has been a central topic of modern, mainly art-based aesthetic theory. With his *Kritik der Urtheilskraft*, Kant initiated an epistemological framework in relation to aesthetic objects by asking how they could be a means of a sensual experience that could not be grasped by means of expression or circumscribed by given concepts. In this kind of reflection, aesthetic objects deal with matters of cognition. Through the notion of reflective judgment, Kant demonstrated how aesthetic media can employ a kind of conceptual reflection that starts from the sensual material and does not know its concept in advance, as it virtually is a meaning that exceeds human expression. The tradition from Schelling and Hegel to Adorno attached this kind of reflection to the work of art and asked how art could be a medium for a representation of an otherwise impossible cognition (e.g., Schelling's idea of experiencing the "absolute" through art). The ability to articulate the aspect of how the work of art can represent more than itself has been one of the major benefits of this kind of theory, and it is far from obsolete today, although it may at one time have been too narrowly focused on art. Besides, it holds considerable potential for critiquing the operations and contexts of aesthetic phenomena—something that has been neglected by the aesthetic theory directly related to design.[39]

Thus, in his influential *Ästhetische Theorie*, Adorno discusses art as a medium that is, paradoxically, inevitably bound to the reality of the given (which, critically for Adorno, is necessarily problematic; as in Adorno's materialist analysis, the given in its fundamental structures is negatively conceived as the result of an economic exchange that leads to human inauthenticity and a leveling of values) while at the same time having the potential to transcend the given and show new meaning potential that might in the end prove subversive or utopian.[40] This transcendence is, of course, a paradox as it cannot in its constitution transcend the conditions of the given. Put another way, although art may encompass a configuration of the "other" of the given, it must always be on the basis of the given. As Adorno (1970) says, "the non-being in the works of art is a constellation of being" (204). In his work, Adorno seeks constantly to address this defining and, hence, unresolved paradox, which contributes to the everlasting energy of his work and demonstrates a structure of the aesthetic medium where, through its own means, it stands constantly on the verge of something else, the "other," the negation of the given. He says that "fantasy" cannot be "that cheap ability to escape being in proposing a non-being as if it existed"; instead it can transform "what the works of art always absorbed from being, into constellations, through which they become the other of being, if only through the specific negation of being." (258).[41] Therefore, the work of art for Adorno is not to be seen as a means of representation but as "apparition" (130), which in itself creates momentary traces of that which is not existing or not yet existing. The work of art can be a medium of the possible-to-come; it may indicate the illusionary character of the nonbeing and the possible. And yet it must always negate itself; this nonbeing can never rise to become being but can exist only within the negated frame of the work of art (Iser 2003).

Still, a common feature of much aesthetic theory has been to conceptualize how art can represent or contain something that is otherwise unrepresentable or incomprehensible, thus functioning as a medium for an otherwise ungraspable surplus of meaning. For Adorno (1970), art evokes a *Herstellung des Mehr*, a production of some-thing "more," whereby the works of art "let themselves be actualized as appearances of expression; they are not only the otherness of the empirical: Everything in them turns into otherness" (126). Thus, art produces its own transcendence of meaning that is not directly represented by the work of art but comes to expression as an otherness (*ein Anderes*) paradoxically conveyed by and separated from the structure of the work of art, in the same way that the work of art is both connected and opposed to the material structures of society. If we extend the reflection from the domain of art, this means that all aesthetic media can contain a function that disturbs linear communica-tion, lets the aesthetic medium appear as an object with a high degree of "aestheti-cism," takes communication in a new direction or attempts to challenge understanding, and perhaps breaks with existing paradigms of understanding.

Following this line of thought, Martin Seel is also interested in the surplus of meaning that aesthetic objects can communicate, but he does not limit himself to the sphere of art, although art is often his main topic. With a focus on the function of human perception in the process of confronting something "other" in a surplus of meaning, Seel claims that the capacity of art is to "bring forward otherwise unrepre-sentable circumstances." Art, in his view, has to do with "ways of human commitment in the real or the unreal, in conditions of the world in the past, the present, or the future. Ways of *meeting the world* are put forward, whereby ways of *meeting the meeting of the world* will be possible" (Seel 2000, 184).[42] Furthermore, this process of ways of meeting the world is not tied to goal-oriented understanding but to a meeting outside the artwork in the human subjects themselves: "Objects of art are a medium for an experience that takes place as a process of an understanding that is not oriented towards a result of an understood. . . . Understanding art is more about an otherwise impossible meeting with otherwise impossible possibilities of perceiving ourselves" (Seel 2007, 38).[43]

Thus, aspects of nonunderstanding or incomprehensibility in aesthetic media engage us in a new understanding; prisms for understanding, new ways of meeting the world, and, reflectively, of meeting this meeting are engaged, which enables new patterns of perception and understanding. Thus, aesthetic objects can function as schemata for a new kind of perception and understanding that transcends everyday perception. In turn, this can lead to a new kind of seeing. Following Roger Scruton (1974), this kind of seeing through an aesthetic medium is a controlled form of "seeing as" that focuses on specific aspects, consciously reflects this seeing, and points to an "unasserted thought" that is otherwise impossible outside the medium of art (115). Scruton claims that "the 'unasserted' nature of 'seeing as' dictates the structure of aesthetic experience" (120). Aesthetic media can be employed to grasp aspects of meaning that are otherwise difficult to handle. Thus they point to or aim to incorporate the added value of transcending meaning.

Furthermore, Adorno points to the ability of works of art to contain aspects of graspable certainty and determination, as well as aspects of the opposite, the indeterminate, and thus enigmatic. In pointing to a truth that can never be directly expressed, he argues that works of art act as a "question mark" that indicates a direction as well as a disruption: According to Adorno (1970), works of art can describe a figure that indicates a "passage in that direction . . . where the work of art breaks off" (188).[44] Thus, "the enigmatic of the works of art is their being broken off [*Abgebrochensein*]" (191). In this kind of reflection, the added value of meaning resides outside the aesthetic medium, which then indirectly points to it and, in the same turn, demonstrates its impossibility as direct presence. However, the impossible meaning gains a sort of representation as the energy of the aesthetic medium is focused on a point outside its capacity as a medium; the aesthetic medium may also indirectly point to the other side of the borderline in a reflective movement that points to its own limitation and thus the borderline of the possible.[45] Adorno (1970) states this in the seemingly paradoxical formula of solving the enigma of art by pointing to its foundation: "To solve the enigma amounts to indicating the reason for its insolvability: the gaze with which the work of art looks at its beholder" (185).[46] Instead of remaining in a safe position as viewers comprehending an object, we must try to make this relation dynamic and shift our perspective, making our own position vulnerable to the meaning that meets us, much in the way that Merleau-Ponty suggests through the notion of the all-encompassing *chair* (flesh). Reversing the positions of viewing offers us a perspective on ourselves from an otherness, an alterity of meaning, which at the same time points to a borderline of meaning and understanding. In this way, then, we are able to glimpse this outside of meaning indirectly.

As objects of everyday life are often intended to operate discreetly by means of smooth functionality, it may perhaps be difficult to see design in this context of an aesthetic negation of reality and proposals of new models of understanding pointing outside meaning. We may, however, ask the same type of questions of design, regardless of the difference in constitution as medium: how it is capable, as a medium, of pointing in a direction where it must break off, that is, how it points to the borderlines of understanding in challenging given conceptions. Next, it is worth asking designed objects the difficult question concerning how they define a relationship with reality within the relationship of physical manifestation or idea, how they can be seen as media for meeting the world in new and reflective ways where new kinds of experience and forms of experiencing are evoked, and how they point, if possible, beyond themselves to some form of meaning that is not yet existing or cannot yet be conceived.

In the case of Panton, the conceptual framework of inquiring about the aesthetics of communicative structures can lead to different levels of questioning. First, it is obvious that for Panton, it is not enough to inquire about the sensual effects of ambience. One must also inquire about the idea content, which in this case has to do with proposing a utopian vision of new modes of being and living in and with design. In the historical and cultural context of the 1960s, Panton's design can be seen as a provocative response to a climate of pervasive cultural conformity, with little room for alternative ways of living. In this broad ideological context, Panton's design in a sense proposes a new model for life. The design makes a proposal for a way of engagement and meaning that in its full extension is not yet existing and whose nature the design can only indicate: What would it be to live according to this design? Second, we can ask how Panton's design proposes new orders of experiencing and meeting the world. Only by raising this question can we fully appreciate the radicalism of his design: it not only contains a pure idea as a nonobliging experiment; it performs and executes the utopian potential of this idea. Panton's design contains a strong and ideologically biased idea of living differently but expresses this idea through a physical manifestation. In short, his design tries to enable us, "afford" us,[47] to live in new ways that could hardly be imagined before the realization and presentation of the design. In this sense, his design also encompasses a dimension of implying an irreversibility of a before and after—the way we think of and experience design can never be quite the same again. Thus, it performs the new kind of being that it states on an ideological level. In and through its physical manifestation, Panton's design not only suggests an idea of living differently: it fundamentally challenges our very understanding of design.

Reflecting Ideas

On an abstract level, we may ask a number of questions regarding the relationship of design to its content of meaning. I will argue that aesthetics in design within this context concerns how design relates to meaning and modes of understanding. It is not enough to ask what the meaning of a specific design is on a conceptual level (the "idea"); we must also ask how it performs or reflects this meaning in its physical form and how it relates to the kind of self-reflective aesthetic function where it displays a surplus of meaning. In this sense, discussing aesthetics in design is a way of consciously focusing on dimensions of meaning in design but also, on behalf of the designers, on the construction of meaning. How can a surplus of meaning be invested in design, and how can it be reflected in an actual design?

Panton suggests one possible direction by letting the basic idea be so pervasive and effective in his design that it not only enables the sensual relationship by creating an ambience but also produces a surplus of meaning on an ideological level by pointing to a different way of life. Another way of approaching aesthetics is to maintain a surplus of meaning but have the idea be more indirectly mediated in the design, that is, less directly performed or displayed in the sense of implying a new overall structure of meaning through the design.

This principle can be observed in a series of chairs by the Danish-English designer Louise Campbell (see also the further discussion of the chairs in chapter 5). Two of them are one-off chairs, *Honesty* (1999, figure 3.5) and *Bille Goes Zen* (2003, figure 3.6); the third, *Veryround* (2006, figure 3.7) is manufactured in a limited number by Zanotta, Italy.

Figure 3.5
Honesty. One-off chair in ash made by joining two identical but differently scaled layers, 1999. *Design:* Louise Campbell. *Photo:* Erik Brahl.

Figure 3.6
Bille Goes Zen. One-off chair in ash named after the cabinet maker Lars Bille Christensen, 2003.
Design: Louise Campbell. *Photo:* Erik Brahl.

Although the materials vary (the first two are made in ash, and the third in 2 millimeter powder-coated steel sheet frame), all three chairs are mediators of the same principle. The construction is based on two identical but differently scaled circular layers revolving around a central focal point. Assembled, the layers produce an expanded, three-dimensional circular structure that rests directly on the floor. Viewed as a continuous series, the chairs represent an ongoing meditation on—and a perfection of a principle of—construction where the most recent, *Veryround*, appears as the current culmination. It is not only round in its overall outline but also at the level of detailing, compiled by 260 identical circular modules in different sizes.[48]

Campbell's chairs represent a play with construction and form. The form does not rationally follow the functional premise of being a chair made for sitting; instead, it follows the experimental principle of the two-circle structure. In this sense, the chairs are attempts at bringing a rather abstract idea to life. The idea does not remain abstract; it is (as with most design) sensuously laid out in tangible materials, claiming a presence in actual space. Normally the sensuous qualities of design produce the extra element of the design that is often regarded as "aesthetic." Here, the designs are superbly

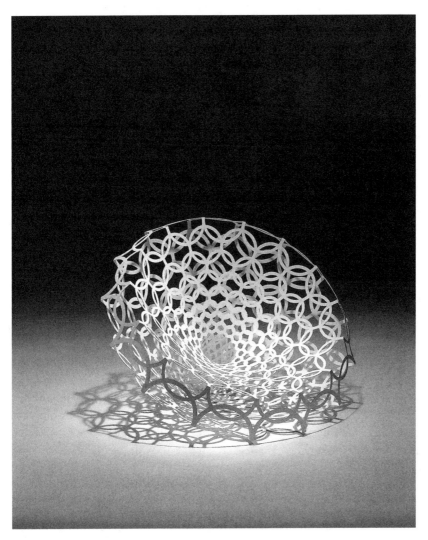

Figure 3.7
Veryround. Chair made in laser-cut 2 millimeter powder-coated steel sheet frame. The chair consists of 260 identical circles in different sizes. *Design:* Louise Campbell. *Photo:* Zanotta.

executed and, in the case of the first two chairs, brilliantly handcrafted. But more than anything else, it is the idea of the formal and nonfunctional principle of circularity that creates a surplus of meaning in this design.

As with Panton, the idea pervades and determines the design, and in both cases there is an almost perfect integration of idea and physical manifestation. The idea is relevant only insofar as it is put to work; the physical expression of form has little relevance without an idea or meaning content. In my view, this is a hallmark of aesthetics in design. But where Panton's design reflectively points to the fact that there is some kind of idea operating in and through the design (clearly evident in the way his design, with a direct and aggressive appeal to the senses, performs the pointing to the utopian idea of a different way of life), in Campbell's chairs the idea is a more subtle experiment of pure form. The idea, of course, is the overall formal and nonfunctional principle that governs the design; however, it works simply through the design and does not reflectively point to itself as idea.

This structure of investigating how an idea can be reflected in the design and how it can create a surplus of meaning (the overall aesthetic question of how design relates to meaning on a general level) can not only be described in design; it can also be used more actively (by designers) as a tool for reflection in the design process. In relating these two aspects of design as an aesthetics of communicative self-reflection, where the x-axis represents the relation to aesthetic function (the degree of surplus meaning in relation to functional qualities) and the y-axis represents the reflection of the idea, it is possible to see how different kinds of design communicate aesthetically in different ways (see figure 3.8). This coordinate system encompasses different modes of aesthetics. Functionality is not opposed to "aesthetics" as such, but as illustrated with the two axes, it has its own kind of aesthetics with a nonsurplus in the appearance of the sensuous relationship.[49] Designs in this category include the purely functional design of everyday objects that may also reflect their idea content in different ways. At one end of the spectrum is anonymous design, where we simply see through the inherent idea; at the other end of the spectrum is the sort of functional design that displays its idea in a way that reflects only that there *is* an idea but also, through this mechanism, often explains itself in a process of "natural mapping."[50] Likewise, there may be (as described in the cases of Panton and Campbell) different modes of aesthetics linked to a great surplus of meaning and appearance. At one end of the spectrum is the purely conceptual design, which does not, however, entirely circumscribe the modality of Panton's highly sensuous experiments but is prevalent when the conceptual aspect is formulated at the ideological level. The other end of the spectrum is where most "lifestyle" design is found, a type of design that uses a high degree of outer appearance with a surplus of appeal to the users, or rather consumers, and where the underlying idea does not have to be reflectively stated. Campbell's design is more experimental than lifestyle (although *Veryround* does have its place in the international circulation of high-end furniture), but she operates with the same approach of indirectly putting the idea to work. The experimental focus of her series of chairs is to challenge the relationship of idea and physical manifestation so that the idea does not take over but acts like Merleau-Ponty's inner structure, manifesting and concealing itself at the same time. In Campbell's case, aesthetics in design is expressed as an ongoing dialogue of outer appearance, constantly hiding and revealing its meaning content.

To sum up, this theoretical framework can be used in analyses and discussions of aesthetics in design (e.g., Where can we place Philippe Starck's *Juicy Salif*? How does it reflect the idea of a lemon squeezer?), but it can also inform designers who need to deal with the challenges of the aesthetic in design on a practical level. The two aspects of aesthetics in design that have been put forward so far—design as a structure of sensual appearance and design as an act of communication that may contain an aesthetic coding that lets an idea or meaning content be physically manifested and reflected in a variety of ways—can lead to a more theoretically focused inclusion of aesthetic matters in the process of designing.

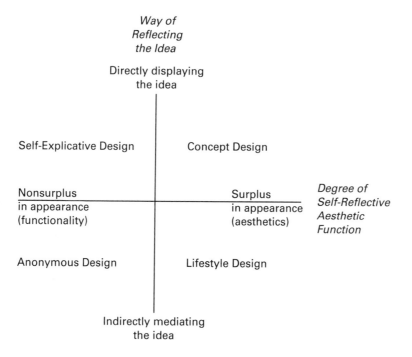

Figure 3.8
Framework for conceiving aesthetics in design as formulation and construction of meaning.

As a next step, it is important to look into the distribution of the sensual and conceptual material of design and how it engages in a discursive context of organizing meaning. With the object again as the point of departure, the perspective now shifts to the level of context that design objects participate in and have the potential to radically change.

The Contextual-Discursive Platform: Aestheticization

In his phenomenological reflection, Merleau-Ponty deals with two interlaced structures on the level of actual experience: that of the perceiver and the perceived and that of the visible and the invisible. Regarding the dominant artificial material culture of late modern societies, it seems relevant to expand Merleau-Ponty's original model with a third interlaced structure of experience that focuses on the object and its influencing contexts.

Merleau-Ponty, as I have already noted, focuses on the conditions of experience itself, whereas the question that we might raise from the perspective of design is how objects shape and condition experience. This reversal from the experiencing subject to the framing and conditioning objects has also been discussed as postphenomenological (see Verbeek 2005, the discussion of Verbeek's notion of materialist aesthetics later in this chapter, and the discussion in chapter 10), that is, as the inauguration of a radical new paradigm in relation to phenomenology. My point here is not to transcend the basic assumptions of phenomenology but to supplement them with the logic of a central element that constitutes the frame of experience: our surroundings and their design and, in extension of this, their aesthetic logic. Thus, my aim is both to remain within the general framework of phenomenology and to expand it with a notion of how experience is constituted on behalf of the world and context of objects that enter into an interlaced and dialogical structure with the experiencing subject. I am interested as well in the argument on a general level. This means that I do not address in this section how various contexts have created specific conditions for constituting the aesthetic character of the object but focus instead on the creation and distribution of the aesthetic on the level of the generalized object: the ability of design objects to frame experience. In the connection of experience and the power of the influence and structure of objects, it becomes clear that aesthetics is not merely about the superficial styling of objects but is in fact something that has epistemological, and thus ethical, implications. When we choose to design the world in certain ways, we also choose strategies of sensual appearance (the first platform), frames of understanding (the second platform), and the distribution of the aesthetic (the third platform), all of which have consequences for the mode of the filter through which we experience our surroundings.[51]

This discussion follows a series of steps. First, I employ Jacques Rancière's aesthetic theory to introduce the field of aesthetics regarding the function of aesthetic objects as distributed within the framework of power and discourses that transmit as well as permit power and knowledge. Next, I explore how this relates to the prevalent framework of the aestheticization of everyday life, which may even reach such a degree of saturation that it is reversed in what has been called *an-aesthetics*. In playing at the meaning of anaesthetization, the term *an-aesthetics* refers to a situation where too much of an aesthetic effect leads to insensibility and a feeling of numbness. Finally, in the conclusion to this chapter, with a reworking of figure 3.8 in figure 3.10, I relate this issue to the overall discussion of how design objects can be addressed as aesthetic.

The Distribution of the Aesthetic

A central point in Rancière's aesthetics in the work *La Partage du sensible: Esthétique et politique* (2000, translated into English as *The Politics of Aesthetics*, 2004), is to investigate aesthetics as a matter of power and politics in determining "what presents itself to sensory experience." Thus, aesthetics can be seen as "a delimitation of spaces and times, of the visible and the invisible, of speech and noise, that simultaneously determines the place and the stakes of politics as a form of experience." Aesthetics is political and ethical in the sense that it deals with the creation and distribution of sensual material and addresses how artistic practices, in their ways of doing and making, contribute to the "modes of being and forms of visibility" (Rancière 2004, 13). It is on this basis that Rancière points to a new paradigm of aesthetics, which he introduces in this way:

First of all, elaborating the very meaning that is designated by the term aesthetics . . . [this term] denotes neither art theory in general nor a theory that would consign art to its effects on sensibility. Aesthetics refers to the specific regime for identifying and reflecting on the arts: a mode of articulation between ways of doing and making, their corresponding forms of visibility, and possible ways of thinking about their relationships. (10)

In this way, Rancière aims to discuss what possibilities are determined by works of art and how they are determined: Thus, in Rancière's conception, aesthetics deals with the constitution and regulation of the space of possibility evoked by artistic media.[52]

In this way, the analysis of aesthetic media has a kinship with discourse analysis in the tradition of Michel Foucault: Here, the focus is on the organization of knowledge in discourse, which structures our access to knowledge. Discourse is organized according to mechanisms of control and regulation (not everything is possible at all times), while simultaneously acting as discontinuous practices without reference to a defining center. They come into being in a dispersion whose frame is not pregiven but evolves as the decentered and decentering movement of the discourse investigates its own conditions as discursive practice (Foucault 1969). In this way, discursive knowledge is not fixed; it is constituted as becoming and explorative. Consequently, Rancière's (2004) perspective on the formation of knowledge not only aims to scrutinize how aesthetic media behave as transmitters of possibilities but also how they produce possibilities in defining domains of the sensual experience. In their way of pointing to new modes of experience, their acts of "distinguishing a sensual mode of being specific to artistic products" (22) and disseminating experiential knowledge, aesthetic media can promote a "recomposition of the landscape of the visible, a recomposition of the relationship between doing, making, being, seeing and saying"; thus, "artistic practices . . . represent and reconfigure the distribution of these activities" (45). This means that aesthetic media have the ability to radically reconfigure and transfigure the territories of "the visible, the conceivable, and the possible" (41): they can lay out possible models for accessing the world in new ways.

Seen in this light, design, despite its diversity of expressions, can be regarded as a medium that often has a direct impact on reality. By contrast, works of art evoke a more indirect effect on our modes of experience. Rancière also links this to politics, as the first level of operation in politics often involves claims and statements about reality:

Politics and art, like forms of knowledge, construct 'fictions", that is to say, *material* rearrangements of signs and images, relationships between what is seen and what is said, between what is done and what can be done. . . . Political statements and literary locutions produce effects in reality. They define *models* of speech or action but also regimes of sensible intensity. (39, first italics his, second italics mine)

Design also produces effects on the symbolic level of rearranging signs and images and of proposing new models of accessing the world (as in Panton's interior designs). In addition, it effects a more direct appeal to the senses, cognition, and notions of organizing meaning in relation to people's lives. Design embodies the principle of distributing the sensible through means of aesthetically appealing artifacts. Through their appeal to the senses and their potential challenge to our understanding, design objects operate as media for staging indirect models as well as immediate and direct sensual and cognitive impact. Consider the basics of an ordinary living room with its appeal to the senses (e.g., with a sofa with large cushions, which promise relaxation), its challenge to our understanding (e.g., with a playful design detail, such as an intriguing chair or lamp or a seemingly soft cushion that is actually hard), or in the organization and delimitation of what is visible versus invisible, possible versus impossible (what action is enabled through the overall constitution of the room's content and arrangement of furniture, its colors, and the staging of ambience).

Strategies of Aestheticization

Aestheticization is a mode of distributing the sensual with an emphasis on the overall impact of aesthetic media on experience. In this conception, it is a concept with a high degree of sensual appeal and aesthetic coding in the surroundings of human beings and the transmission of this process through specific media. In this context, I point to design as a common designator for the mass media of the objects, interiors, and surroundings that we engage with.

Aestheticization can be viewed diachronically and synchronically. In a diachronic reflection reaching back in history, aestheticization is primarily related to the rise of modernism and mass culture in modern, especially Western, societies. According to Mike Featherstone, whose book *Consumer Culture and Postmodernism* (1991) is seminal on the topic, this aestheticization is a result of a historical process where the boundaries of high culture break down and devices and form repertoires of art enter the domain of everyday life. Featherstone points to three ways of addressing the aestheticization of everyday life: first, historical avant-garde movements such as the Dadaist and the surrealist movements tried to "efface the boundary between art and everyday life"; second, attempts have been made to turn life into a work of art; and third, and most important, modernity has produced a new culture and a commercial manipulation of images—especially through the medium of advertising, which found expression in Paris in the nineteenth century,[53] where the massive effect of "the displays, performances and spectacles of the urbanized fabric of daily life" entailed a "constant reworking of desires through images": "Hence the consumer society must not be regarded as only releasing a dominant materialism, for it also confronts people with dream-images which speak to desires, and aestheticize and derealize reality" (66–68). This notion, of course, hinges on the role of the image and an acceptance of the power of the image to alter conceptions of reality. In this way, Featherstone follows Baudrillard's analysis of the effect of the dominance of images in effacing the difference between image and reality and, as a consequence, creating a new, hyperreal, superficial, and "aestheticized" version of life (68).[54] In this idea, aestheticization comprehends the "direct impressions, sensations and images of the consumer culture 'dream worlds'" (72). This process is, according to Featherstone, not only a result of a postmodern culture of the sign that lets superficial signifiers circulate in an erasure of the sense of reality; it can also be traced back to the culture of the carnivalesque and the medieval marketplace, where meaning was also staged and arranged in order to appeal to the public on the level of aesthetics and appearance in an attempt to draw them in.

Apart from acknowledging the historical heritage of seductive image cultures, we may also examine the mode of operation in aestheticization synchronically and systematically. Important questions include those of ontology (the effect on and consequences for the being of things), extension (the reach of aestheticization), and structure (the organizing principle of aestheticization).

First, the question of ontology is very much in line with Featherstone's reflection in following Baudrillard. The question is whether the prevalent aestheticization produces an effect of (image-dominated) simulation that creates new unreal (counter-) images of reality, and if so, what their effect is. Does aestheticization result in the creation of superficial simulated meaning that precludes access to a "more real" reality behind the appearances? It is part of a critical approach to a concept such as aestheticization that we attempt to look behind it. In this way, Featherstone analyzes the mechanism of aestheticization. Likewise, in his analysis of the *Alltagsästhetisierung* (everyday aestheticization), the philosopher Ernst Oldemeyer (2008) operates critically with a differentiation of the world of appearance of aestheticization, *Scheinwelt der Alltagsästhetisierung,* which he sees as subsequent to and a consequence of the aesthetic strategies surrounding goods, *Warenästhetisierung,* and the "actual lived life of most people" (24).

Thus, the premises of this approach are that we have the critical and analytical capability to separate the real from the fake, reality from the world of appearances. But this critical opposition of real versus simulation may also produce an incorrect perspective on the ontological effect of aestheticization. It may be less a matter of producing a new hyperreal level of reality than it is the result of creating the pervasive and omnipresent artificial cultures of images and of design aiming for the highest possible sensual appeal, even if this is also part of the picture that can be encountered in a very concrete sense, for example, in theme parks with their fabrication of a simulated counterreality. Aestheticization may be more a matter of examining how the interface that we apply when we meet the world is changing as a result of strategies of making objects and surfaces more sensually appealing, applying aesthetic coding, and asking how this process affects experience.

In this sense, aestheticization is not so much about the artificial and superficial creation of hyperreal meaning, which will always be at a distance to something more real or authentic, and more about staging and distributing meaning in a way that changes the conditions of experience. Design is everywhere, and the fact that it constantly enters and pervades new areas of our everyday surroundings (however diverse they may be)—from the interiors of houses and staging of urban cityscapes, to small electronic devices such as smart phones and tablet computers, and the organization of services according to design principles of function and aesthetic appeal—is not evidence of the creation of a particular domain of artificial form and appearance in the realm of advertising or commercial goods; rather, it is a structural change in the general appearance of the world and its organization of meaning. Tablet computers, for example, are vehicles of aestheticization, not because they contribute to the creation of the overall number of beautiful forms in the world (even if Apple might think that its iPads do that), but because they, following Rancière, "determine what presents itself to sensory experience" when they serve as media for knowledge and entertainment and become devices for a discursive structuring of knowledge and through this process enable and condition experience.

The question of extension next deals with the degree of pervasiveness of design and whether the aesthetic is just one large, undifferentiated mass of sensual appeal. How far does aestheticization reach, and how does it permeate the world of material objects? On the one hand, we might state that aestheticization is ubiquitous: not only are we surrounded by things that strive for sensual appeal, but even the immaterially operating knowledge society depends on materially present objects, just as all software depends on hardware in order to be realized. Konrad Paul Liessmann (2010) states that we live in a time of light materials, as "things lose their weight and materiality through modern production technology. . . . It is as if all matter [*Stoff*] has changed into a sovereign play of forms" (18–19). As a means for things to obtain presence and relevance for us in their play of form and matter, aestheticization is noncircumventable. Yet things are not just things; they are differentiated in a wide variety of ways. In relation to design, I address this issue in the next section.

Furthermore, the field of aestheticization demonstrates borderlines concerning degrees of the aesthetic, where there is too much or not enough of the aesthetic. This reverse side of the aesthetic has been described by Wolfgang Welsch (1990) as *an-aesthetic*, a state of being where the "elementary condition of the aesthetic, the ability to feel, has been negated" (10). The an-aesthetic should not be seen as the pure negation of the aesthetic but as its condition and border, as it is part of a dialectic with the purpose of demonstrating what the nature of the aesthetic is—in Welsch's view, the ability to feel. In this conception, the an-aesthetic ranges from the "zero phenomenon to the hyper phenomenon of the aesthetic" (11). Thus, the an-aesthetic can be detected when aestheticization becomes excessive and we are overwhelmed by overly designed things with excessive detailing; that is where aestheticization becomes nauseating. A lack of the aesthetic can also occur when nothing has any particular appeal or coding, and everything is bland and ordinary. Thus, the aesthetic can be intensified to the degree of hyperintensification or deintensified to the degree of nothingness. With regard to the pervasiveness of design as an aesthetic medium, it can have different impacts and effects, depending on whether we are dealing with one end of the spectrum—overdesigned lifestyle trends or theme parks—which causes dizziness in a constant attraction of attention, or with the other end of the spectrum with everyday objects of anonymous design that we barely notice. Alternatively, we may also focus on the main aspect of design as creating a dominant and omnipresent culture of the aesthetic as the filter through which we experience the world and our interface for meeting the world. The main point in this context is that design creates a pervasive structure of aestheticization that shapes the condition for us, our action, and our behavior.

In this way, the issue of the pervasiveness of the aesthetic leads to the question of how it is organized and what characterizes its principles of organization. This is an almost impossible question to answer because the aesthetic is such a vast field with a wide range of appearances. Still, something can be said about its fundamental structure.

In a reflection on the pervasiveness of the aesthetic, Liessmann (2010) points to the aesthetic experience of everyday life as it oscillates between disappearance (the beauty of it has always already faded) and renewal (it returns). I view this structural dialectic as a basic factor for the way in which aesthetic media enter the overall field of the aesthetic, that is, how aesthetic media can play a role in and contribute to the overall level of aestheticization.

Due to the permanent impermanence of the field of aesthetics, it becomes a defining factor for all aesthetic devices to cast themselves as something that matters within the field. They apply the power of assertion, postulating importance and gaining it not with reference to a solid foundation but through an act of pure assertion. Thus, the organizing principle of aestheticization is fundamentally marked by groundlessness, instability, and productive acts of assertion. Nothing is necessary about the aesthetic, and each act of the aesthetic has to stake its claim, whether in the case of new products, urban settings, or new interfaces that enable technological black boxes to transmit their mode of operation to the outside world. An example is the medium of the neon sign, in itself a medium that evokes presence and materiality on the basis of insubstantial matter—in fact, a type of gas in the glass tubes of the sign. Neon signs claim to have an effect on the cityscape and emit messages of desire and hope (as the classic Coca-Cola sign says, "Enjoy"). They institute an order of meaning that people can use as a mirror to reflect themselves (they are the ones enjoying) and point to levels of meaning that are always out of reach (the enjoyment and the desire can never be fulfilled).[55] As a paradigmatic example of an aesthetic medium, the neon sign is based on instability (due to the gas) and created with the power to assert itself in the open space of possible entrances to aestheticization.

Design and Aestheticization

The next step in examining the organizing principle in aestheticization is to relate the discussion more narrowly to design. This involves questions that take their starting point in the object; how they enter and affect the field of the aesthetic and how they contribute to the organization and distribution of meaning and knowledge.

I address this in relation to three dichotomies: the material character of the design, that is, its material or immaterial extension; the type of reflection in the aesthetic medium, that is, whether the idea of the design is directly or indirectly reflected, as I noted in relation to figure 3.8; and the character and type of representation, that is, whether the design has a tendency toward the real, or whether it points in the direction of new models or simulations of reality.

The question of the materiality of design relates to the means by which design enters the field of the aesthetic, that is, how design, in its act of entering the aesthetic through various devices, also contributes to the structuring of this field. Thus, the perspective here is how objects of design shape and condition experience and how design is part of the distribution of the aesthetic material with consequences for a discursive enabling of meaning.

A starting point for this discussion is Peter-Paul Verbeek's actor-network theory–influenced notion of "material aesthetics" (Verbeek 2005). A pivotal element in his notion of aesthetics is that it focuses not on works of art but on "useful objects" (210) and our bodily interactions with them. Thus, the point is that the "meaning of aesthetics in design then comes to include not only style and beauty but also the relations between people and products, and the ways in which products co-shape the relationship between people and the world" (212).

Thus, in Verbeek's view, design objects not only make the world appear more beautiful but also contain a fundamental mediating role with regard to the specific shape and character of human "experience and existence" (211): "Artifacts inevitably mediate the relations between humans and their world, and therefore also the relations that humans have to the artifacts themselves" (218). Playing this central mediating role for the shaping of experience, the objects entail an "ethical dimension as moral considerations are transformed, shaped or even taken over" (216).[56] Verbeek summarizes the spheres of morality in design in a way that resembles my entry into the discussion of the possible in design with a dimension that lies prior to the creation of the object and a dimension that takes the object as its starting point:

Things carry morality because they shape the way in which people experience their world and organize their existence, regardless of whether this is done consciously and intentionally or not. . . . . Design has two types of moral dimensions. First, designed products play a mediating role in people's moral considerations, and second, the design process may involve moral choices with reference to this mediating role. (216–217)

I believe that with his concept of material aesthetics, Verbeek has delivered one of the most important contributions regarding the sensual impact of design. He relates the material impact of objects to experience and the conditioning of experience, and he demonstrates how we can escape the "aesthetic cage" of outer styling in design.[57] The distribution of the sensual and material is ethical as well as political (as with Rancière) in its consequences. Thus, an integral part of design aesthetics is its ability, by sensual means, to mediate experience, just as Panton's interiors create new visions of experience with broad moral implications (by instituting new ways of interacting with each other) or the medium of the neon sign stages and transmits desire.

What Verbeek lacks, however, is a reflection on immateriality in design. Of course, all immaterial design must have a physical manifestation. But design is a transmitter not only of sensually given meaning but also of immaterial ideas, knowledge, and discourses staging and dispersing knowledge.

An emerging field of design where this is evident is design in relation to ubiquitous computing (or pervasive computing), where digital, miniaturized, and often wireless technology is employed to generate an immaterial stream of information that restructures our surroundings and creates a new distribution of knowledge.[58] In the flow of data, knowledge not only remains immaterial in the sense of the framing that takes place within a discourse; it is also mediated and shaped by the structures of information and their almost invisible devices. In this way, the immaterial becomes informational and related to media. Ubiquitous computing involves a communication with effects that lie beyond human interaction, as the objects may even communicate with each other. As Darren Wershler (2010) states:

Cell phones, the Global Positioning System (GPS), matrix codes, (i.e. two dimensional barcodes), metadata, and radio Frequency ID tags (RFIDs) are all components of an Internet of Things that is insinuating itself into formerly mute objects, making them garrulous. Fitted with these technologies, things *do* talk to each other constantly, in codes and machine languages, at incomprehensible speeds, outside the realms of the audible and the visible. (200)

Thus, the flow of self-sufficient data is changing our relation to our surroundings; it instills an invisible subtext, rendering our interaction both physical and digital. However, at the same time, a series of material touch points is needed. QR codes (figure 3.9), or numeric "short codes" (see Wershler 2010, 209) function as entry points to the digital stream of information, while the smart phone with its scanning device for QR codes offers a means of materially decoding the coded message.

My point is that there is a spectrum of material and immaterial structures of sensual appearance and discursive, informational knowledge that influences the ways in which design stages and has an impact on experience. Depending on type and material extension, design can enter the field of the aesthetic in several ways; a general typology, however, is the spectrum of the material and the immaterial. A key point is that in

Figure 3.9
QR code. Scan it and see what it hides.

most, if not all, cases, both material and immaterial effects are involved when design (objects, solutions, services) enters the human domain of creating and evoking meaning. They become part of the aesthetic, thus part of the overall process of the distribution of meaning by means of aestheticization—both by a sensual staging of experience and by shaping the discursive and informational setting of knowledge and meaning.

Next, the dichotomy of material or immaterial can be set in relation to the dichotomies regarding reflection and representation. Considering the degree of reflection, design objects can enter the field of the aesthetic either knowingly and with explicit reflection or discreetly and anonymously. All design objects partake in aestheticization; they simply differ in the degree of awareness they claim to have about this process. This also affects the kind of representation that the design involves. Design with a low degree of reflection has a tendency toward realism, that is, toward confirming the natural and given condition of the existing reality, while design with a high (and even artistic-like) degree of self-reflective bias may open the realm and the boundaries of reality to investigation and exploration in a process of simulating new possibilities of the design.[59]

Seen as a span of reflectivity and simulation versus nonreflectivity and realism, these considerations can be combined, as they are in figure 3.10, with the spectrum of materiality versus immateriality in a coordinate system where the first span is represented by the *y*-axis (linking back to the modes of reflection in figure 3.8) and the second span is represented by the *x*-axis (pointing forward to figures 9.2 and 9.3). This lets us visualize various design approaches toward the field of aestheticization; approaches of materially confirming existing object design (lower left corner), of distributing but not creating new knowledge (lower right corner), of challenging the distribution of the sensual material (upper left corner), or of challenging the distribution of discursively mediated knowledge (upper right corner).

In essence, design can both contribute to and perform the act of aestheticization using different strategies. It can enter the field of aesthetics without challenging its frame; in its (virtually) nonreflective realism, it can obtain a status quo of the sensual or perhaps even contribute to an augmentation of the aestheticized domain of the

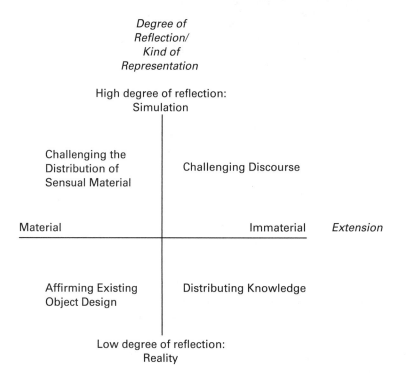

Figure 3.10
Framework for the approaches of design toward the field of aestheticization.

given. Examples of this include the kind of anonymous design that characterizes many everyday utensils, objects, and devices and the constant flow of new lifestyle devices that may be reflective with regard to their formal appearance (as part of their strategies of differentiation on the market) but not with regard to reflecting on the field of the aesthetic as such. On the immaterial level of knowledge, examples of nonchallenging strategies can be seen in incrementally innovative solutions, for example, in service design (as in organizing a postal service without rethinking the frame of the postal service itself) or information design (epigone market followers, for example, in the field of mobile phone technology).

Or design may challenge the ontology, the extension, and the structure of aestheticization. When design challenges the distribution of the sensual, design objects may be employed to question their own contribution to the creation of the aesthetic and their participation as material devices in the distribution of the sensual. That is indeed the case with the critical design movement, which has explored the impact, structure, and texture of objects in order to let them raise questions that are not normally raised by design (the omnipresence of electronic radiation in the case of Dunne and Raby's 2001 Placebo Project; figure 9.1). Another example is the deconstructive graphic design that puts its own medium and functional aspects (e.g., readability) at stake.[60] But this category also includes the kind of experimental furniture design explored by Louise Campbell where the chairs, in reflecting the circular principle, raise the question of their own entry into the aesthetic domain of objects. And it includes design that challenges its own distribution of meaning. As a tendency, this is evident in Campbell's chairs and even more in Panton's interiors, which, by generating new conceptions of living and interacting, push the boundaries of the ability of design to entail, contain, and transmit discourses of meaning. Thus, Panton's design ultimately aims at changing and transfiguring the given characteristics of the aesthetic domain; it aims at constructing new schemata for sensing and understanding our surroundings, and in this act, it points to a radical transfiguration of how the aesthetic frames and conditions experience.

Or the process of entering and, if possible, changing the ontology, the extension, and the structure of aestheticization by challenging the transmission of discursive knowledge through design is evident in design that seeks to push the boundaries of this transmission of knowledge. That is evident in conceptually biased design that aims for a radical and utopian change of the given as in the antidesign and radical design movements of the 1960s, which protested the focus on styling in commercial design and sought to evoke new (impossible) possible futures in and through sketching. On a more mundane level, it is evident in the ambitions of products and services that strive for radical innovation; a radical innovation on the level of a product type can be seen in combined product-service, for example, smart phone apps that open the electronic device to a vast range of new possibilities and render it an open-ended structure for a variety of discourses: Through apps, the digital device of a smart phone or a tablet computer becomes a medium of discursive concentration as well as dispersion.[61] Smart phones aestheticize not because they look good but because they propose new models of structuring experience.

Thus, design has an aesthetic impact on sensual, conceptual, and contextual levels. In this reflection of the aesthetic—and the aesthetic as a concept that goes beyond superficial styling—design is opened to possibilities in a variety of directions. In the following chapters, I use the concepts of the imagination and the imaginary to explore how this evoking and engaging of possibilities is enabled and takes place, and how the evoking of possibilities plays a central role for the constitution of design as a medium.

4 Imagination

In this chapter, I introduce the general concept of imagination. I focus primarily on the historic idea of imagination but also extract elements from the tradition that can be made relevant for a generic reflection on design.

As a basic premise, imagination is vital in design, as it is in all human thinking and creation. When we imagine, we obtain a visually oriented abstraction that can take us in new directions and lead us to examine new possibilities. Consequently imagination is a general human capacity; without it, we would have only "dull materiality," to use the words of the French philosopher Jean-Paul Sartre. At the same time, imagination initiates, in John Dewey's (2005) words, a "venture into the unknown" (284): to engage the imagination is to render meaning open and search for new possibilities. Thus, the sociological philosopher Peter Murphy (Murphy, Peters, and Marginson 2010) states: "The work of the imagination does not just represent 'what is absent'. It also positions objects that otherwise could not exist" (28). Through imagination, we get to the other side on what is given in the world of reality. Through the formative structure of imagination, we can apprehend an image that eventually can be transposed to the creation of an object. Whether imagination is an exclusively human capability may be an open question (other intelligent animals also stray away from dull materiality and pure instinct), but it is surely a genuinely human capability that has always been—and continues to be—a driving force behind the making of the modern world. Without the ability to imagine new possibilities, there would be no expansion of the notions and concepts of what it means to be human.

The imagination is not only a specific capacity within the human consciousness; the assertion of it has a history that has given rise to different ideologies of the imagination. Of particular interest to design is the notion that links imagination with the productive force of creativity and with the concept of human consciousness as freely able to produce images and meaning more or less related to reality: "In order to create, one must have the ability to *imagine*. Imagination is required within all fields of design,"

(Stolterman and Nelson 2003, 165). The link between imagination and creativity is rooted in English empiricism and European romanticism. Since the romantic era, imagination has been celebrated as a locus of human creativity, that is, as the seat of a limitless and transcendent mental activity that can lead to radically new creations by staging, setting, transforming, coalescing, synthesizing, and blending meaning (Casey 1976; Kearney 1998; Coleridge 1984; Fauconnier and Turner 2002; Wunenburger 2003, Murphy, Peters, and Marginson 2010).

Concepts of the Imagination

As a concept, imagination dates back to antiquity. Under the term *fantasy*, Aristotle and Plato analyzed its capacity for imagining things, rendering visible and evoking appearances and dream images, all meanings that are implied in the Greek word. In medieval times, the word was adopted as *phantasia* and, at the same time, translated into *imaginatio,* with the latter implying the role of the image in imagination. Imagination as a concept also carries with it the ontology of the unreal through the derivation of the imaginary.[1]

It was not until later, in the movements of the Enlightenment and romanticism in the eighteenth and nineteenth centuries, that imagination was imbued with special powers and given a special place within the human mind and spirit. Perhaps the "Enlightenment created the idea of imagination"; however, it was in romanticism that imagination was proclaimed and charged with aspirations of being an active and dynamic source of inspiration as "a force, an energy, not a state of being" (Engell 1980, 3, 6).[2] The investigation of imagination as a matter of epistemology was pivotal to the Enlightenment and its ramifications in English empiricism, with its interest in the sensual foundations of and mediations between body and mind for authors such as Hobbes, Locke, and Hume as well as in romanticism. This applies if the human mind is seen as merely reflecting reality, as in the empiricist concept of reproductive imagination. Here, all creations of the imagination have some form of sensual equivalent in the outside world, although the equivalent may be temporarily displaced (as in memory) or result in new, nonexisting, and previously unseen amalgamations based on existing elements (as in the centaur, which combines a man and a horse). Or it applies if in its creative operations the human mind is somehow capable of transcending reality, as in the radicalized version of the romantic notion of "productive imagination," a concept originally devised by Kant (1990, B151) and later adopted by the romantics.

This view of human imagination quickly leads to considerations about the powers and limitations (if any) of human creativity. Thus, romanticism shaped a series of fundamental concepts related to imagination and its capacity as creative, productive energy. In this chapter, I articulate these concepts as opposite pairs in order to employ them as a basic taxonomy for the operations and workings of the imagination that can also be applied in relation to design.

The basic purpose of stating the structure in dichotomies is twofold. First, imagination per se cannot be grasped or analyzed directly; we cannot place it on the table and dissect it.[3] But we can attempt to describe its elements of operation indirectly. Second, the complexity of the imagination is stated by its participation on both sides of the respective dichotomies. It is, for example, both a movement of internalization, where the fullness of the image is posed with enthusiasm and a belief in the transcendence of meaning, and a process of externalization and reflection, with an understanding of the emptiness of the image and the constitutive immanence of all meaning.

Internalization-Externalization

Romantic authors such as Percy Bysshe Shelley, S. T. Coleridge, and Novalis, all contributed to the establishment of a discourse of creativity as something rooted in a mental setting in relation to the appearance of the world. Thus, a basic principle in romanticism is internalization, the "inward sight," to use a phrase from Shelley's 1821 treatise, *A Defense of Poetry* (Shelley 2002, 533), where the romantics, in a process of reverting the structural relationship of inside and outside, sought to discover the wonders and freedom of the inexhaustible and unbounded inside consciousness and let the inside serve as the central basis for conceiving meaning and apprehending the world.

At the same time, a central insight of romanticism is that imagination must be externalized in a medium if it is to have any effect.[4] Novalis (1965), who famously said that "the secret way is going inward," noted that this inward journey had to be complemented with an outward gaze: "the second step must be an active, outward gaze—a self-active, unexpended perception of the outside world" (422).[5] The gaze must be directed outward, toward the world, but it has to begin with a detour to the inside of consciousness. The gaze must be tinted by the operations of consciousness as it "dissolves, diffuses, dissipates, in order to re-create" (Coleridge 1984, 304) and thus serves as a locus for the creation of new meaning. It must also be mediated, for example, in works of art, the preferred medium in romanticism, in order to have any effect. Thus, the romantics discovered that aesthetic media can be regarded as interfaces of our meeting with the world, as they create and employ schemata for the way in which we apprehend and comprehend the world. Whereas the romantics worked with texts and paintings, contemporary culture accesses the same sort of interface through the sensually mediated imagination of design. Thus, imagination in design should be investigated as structures of meaning that may originate in a mental concept but are effective only on the level of the actual design.

As a model for creativity in design, the structure of internalization and externalization is informative in several ways. First, we see that the creation of new meaning may occur in the formative powers of imagination in the mind (in this way, the detour of internalization is necessary because it provides access to a potential exploration of the premises of experience and cognizance), but it comes to itself only in the meeting or refraction of inside and outside. Second, we see that this must take place in a medium that is not necessarily art.

This double condition of imaginative mind and reflective medium is also central to Dewey's theory of aesthetics in *Art as Experience* (2005) in which he explicitly and in a post-romantic manner links aesthetics with imagination: Imagination is something to be explored, reflected on, and communicated within the aesthetic medium. Then he states the engagement with imagination as a method of obtaining the new, based on the refraction of mind and world, of inner and outer vision. In his view, imagination "is a *way* of seeing and feeling things as they compose an integral whole. It is the large and generous blending of interests at the point where the mind comes in contact with the world. When old and familiar things are made new in experience, there is imagination" (278).

In this way, the unknown and unfamiliar become natural and familiar; Dewey (2005) writes that "the far and strange become the most natural inevitable things in the world" (278). He then points at the dialectics of the old and the new and proclaims that "the conscious adjustment of the new and the old *is* imagination" (283). Art, he said, is being privileged as a medium for expressing the "meanings that are imaginatively evoked" (285) and for serving as a frame of the unifying, imaginative vision. In another definitive formulation, he states that imagination is the interaction of inner and outer vision and says that "as imagination takes form the work of art is born" (280). Thus, in Dewey's view, imagination is not so much a special faculty to be designated somewhere in the human consciousness but an ability that "holds all other elements in solution" (286). This synthetic operation in the shape of "meanings imaginatively summoned" can obtain "material expression" of the work of art and hereby interact with the self of the receiver (285). Ultimately, the term *work of art*, in accordance with Dewey's own experience-oriented theory, can be replaced with *design* or other material expressions with aesthetic qualities: We can experience that aesthetically, which obtains meaning through imagination and thus offers an expansion and condensation of experience (Balmer 2009).

Furthermore, the dialectic of internalization and externalization offers a more precise concept of imagination in design, that is, how creativity through imagination not only takes place in the analytically inaccessible minds of designers (Liddament, 2000) but finds its way into and thus is traceable in their design. To illustrate, the process of internalization and externalization can be seen in designers' models or prototypes; they start with an idea or image of the design and then attempt to develop and produce in a mutually informative dialogue with the requirements of possible forms and materials. The designer Louise Campbell said that only to a certain point can a designer think forward because he or she always has to test the idea in three dimensions and in a material form: visual, tactile, and concrete (Folkmann 2007b, 51). In her model work, an imaginative idea for a new design may spring from a blank space but can prove itself only in the explorative process of experimenting with model work: A central part of the imaginative thinking of a designer is to externalize inner thoughts. In fact, the inner idea may not be clear in the sense of a vision or a final design. Campbell says, "I have never got an idea out of the blue with a clear vision of a final design. Instead, I get ideas of directions to explore. [The point is] to see possibilities, to know how to grasp them and to let them lead you rather than drag them in a pre-determined direction" (Duedahl 2012, 6). In this way, ideas do not exist as complete mental entities that need to be dug out of the mind but develop and unfold in a dialogue with their possible expressions. Thus, the structure of internalization-externalization may form a general model for an overall framework for discussing concepts of imagination in relation to the work of designers and to design objects.

In reflecting on the position of imagination in the internalization-externalization framework, several questions pertaining to the issue of knowledge take on urgency: When we apply the inward gaze, what can we possibly know? What is the contribution of new meaning from the imaginative operations of consciousness? In phenomenological discussions, it has been pointed out that a mental image will always be less than worldly perception, because we can project as an imaginary image only what we already know (Sartre 1940). Even romanticism's main apologist of the imagination, Coleridge, pointed out the impossibility of *creatio ex nihilo*, as all faculties of consciousness rely on experience. Nevertheless, imagination holds the potential to transform the material that it might receive from experience, and through the "negation of the condition of being in the world" it can posit "an anti-world" (Sartre 1940, 261), potentially offering new conditions of meaning. The main point is that something happens to meaning when it is internalized; in addition, the boundaries of what is knowable and what is not are blurred. Imagination, then, can be seen as a mental structure that negotiates known and unknown (see chapter 7).

The Image: Fullness-Emptiness

A central legacy of romanticism is the notion of imagination as a creative, productive power that leads to an abundance of new creations. All representations of historical events and movements are marked by their afterlife and subsequent assessment and, roughly speaking, the resulting interpretive constructs. That is also the case for this notion, which is clearly the assessment of a later time based on the rich textures of romantic literature with authors such as (in an English context) Keats, Shelley, and Wordsworth. However, imagination leads not only to abundance but also to its reverse: the emptiness of representation. That is evident if we take a closer look at the role of what is often considered a key product of imagination: the image. Mental imagination is attached to the production of imaginary meaning in the form of images,[6] and, conversely, the perception of images also requires creative imagination: we always compare the outer images with the inner ones (Wettig 2009).

Thus, it is worth examining the character and status of the image in the process of imagination, especially because the ability to create images has been held in such high esteem within the context of artistic creativity. In his seminal study on artistic creation, *Visual Thinking* (1969), the German-born art theorist and psychologist Rudolf Arnheim points to the "imaginative power of visual thinking as performed by artists" (Mareis 2010, 6).[7] In brief, Arnheim meant that "truly productive thinking in whatever area of cognition takes place in the realm of imagery." With this focus on the "truly creative aspects of the mind," he claims a productive role of the visual capacity as an otherwise overlooked complement to rational, discursive cognition (Arnheim 1969, v–vi). With its differentiated view of various aspects of imagery, such as mental images, symbols, signs, and abstractions, Arnheim's work can contribute to a deepened understanding of the importance of specific visual strategies and representations in perceptual processes. In this sense, it complements the abstract notion of the visual in philosophical epistemology as in Kant, where it operates in cognition as mere abstract analogs for things perceived (Kant 1990). Recently, however, Kathryn Moore (2010) has questioned the concept of visual thinking as a(n) (art-)specific "sensory mode of thinking" (11). In response to Arnheim's justified claim of the importance of visual thinking, Moore objects to the dominance that visual thinking has, in her opinion, acquired today within the field of design. She criticizes visual thinking for applying a quasi-metaphysical preconception of a special and in-depth approach to creative processes. Instead she takes her starting point in a pragmatic approach to actual seeing and designing on the basis of perception and knowledge:

Collapsing the visual, intelligence and language and many other fragments of consciousness into a holistic concept of perception takes the supernatural element of aesthetic experience out of the equation, exposing as a myth the part of the story suggesting that a deep-seated sensory resonance or recognition of a universal truth is needed to quicken the pulse. The surprising revelation is that the breathtaking nature of the aesthetic experience is dependent on and limited by what we know. (69)

As Arnheim rightly addresses the role of the image in (artistic) cognition that has been suppressed in discourse on rationalism and intellectualism, Moore is equally right to reject the metaphysical implications of an extreme celebration of and belief in the role of the visual in the kind of cognition that lies behind design processes. She criticizes the idea of a presence in the designing consciousness, but as she then takes the discussion in the direction of a vague concept of an acknowledgment of actual visual processes in design, it is worth casting a phenomenological glance at the workings of image in the process of imagining. This may contribute to understanding the specific ontology of the imaginary image, to the *designo interno*, a concept that Arnheim (1969) attributes to the Italian Renaissance painter Federico Zuccari in contrast to the *designo esterno* of the canvas.

The idea of an imaginary presence of abundant meaning in the mind has been severely criticized. First, the empirical foundation of the mental image has been questioned. The empiricists saw the image as a direct representation of the perceived reality, as a "decayed sense" where, as Hobbes says in *Leviathan* (1651), "after the object is removed, or the eye shut, we still retain an image of the thing seen, though more obscure than when we see it" (Hobbes 1998, 11), whereas the phenomenological tradition points to the consequential disappearance of the object. Thus, Sartre (1940) criticizes what he calls "the illusion of immanence," that is, the notion that imaginary images actually exist with a presence in consciousness and, furthermore, that the actual object is considered to be present in the image. The question is, then, what the consequences of the disappearance of the object are: The object is not actually there, but the consciousness has the freedom to produce new images on the basis of it.

In his short text "Two Versions of the Imaginary" (1955), the critic Maurice Blanchot delivers an important analysis of the imaginary and points to two dimensions of it based on the ability of the imagination to let the object disappear, that is, to negate the object and create an imaginary image of it instead. The first dimension is that the negating inner visualization of the object can lead to a process of idealization and concentration of the essential and the truth of the object; the object is raised to a "higher meaning" (Blanchot 1989, 260). The underlying assumption behind this kind of imaginary is a mimetic understanding of the image, which implies that the object of the image is merely given and that the image expresses the essence of the object. Furthermore, in this model of the imaginary, we recognize the traditional notion of the tendency of artistic means to idealize, whether the art is pictorial or literary. The artist can, through her composition of a given material and the process of the mental image, obtain a "better" and more "essential" representation of reality. Blanchot, however, unmasks this operation as illusionary and manipulative. Through the power of the idealizing movement, we can define the distance that develops between the object and the image and produces the idealization.[8]

Blanchot (1989) then claims not only that the imaginary posits a productive distance, but also that the distance is inherent in the object; it is "in the heart of the thing" (255). In its production of the imaginary, imagination not only makes the object absent; it also paradoxically makes the absence present. The imaginary displays a presence of the absent object; the object is made present *as* absent. In this way, Blanchot compares the image with a corpse that in its presence (the body) of something absent (life) is simultaneously here and nowhere. The image, so the argument goes, in its constitutive strangeness (being here and nowhere at the same time) affirms the possibility of a meaning beyond the world that is not positive-transcendental and full of presence but quite the opposite. Blanchot says that the image not only produces nonunderstanding but a withdrawal from every kind of meaning (260). In emphasizing the dissolution of the relationship to the world, Blanchot concludes:

We have spoken of two versions of the imaginary: the image can certainly help us grasp the thing ideally, and in this perspective it is the life-giving negation of the thing; but at the level to which its particular weight pulls us, it also threatens constantly to relegate us not to the absent thing but to its absence as presence, to the neutral double of the object in which all belonging to the world is dissipated. (262)[9]

For Blanchot, the imaginary space of the image carries with it a risk of detachment from all meaning where "the *meaning* does not escape into another meaning, but into the *other* of all meaning" (263).[10] This is, however, an unavoidable risk of the imaginary image; it always contains the possibility of presence turning into absence. Thus, Blanchot demonstrates precisely that the reverse of the idealizing movement in the negating suspension of the object is the loss of all meaning and of any relationship with meaning.

Blanchot's reflections state the double structure of the image and the imaginary as containing the positive as well as the negative; the image is potentially presence and absence. The issue here is how we should view the implications of Blanchot's analysis. I think it is important to comprehend the negation and the emptiness as constitutive parts of the image, which should keep us from positing the image as a structure entirely constituted of overflowing meaning. At the same time, this understanding of the image should be made productive in our understanding of the emergence of new meaning on the basis of negation. In her comprehensive study of the role of imagination in the age of visual media, Sabine Wettig (2009) tries to replace the notion of imagination as based "on something absent" with the notion of imagination as a process of simulation and the virtual that can bring things to new kinds of mental representation as ideas or perceptions (176). Wettig's point is that our thinking is based on images; they form the "background for the possibility of thinking," according to which our perception is organized and new images can be produced (165). Wettig summarizes her basic points about the complexity of the imaginary of images in this way: "The doubling of the present and the perpetual redefining of the real, the imaginary, the simulated, and the virtual in their indistinguishability seem to promote a new construction of reality" (140).

Thus, the imaginary and the potential virtuality of the image enable new perspectives on reality, which are focused not only on the actual but also on the virtual and, hence, the possible. As a locus and medium for creative imagining, the image can take us in new directions and serve as an important source for the production of new meaning. This is an established insight reaching back to the romantics. The phenomenological point is to acknowledge the double nature of the images as a focal point for the creation and disappearance of meaning. This operation of the productive imagination is at the heart of a phenomenology of imagination aimed at design.

Enthusiasm-Reflection

A prevalent structure in the romantic conception of imagination as a model for creative dynamics is the mutual interaction and dependence of an expansive, centrifugal movement of creative, inspirational enthusiasm that brings the imaginings far beyond any given constraints and a centripetal contraction in the moment of awakening from blind enthusiasm and obtaining reflection. As a matrix for enabling and maintaining imaginative vision, the framework of the duality of enthusiasm and reflection reaches beyond romanticism. For example, it is reflected in Nietzsche's reinterpretation of this dualism as a dynamic that instigates culture in the polarity of the ecstatic Dionysian principle and the prudent and clear-headed principle of the Apollonian in *Die Geburt der Tragödie* (1872). It is also detectable in various models of idea generation and creativity, as in Henri Poincaré's (1982) famous model where phases of incubation, a more or less sudden illumination as a breakthrough of an insight of the "new idea," and verification succeed each other. It is, however, in romanticism that the structure finds one of its most incisive and consequential formulations.

In romantic thinking, the opposite of enthusiasm and reflection is regarded as a dynamic exchange of production and destruction that never ends but oscillates in ongoing alternation. Thus, the structure describes the production of an illusory vision that is consciously complemented by the sober retraction of the illusory moment of the vision. Friedrich Schlegel (1988), the main thinker of early German romanticism, *die Frühromantik*,[11] speaks of a "continuous alternation of self-creation and self-annihilation" (2:109); applied to a proposed illusion, this means that the illusion is not simply canceled in order to disappear but is negated, annihilated, in order to be maintained and even raised to a higher level. The logic of operation lies in the idea that all imaginatively proposed visions are illusory and must be exposed to reflection lest they vanish into thin air. They are redrawn to demonstrate the limits of the representation of the vision and thereby point to the other side of limitation and the fact that there is always more to be said and imagined. In a romantic context, the point is to reach a level of meaning that lies beyond all semantics (Frank 1989). This operation has been labeled "romantic irony." If we compare, rhetorical irony is to say one thing and mean another, while romantic irony is the ability to obtain a critical, reflective awareness, knowing that it is always possible to say more than speech allows and that it is possible to push to the boundaries of representation: The vision is framed by reflection and thereby maintained and made possible in a new way.[12] Hence, Schlegel (1988) speaks of enabling *"echappées de vue ins Unendliche,"* glances in eternity (2:125).

In Schlegel's conception, the oscillation of self-creation and self-annihilation is primarily intended for linguistically mediated utterances. However, its basic structure is that of opening up in enthusiasm and withdrawing in reflection. This also applies to the structure of internalization-externalization: if the obtained vision in the inner space of the mind (the moment of self-creation) is to be maintained, it has to step outside itself and become externalized in a process of leaving the inner space of the mind (qua self-annihilation); that is, it must be modified and marked by a medium. Imagination and inward creativity must be communicated, to use Stolterman and Nelson's (2003) design-oriented phrase: the "designer's formative powers are needed both in the process of coming up with the unexpected idea and in giving shape to that idea so that it can be communicated" (179). Thus, reflection and communication are crucial to imagination and in relation to design. What makes the concept of enthusiasm-reflection in romanticism appropriate as a general model for this specific structural principle of imagination is not only its emphasis on the equal importance of both sides of the movement but also its meta-reflective perspective on the overall movement: Knowing that we can propose visions in imagination and that they have a limit and must be refracted in a medium lets us gain knowledge that lets imagination evolve on a higher level.

Immanence-Transcendence

By employing imagination, we can, in principle, encompass everything. As a vehicle for transformation inside the mind, imagination can act as a catalyst for synthesizing, coalescing, and unifying meaning that is otherwise fragmented or disparate. Since designing can be seen as containing and partaking in a synthesizing activity, it may be worthwhile to take a closer look at the formulation of imagination in relation to synthesis.[13] The main ideologist of synthesis through imagination in romanticism, Samuel Taylor Coleridge, describes the poet as someone who productively "diffuses a tone, and spirit of unity, that blends, and (as it were) fuses, each into each, by that synthetical and magical power, to which we have exclusively appropriated the name of imagination," whereby a "reconciliation of opposite or discordant qualities" (Coleridge 1984, 2:16) can be achieved. Thus, the imagination in Coleridge's description is "esemplastic," a word that Coleridge appears to have coined from the German *In-Eins-Bildung*.[14] However, the important point is not only that imagination is capable of synthesizing; even more important are the structure and process of this operation.[15] Taking the actual dynamics in the coalescing power of imagination into account, cognitive science has explored the many ways in which the mind creates new meaning. Most notably, the theory of blending has demonstrated how new concepts develop based on the fusion of other concepts (Fauconnier and Turner 2002).[16] From the perspective of romanticism, this work can be seen as a comprehensive elaboration on Coleridge's original concept of imagination. In this context, however, the emphasis will not be on the actual blending of concepts as a mental operation, although it is relevant, especially to research into interaction design (see Markussen 2010) and although that is a key concern for Coleridge himself.[17] Instead the emphasis will be on the structural components forming the base of imagination in its process of an ontological transformation of reality.

First, synthesis is not easily achieved; it always takes place in the refraction of the inner infinite space of the mind and the constraints of the outside world. There might be a tendency toward unification and idealization, but it is by definition a struggle that ultimately does not change the ontological status of the fixed and dead objects that are to be transformed, as the following quotation, one of the central formulations of imagination within romanticism, notes:

The imagination then I consider either as primary, or secondary. The primary imagination I hold to be the living Power and prime Agent of all human Perception, and as a repetition in the finite mind of the eternal act of creation in the infinite I AM. The secondary I consider as an echo of the former, co-existing with the conscious will, yet still identical with the primary in the kind of its agency, and differing only in degree, and in the mode of its operation. It dissolves, diffuses, dissipates, in order to re-create; or where this process is rendered impossible, yet still it struggles to idealize and to unify. It is essentially *vital*, even as all objects (as objects) are essentially fixed and dead. (Coleridge 1984, 1:304)

Prior to "imagination" Coleridge sees "fancy," which by receiving "all its materials ready made from the law of association" is entirely bound to and limited by empirical experience. Without going into the references to contemporary philosophy, which might make the paragraph hard to decipher,[18] the crucial point here is that Coleridge describes a concept of a transcendent imagination that is capable of recreating the dissolved while being simultaneously bound to the empirical being of the world. Coleridge's statement has often been cited in support of the ability of imagination to transcend all existing meanings, but it is important to note here that his concept encompasses both ends of the spectrum of empirical foundation and imaginative flights.

I believe that the empirical foundation describes a basic feature of imagination. Even more, this characteristic is relevant to design as a medium that is often bound to material manifestation. Nonetheless, this is relevant to conceptualize as a basic, general component for a concept of imagination because there exists in romanticism and beyond a wealth of notions of the visionary imagination that seek to loosen the ties to reality and fly into the open space of new creation. This is not only a deviation from the original concepts of imagination in romanticism; it also weakens the concept by detaching itself from any kind of relevance or attachment.

Within romanticism, it is possible to find concepts of a rational approach to creative activity that relates to existing reality as well as an indulgence in mystery.[19] Coleridge's statement of the secondary imagination as "co-existing with the conscious will" hints to the latter, as it implies that secondary imagination is somehow beyond the control of conscious volition. In addition, William Blake's notion of a "four-fold vision" has been an inspiration for concepts of creativity, as it leads from perception through phases of analysis, abstraction, and a recognition of the self to disintegration, opening, and surrendering in a stage of a decentering of the creative subject: "One must be willing to give up images of what exists 'out there' and be willing to encounter a new way of thinking and imaging in discoveries what can be" (Ainsworth-Land 1982, 15).

This transcending openness, which in a mystic reversion of subject and object renders the subject passive or even annihilated and thus open to a flow or a passage of new meaning, has also found its way into theories of management.[20] Most recently, transcendence of the subject has been the pivotal axis in C. Otto Scharmer's *Theory U* (2007), where a "letting go" leads to a "presencing" "where we approach ourselves *from the emerging future"* (163), thus enabling a new, unforeseeable. and emerging knowledge that ultimately it is productive to manage.[21] Although romanticism itself was progressive and future-oriented, in a romantic context, it would most often not be the temporality of a "future" that emerged[22] but rather the world or the cosmos in a nontemporal emergence, aiming to "'let go,' to disintegrate, to open oneself up to the spontaneous flow of arising thoughts and images" (Ainsworth-Land 1982, 24). Seen within the context of this tradition, Scharmer's trick is to instrumentalize the openness of spiritual transcendence for the purpose of refining strategies of management. At the same time, however, with this idea of management by spiritual openness, Scharmer grounds transcendence in a sort of empirical foundation. This points to a general aspect of transcendent imagination: all imagining subjects are always immanently embedded in contexts that circumscribe and ultimately condition their imagining.

The polarity of transcendence and immanence can be described in terms of possibilizing and actualizing. In *Imagining: A Phenomenological Study* (1976), the philosopher Edward Casey proposed the term *possibilizing* to describe the act where the imagination opens the door to "pure possibility," which is autonomous, in contrast to instrumental "hypothetical possibility," and emerges in the autonomous operation of imagination (206). Hence, the "function of possibilizing cannot be reduced to the projection of alternative means to a preconstituted end, an end determined by the demands of representation or expression" (206). Casey situates this process within the communication of the aesthetic medium—art, to be precise—which also offers a framing of the possible in the new setting of experience:

The possibilizing activity of imagination in art opens up an experiential domain that would not otherwise have been available either to the artist or to the spectator. This domain is one in which *everything is appears as purely possible.* Within the medium-bound, spatio-temporal limits of a given work of art, the domain of the purely possible emerges whenever imagining is functioning autonomously. (206)

On the one hand, then, possibilizing opens the space of meaning and attributes it with a tendency toward transcendence where the "possibilities are themselves ends" (Casey 1976, 231). On the other hand, the aesthetic medium plays an important role in actualizing the possible, that is, in embodying it and thus giving it an expression within the context of empirical immanence.[23] Of course, going beyond the aesthetic medium of art, this also applies to design as a dialectical interrelation that engages a sense of pure possibility and gives it expression, and even direction, within a logic of projection in the medium of design (see chapter 10). Enhancing Casey's notion, the moment of possibilizing can be described as an active search for new possibilities; "to possibilize" is to transcend the existing elements of the given and open the imagination to the potential of pure possibility. Thus, possibilizing is close to Musil's notion of *Möglichkeitssinn* (see chapter 2), as things might always be different, and we can make new discoveries in the element of the nongiven or, rather, the not-yet-given.

In essence, in its position within a spectrum of empirical immanence and visionary transcendence of the concrete and the abstract, imagination describes the figure of a spiral. It clearly demonstrates a vertical movement of elevation, rising above the disparate parts of empirical material in a search of synthesis and creation beyond conscious volition. But it is also anchored in the horizontal grounding of empirical matter. The actual things of the world not only prevent imagination from flight into complete abstraction, but conversely, imagination evokes an alteration and transformation of the material that becomes the starting point for the imaginative process. Things do not stay the same throughout the process of imagination. They do not lose their empirical foundation, but they may change in meaning as a result of the power of the imagination to create a space of internalization, enthusiasm, abstraction, synthesis, and transcendence. To illustrate, matters of form or material may undergo transformations of effect and extension in the imaginative process, but they remain bound by certain constraints.

The structure of imagination is that of letting transformation take place in and through a specific medium—in this context, the medium of design. Imagining a new chair (or any other kind of design object) does not mean that the chair evaporates into thin air, not least because the process of imagining is part of a design process that will ultimately result in a new design of an actual, physically present chair. Of course, part of the process takes place in the mind without any claim of a result. On the whole, however, the dynamics of imagination operates with the empirical foundation of chairs (the idea of a chair, the knowledge of existing chairs, the cultural contexts of chairs, and, in most cases, the client brief) as the basis for an abstraction whereby new syntheses of, for example, applied materials, crossovers of functions, and interpretations of contexts for chairs can develop. This dynamics of "unrealizing" abstraction forms a central element of the phenomenology of the imagination that I examine in the next chapter.

5 A Phenomenology of Imagination in Design

In the previous chapter, I described basic aspects of the structure of imagination under the topics of internalization-externalization, fullness-emptiness, enthusiasm-reflection, and immanence-transcendence.

In this chapter, I develop a concept of imagination that is able to enter into a dialogue with the processes, workings, and operations of design. This conceptual framework can be labeled a *phenomenology of imagination in design*. Its structure relates to the concept of aesthetics presented in chapter 3 and points forward to the rest of the book. Accordingly, I describe it in terms of its sensually, conceptually, and contextually oriented impact:

• The sensual base of the imagination is related to a process of internalization where imagination is effective in consciousness and through the act of negation produces imaginary meaning. The internal production of meaning leads to the discussion of imagination in relation to design practices through acts of "schematization" (chapter 7).

• The conceptual dimension of imagination unfolds in an act of unrealization where the given and actual are at stake at the border of the possible and the imaginary. It is conceptual in the sense that it challenges what meaning is. Through the act of unrealization, new dimensions of meaning are explored, and the imaginary gains in importance as a vehicle and principle of meaning (chapter 8). This facilitates the production of symbolic meaning in design (chapter 9).

• The contextual aspect of imagination is founded in the process where design objects become artifacts with a potential transfigurative effect on our life and ways of experiencing and understanding. On the level of design phenomenology, or in the perspective of a postphenomenology that is oriented toward the role of artifacts in mediating the human relationship with the world (Verbeek 2005), design objects are employed as structures of aesthetic schematization that mediate and create human action (chapter 10).

I enter a conceptual analysis of the phenomenology of imagination by introducing and discussing the operations of negation, unrealization, and transfiguration and explain them mainly through phenomenological theory but also in course of the discussion related to design. In chapter 8, I focus more narrowly on the nature of the imaginary in design and point to the structural condition of its formation on the basis of imagination.

Negativity

The role of imagination is to transform meaning. Without the imagination, there would be no generation of new possibilities. The transformation of meaning through imagination is a process of several steps. The first step goes through the sensual phase of internalization, which performs an overall and comprehensive negation of the object that is being internalized.

When we imagine, the object is not actually there. The imagination is the catalyst in this logic of negativity whose product is the imaginary, and it is this negativity that opens up the space of what is possible. Imagination is famous for its ability to create rich and full presentations; at least, this is an extreme consequence of the ideology of creative imagination. However, when we consider the imaginary as a vehicle of meaning, it is a vehicle where meaning must be annihilated in order to be transformed. Through negation, the meaning of an object can be altered, manipulated, and fused with other layers and dimensions of meaning (e.g., in an imaginative process, the objects of a table and a chair can be negated as concrete objects, or types of objects, and reimagined in a crossing or a fusion—see the example of Hammerstrøm in chapter 7—in the same way the centaur in its combination of a man and a horse is a reimagining of both).

Furthermore, it is crucial for the process of transforming meaning to state that there would be no meaning without negation. Spinoza claimed that negation is needed if we are to determine anything, *omnis determinato est negatio*, and we may follow his argument: "Without nothing, without negation, without permanent annihilation no semantic determination, no predication, no relevancy and no meaning" (Hörisch 2009, 135). In direct conjunction with the imaginary, it can be said that "the imaginary is posed by a consciousness as content that is concrete but absent, not actualized": by the ability of negation, the "imaginary allows us to detach ourselves from the immediate, the present and perceived reality, without shutting us into the abstractions of thinking" (Wunenburger 2003, 63). Focusing on negation, we may get closer to the performance of the imaginary in design.

In this endeavor, I will draw in particular on one of the French phenomenological philosophers, Jean-Paul Sartre. The key text in this context is his early book *L'imaginaire*, which was published in 1940, with the subtitle *Psychologie phénoménologique de l'imagination,* prior to his later famous existentialist philosophy. Sartre closely relates the imaginary to freedom: the imaginary is a product of free imagining; that is, we are free because we can imagine, and simultaneously, we can imagine because we are free (Kearney 1998). Thus, to Sartre, the basic premise is that the imagining mind intends and posits its object as a nothing, *comme un néant*; the object is placed in a "position of absence or inexistence" (Sartre 1940, 30).[1] Consequently, consciousness *unrealizes* the object of the outer world. According to Sartre, there is no production of a new unreal world in the mind; unrealizing by imagining means creating a form of poverty within consciousness, as there can only be less meaning inside than outside consciousness.[2] Thus, creating an inner world with individualized objects and environments is impossible (150). What remains is a negation of the world that points to a different way of conceiving what "world" is. Thus, Sartre states that unreal objects are like "strange beings that escape the laws of the world" (260) and that they oscillate in "perpetual evasion" between appearance and disappearance. He says that unreal objects, *objets-fantômes*, "give us the opportunity to escape from all the constraints of the *world*; it seems that they present themselves as a negation of the condition of *being in the world*, like an anti-world" (261).[3] Thus, he ascribes a central mental capacity to imagination. The production of the imaginary through negation serves as a basic condition of our capacity for abstraction and conceptualization beyond the singular material. In this way, from the point of view of consciousness, the world is always imbued with imaginary meaning.

In relation to design, it might be productive to focus on negativity and the process of negation to see what happens when something is turned away from having an existence in the physical world, that is, turned into something imaginary. This is a process that can be seen in more immaterial kinds of design, for example, in Web design with its destabilization of the extension of physical space, whereby the immaterial, imaginary space of the computer screen makes the new space actual and concrete. In negating the "real" reality, the visualization of something quite new and never seen before is made possible, and this visualization of imagination expands the space of possibility, for example, in "second worlds," or the imaginary worlds of games. In addition to this direct application, negation is a basic condition of the production of all meaning, including meaning in design. Every act of creating a new object starts with annihilating the previously given.

Sartre has of course been criticized with claims that this idea of pure negation leads to a ghostly as well as ghastly counterworld.[4] To Sartre, it is important to emphasize that the real world and the imaginary are mutually interdependent. Sartre's basic point is that "everything imaginary appears 'on the foundation of world,' but conversely, all apprehension of the real as world implicates a hidden surpassing towards the imaginary" (1940, 361).[5] First, the imaginary has its foundation in the world; that is, it is situated within the world. Second, our capacity for comprehending the world is based on our faculty of imagination to negate, annihilate, and create distance to the otherwise dull materiality of the present world. The effect of this operation for the constitution of new meaning will be developed in chapter 7 under the heading of "schematization," that is, how imagination produces schemes within the framework of internalization (and the complement in externalization) that enable new meaning by combining sensual material and conceptual meaning, and, importantly, how this can be developed in the setting of the design situation.

Unrealization

As a product of consciousness, the imaginary simultaneously surpasses the world and is contained within it. The act of unrealization can be engaged not only to describe the process where the imaginary meaning is detached from the world of reality but also the productive moment of this detachment. It is the formative aspect of the phenomenological process of imagination where it not only negates meaning in a sensually and bodily anchored act but also attempts to relate imaginary meaning to the actual and take it in new directions.

Through unrealization, meaning is created at the verge of reality and the imaginary, of actuality and possibility. In its productive, unrealizing moment, the imaginary can be a "production of another world" and something "which opens itself to possibilities" (Wunenburger 2003, 63). Therefore, to relate meaning to the sphere of the imaginary in the process of unrealization means to experience negation and open up a new dimension of possibility at one and the same time. As a vehicle for meaning, the imaginary thus enables a complex relationship of negation and positioning, of absence and presence. On the basis of negation, something new may come into being.

Seen as a basic structure for designed objects, the framework of the imaginary opens up the closure that may characterize objects on a physical level. Through the prism of the imaginary, I claim that design objects are permeated by structures of negation. First, they are products of a process of negation: in their becoming, they are products of an internalizing mind that externalizes itself (or, often in collaborative design processes, several minds externalizing themselves). Through the act of internalization, negation is employed, so the process of negation in imagining is a premise for the development of design objects. Second, the product of this process, the imaginary, stays with the design object as a structure of meaning. Through the imaginary, the human mind creates a structure of meaning—on the basis on negation and on the verge of positioning of new meaning—that operates as a formative meaning structure for the design object. At the same time, the imaginary meaning is detached from its moorings in the human mind as it is externalized in a design object. Hereby, the formative principle of negation follows the objects in their externalized materialization.

The imaginary may then be used to conceptualize the complex relationship between a mental process of immaterial imagining on the one hand and the realization in a physical, concrete, and material medium on the other. Thus, the imaginary in design can be applied by theorizing the inner dynamics of expanding the space of possibility in design. Thus, we can focus at the implications of the process of creative imagining for the constitution and ontology of the object and for the object's ability to "possibilize." In essence, reflecting on the imaginary in design may reveal that objects are always more than their materiality. Productive for the understanding of meaning production in design objects, they come into being in an interplay of negation and positioning, of annihilating absence and the creation of a new presence.

To anchor the notion of unrealization in phenomenological concepts, I turn to Merleau-Ponty. Within the framework of a general phenomenology of experience, Merleau-Ponty elaborates on the relation of real and imaginary on the level of subject-object interaction or, to use his own terms, the visible and the invisible. He proposes a concept of the imaginary where it relates to the real. As I noted in chapter 3, the experiencing subject for Merleau-Ponty cannot be separated from the experienced world; subject and object are thus reciprocally intertwined, and hence the human mind, the locus of experience, is always incarnated in a body, in a concrete world of things and in intersubjective relations. In his working notes for the book *Le visible et l'invisible* (1964), Merleau-Ponty (1964) criticizes Sartre for being too obsessed with negativity (314). Instead, he claims the primacy of the visible as part of the invisible: "This visible that is not actually seen is not the Sartrean imaginary: the presence within or of the absent. It is the presence of the imminent, the latent and the hidden" (298).[6] His point is that the visible in the world that we experience always has its double in the invisible in the form of an "inner brace" (193) and that this invisible cannot exist as something that is not directly involved with and participating in the visible. To Merleau-Ponty every concrete, visible manifestation always carries with it an invisible idea or meaning. The ideas (and there are always several) are not accessible without bodily experience, and at the same time, the ideas cannot be fully expressed in their physical manifestation. The ideas are inexhaustible with regard to their manifestation.

Focusing on the relationship between the real and the imaginary, Sartre and Merleau-Ponty agree that there is a relationship, but they disagree on the nature and structure of this relationship. While Sartre claims the essential poverty of the imaginary due to the process of negativity, Merleau-Ponty detaches the concept of the imaginary from consciousness and casts it instead as a more general and structuralist notion of an idea that is founded on a deeper level. On this point I believe that Merleau-Ponty provides the more productive concept.

Furthermore, his concept more accurately defines a next step in the process of the imaginary: When we face an object of design, it is not something that exists within consciousness as a hollow ghost of negation; rather it is the concrete materialization of an imaginary structure. Sartre may describe the first part of the process of the imaginary, the transformative internalization of the outer world in consciousness, while Merleau-Ponty may be used to describe the next step when the imaginary has been externalized and realized in a design. From this perspective, we may try to grasp the traces of the invisible structures of the idea and the imaginary in the object. Furthermore, the visible and invisible structures in the object can be seen in relation to Daniel Miller's (1987) social-anthropologist conception of the bridging roles of the object, as it operates on the levels of both "abstract signifiers" and "concrete signifieds": "Through its extreme visibility and its extreme invisibility" it is engaged in conscious as well as unconscious processes of making meaning (107–108). The implication that Miller draws from this is that the object, through its physical presence and its "materiality, is always an element in cultural transformation" (107). The concept of the imaginary may, however, shift our focus from psychological processes (e.g., the role of the object in ontogenesis) to the question of the influence of mental processes on questions concerning the construction of meaning in objects. In chapter 9, I attached this process of meaning construction to the aspect of symbolic coding in design.

The refraction of objects through the prism of the imaginary as a structure of meaning at the intersection of negation and positioning of new meaning can draw attention to the nonclosure of designed object. Generally all design objects are artifacts that share the act of making sense (Hagan 2007) and are inscribed in and circumscribed by contexts of cultural meaning, whether they interfere with or reflect the larger contexts of society or, on a smaller scale, define themselves in relation to their immediate surroundings or reflect meaning that is intrinsic to design, other design objects or design principles. In this respect, all design objects, whether defined with material closure as static objects or as objects of interaction, may be seen as unfinished. They are always parts of larger networks involving other objects that together play a role in constituting "an embedding environment for the self" while also defining open and unfolding knowledge processes (Knorr-Cetina 1997, 24). Regarded as "objects of knowledge" with an "unfolding ontology," design objects can be seen as "processes and projections rather than definitive things" (Knorr-Cetina 2001, 181–182). This openness may imbue them with a potential for defining, creating, or actualizing meaning.

My point is that this openness can be founded on the level of imaginary meaning, and I will show some examples of this principle.

Generally the many layers of linking in Web design can be regarded as structures of imaginary and potential meaning that at best imitate the associative processes of consciousness. This can be demonstrated by the "Web extension" to Thorvaldsen's Museum in Copenhagen, Tilbygningen.dk (2006; see figure 5.1, design by Oncotype). As media of interaction, Web solutions directly and explicitly engage users. Through their interactive, nonlinear structure, they address meaning as something that evolves in exchanges between the medium and imaginary possibilities activated by users. In this context, Tilbygningen.dk displays all or many of the virtual possibilities that may be activated in encounters with works of art in the physical museum (e.g., knowledge about sculpture, the eighteenth century, and antique tradition as well as references to contemporary questions of identity and artistic creation). In its design, the trace of the user's associative process moving through the Web site is not hidden (as when in linking from one page to another, the initial page disappears) but openly displayed as the nonlinear simultaneity of multiple windows. In this way, the designers, Oncotype, used a basic design principle: to make explicit on the Web site that a new opening of possibilities always closes others and that these are not left behind but are part of the overall space of possibility that is engaged and staged by the Web site and its dialogue with the users. As a consequence, all the layers of imaginary meaning that are activated in Tilbygningen.dk, including the way in which associations might work their way through the layers of meaning, are converted to a principle of form and thus directly and actively put into play.

Design objects with a high degree of materiality may break with the static closure of the object and partake in the structures of imaginary meaning. In their explorative principle, the series of round chairs designed by Louise Campbell and discussed in chapter 3 (figures 3.5 to 3.7) may be illustrative. They can be seen as permeated by an imaginary dimension of what is possible and of how the impossible can be made possible. The chairs form part of an ongoing exploration of the circular as a principle for a chair; the common principle of construction is the central focal point that serves as the starting point for compiling two identical but differently scaled circular layers. The form of the chairs does not rationally follow the functional aspects of being a chair made for sitting; instead, it follows the experimental principle of the two-circle structure, which is multiplied in *Veryround* with its compilation of 260 identical circular modules in different sizes. Here, Campbell's designs not only expand the notion of

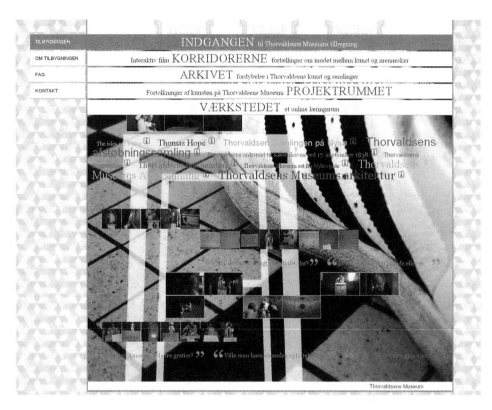

Figure 5.1
http://tilbygningen.dk. *Design:* Oncotype. *Image:* Thorvaldsens Museum.

what is possible in design and how the impossible (of the circular principle) can be made possible; they are also continuously marked by the open possibility of the idea that they are striving to materialize. In this sense, Campbell's designs are "epistemic objects" of knowledge; they have the capacity to unfold indefinitely while at the same time being in "the process of being materially defined" (Knorr-Cetina 2001, 181). Through their constitution as design objects, the chairs entail a potential of meaning that may be actualized and realized within a cultural context: what being a chair means and, regarding the reflective character of Campbell's chairs, to whom. In this way, the design object enables meaning in specific ways that point (back) to its constitution in the imaginary as a negation of meaning and new becoming of meaning in the process of unrealization as well as (forward) to its possible cultural applications. The kind of imaginary meaning that is actively at work in Campbell's chairs points to culturally circumscribed questions of what a chair is, that is, the ontology of the chair as a design object that affords meaning in a certain way and communicates it to an audience.

Transfiguration

While the phase of internalization focuses on the aspect of negation as objects turn into imaginary meaning inside consciousness (with consequences for design process and design epistemology) and the aspect of unrealization touches on the dialectic of the imaginary and the real (with consequences for understanding design objects as bearers of meaning and as ontological entities), the last phase of the phenomenology of imagination follows the objects as they become a medium for actual human commitment on a level of contextual meaning. Ultimately, design (as designed objects or solutions) has an effect as culturally and socially engaged artifacts. Design is, to use a crude abstraction, one of the central material prisms we live our lives through. Thus, in its ability to construct and convey meaning, design can be imbued with a potential transfigurative effect, especially on our ways of experiencing and understanding modern life (with consequences for a specific design phenomenology, a topic explored in chapter 10).

In this sense, one problem with Sartre's and Merleau-Ponty's phenomenological speculations is that they seem detached from any outer cultural and societal context. Merleau-Ponty's notion of the "idea" may, however, be seen as homologous to any kind of cultural meaning at work through its incarnation in the material. Accordingly, in relation to the imaginary, we would then have a space of resonance for cultural meaning that, due to the inexpressibility of the "inner brace" of meaning, cannot be understood as a simple one-directional, one-dimensional transmission of meaning into the present materiality of the object. Rather, it should be viewed as a larger context, or entity of context, of meaning that, like the inexhaustibly expressed idea, paradoxically is never fully expressed although it is always more than its expression.

This kind of ideational structure can be productive for our understanding of the transfigurative effects of design. First, it enables us to reflect on the dimension of the possible in design. What permeates the material appearance of design is not simply one specific idea that comes into being through design but rather a complex of related ideas that comes into being through the interplay of negation and positioning, of absence and presence, which lets meaning come into being at the intersection of actuality and possibility. Second, this dimension of meaning is always imbued with (or circumscribed by) cultural meaning of what is and what might be. In their structure of actualized and potential layers of meaning, design objects point to and interact with contexts of societal or cultural meaning in a variety of ways. Design objects engage in imaginary produced meaning and may contain levels of meaning that are capable of promoting transfiguration on the level of cultural and social contexts.

Examples may vary from the ways in which new ideas of detailing and lightness in furniture design can affect our understanding of possibilities in the production and use of chairs (as in Bruno Mathsson's use of bent plywood in making light and visually appealing armchairs) to system, service, and information design that is deeply embedded in the structure of the presence and absence of combined material and ideational content (one example is Apple's combined structure of hardware and software surrounding the music software iTunes). Design objects both materialize imaginary meaning and enable meaning construction through the imaginary. Design objects mediate ideas and imaginings and make them concrete (thus, design stabilizes and manifests the imaginary); they may also have possible transfigurative effects by being imbued with the immaterial structures of imaginary meaning (whereby the imaginary becomes design).

An aspect of this issue is the principal question of how the imaginary may be conceptualized as an entity that exists outside consciousness. A central entry to this discussion is the aim of the philosopher Cornelius Castoriadis (1975) to transpose and prolong the imaginary as a product of human imagination and as a creative force on the level of society. The imaginary may thus be important in the generative dynamics of creating social institutions (Castoriadis 1975) and may be expanded to include a social version of the imaginary that consumers create on the level of intersubjective meaning (Lash and Lury 2007). Furthermore, imagination on an intersubjective level has been taken up Murphy (Murphy, Peters, and Marginson 2010) in his concept of imagination as an "act of figuration" that with a "power of organization" is involved in "object creation" enacted through a series of "form-generation media" and construction of patterns such as hierarchy, balance, repetition, similarity, and proportion, all residing at the intersection of "the sensuousness of materials and the meaningfulness of explicit forms (26-29).[7] Murphy's take on the imagination is conceived to have implications for a larger scale of social dynamics. As a vehicle for the production of meaning, where the human world can be made a virtual one and the possibilizing dynamics of "as if" can be engaged to push meaning in new directions, the imagination has a social dimension. As a principle of meaning generation rooted in practical reality, it interferes in the social-cultural sphere. In this way, it can be detected how societies at different times can be "more or less imaginative" (Murphy, Peters, and Marginson 2010, 6), that is, show different degrees of creativity and vision in the production of meaning. The European Renaissance, for example, was a period with a flourish of creative endeavors, whereas the contemporary age seen on the large scale, in Murphy's somewhat pessimistic analysis, is a period of few creative achievements.

But what is interesting in this context is that Murphy tries to describe the operative structure of imagination and how it transcends a subjective fixture and can be described as a collective, anonymous effort of creation: "In the first phase of creation, *divergent thinking* opens onto a near-infinite range of materials, possibilities, representations and ideas. In the second phase of creation, *convergent thinking* unites and integrates" (Murphy, Peters, and Marginson 2010, 106). With a reference to Castoriadis, Murphy states that the "temporal schemata of creation" are different from the subjective-psychological time of, for example, memory and expectation: "non-subjective time is a time outside of mind" (42–43). In pointing to the formative act of figuration in imagination, that is, how meaning is produced and catalyzed through pattern building, and how this involves a larger-scale process of meaning creation, Murphy makes a productive contribution to the conceptualization of a transsubjectively operating imagination. His emphasis lies in challenging how societies—more specifically, universities as knowledge-producing institutions—can be more creative, not on the formative dynamics of the creation of objects of a second nature even though he considers this a hallmark of imagination.

However, Murphy's focal point of form-generating media as transmitter between formative structures of creative imagination and actual production of meaning can prove relevant for the investigation of design, as design in its process of development can be seen as externalizing the formative process of active meaning creation. More problematic, in my view, is Murphy's concept of the specific pattern forms attached to imagination—hierarchy, balance, symmetry, and proportion, all of them principles of harmony (even if conceived as dynamic principle of balance), integration, and order. In implicitly applying Coleridge's principle of imagination, he states: "Patterns are the ordered—and ordering—coalescence of contrasts" (46) and claims relevance for similitude, analogy, and synthesis. Murphy claims the just relevance of these principles and does not demonstrate their application. Furthermore, he anchors them in a metaphysical assumption that they are "transcendent in relation to human beings and immanent in nature" (72); they are at the one and at the same time inherent in human imagination and beyond it.[8] In my regard, Murphy here leaves out the element of chaotic-enthusiastic transgression and subversion in imagination: that everything also can be turned into its opposite and hereby point to new configurations of meaning.

On the level of the concrete object, we may argue on principle that the imagination as a matter of consciousness must be externalized; otherwise we would have only psychological and, in principle, inaccessible individual matter, as I noted in the discussion of internalization and externalization. To follow this line of argument, the imaginary is first of all productive in an epistemological act, as the imagination is an inherent aspect of our way of seeing and perceiving as well as organizing and making meaning. Furthermore, we may try to grasp the imaginary when it is not only a part of an inner process of consciousness but takes on an externalized form and assumes the character of something tangible that lies outside our consciousness. In this vein, Dewey (2005) claims that the imaginative operations of a work of art may be to "concentrate and enlarge an immediate experience," but still "the meanings imaginatively summoned, assembled, and integrated are embodied in material existence that here and now interacts with the self" (285). Wunenburger (2003) states in his phenomenological conception that the "imaginary is inseparable from its works, whether mental or materialized," whereby "every materialized product contributes to enriching the representation of the world" (29). This materializing concept of the imaginary lets us reflect on the role of the medium: design as an aesthetic medium for imaginary meaning.

Because the process of mediation always affects the content to be mediated, to reflect on design as a medium of imaginary meaning is to be aware of the meaning production in the process of mediation, the span of imaginary, immaterial meaning, and the specificity of the often material objects of design. Hence, to employ the imaginary as a concept in relation to design contributes to the discussion of what design is (see chapter 8 on design ontology) and how meaning enters design, and vice versa, when design is the medium for the imaginary, how the imaginary is to be seen through the refraction, and the effects of its mediation: what design as a medium does to the imaginary.

First, design offers an often context-bound materiality to the imaginary meaning. In this context, we may see a dynamic span between the origin within a creative imagination and the imaginary conveyed in an object and ask how the imagination works in its mediated manifestations. By using the imaginary as a concept for linking back to productive imagining in a creative person's mind, we avoid an intentional fallacy because the workings of the externalized form of the imaginary will always differ from its principal origin (qua imagination) in the human mind.[9] Then the medium of design engages a cultural potentiality of the imaginary. As a mediator of material as well as immaterial dimensions of cultural and social contextual meaning, design can essentially be conceived as a medium that mediates culture. Design objects are embedded in culture; culture also works through design via the imaginary. Design objects are objects of cultural possibilities with a potential transfigurative effect. Of course, how this works must be specified in each case of design and cultural context; my aim here is to examine the principles in the way that design objects relate to their defining contexts. My point is that we may apply a more theoretical view on the imaginary to determine not only how design is created—as is every human creation— as an externalization of internalized meaning (the topic of chapters 6 and 7). In doing so, on the level of the ontology of the design object, we may also determine how design objects are permeated by imaginary meaning (the topic of chapters 8 and 9). In dealing with design, a domain of predominantly physical objects and a theoretical bias of culture as materially manifest, we may find a new perspective on the way in which we encounter, perceive, and conceptualize design in its potential transfigurative effect (the topic of chapter 10). More specifically, using the lens of the imaginary may shed light on the specific relationship of the imaginary idea and material presence, of negation and position, and of absence and presence regarding meaning and its organization. It is this fundamental constitution of design objects that enables them to address meaning and thus deal with meaning that points to and is circumscribed by a cultural context. We may be better informed of how and why objects are structured by specific dimensions of meaning and contribute to the symbolic coding in the production of cultural meaning. This symbolic coding may ultimately confer a kind of transfigurative power on our ways of using and engaging with design.

6   Imagination and Design Epistemology

The first step of dealing with imagination in design is to focus on the internal process of imagining as a central part of design practice. Thus, imagination relates to cognition and the often experiential knowledge in design. In essence, the questions can be asked as to how designers imagine when they design, how we can detect imagination in design and design processes, and what the mental setting of designers is toward the design tasks they address as they devise concrete, creative solutions to often ill-defined problems.[1]

In the next chapter, I introduce the concept of schematization as an entry into the analysis of processes of imagination in the development of design. Prior to the focus on that concept, this chapter methodologically lays the foundation for how to approach imagination in design as a question of structural coding. Ultimately, it is a discussion that can be anchored within the field of design epistemology that designates a field of an ongoing discussion of how designers act and think and how design work takes place in a tension of imagination, cognitive operation, and concerns of more or less structured methods.

Researching Imagination

Handling imagination is not unproblematic. The romantics tried to discover the wonders and freedom of the inexhaustible and borderless inside consciousness, and philosophically, there have been attempts at using the method of introspection to learn about the operations of the mind. Thus, in his rich but problematic book *L'imaginaire* (1940) Jean-Paul Sartre tried to close his eyes and use himself as an object of reflection. In addition to the inherent methodological problem in being both the observer and the observed, Sartre was also faced with the problem of gaining true and valuable knowledge from the inside of the mind. It should be noted that the romantics never believed that they could gain direct access to it (although some believed in access by means of drugs); instead they viewed the powers and dynamics of the imagination as something that might possibly be extracted and liberated as an important human capacity. For this reason and for its nuanced reflections on the topic, romanticism is still important for contemporary discourse on the imagination (Casey 1976; Kearney 1994; Folkmann 2006a).

Seen in a research perspective, the effort to get behind the workings of the imagination has led in various directions, which may be placed on a spectrum ranging from empiricist-positivist to philosophical-epistemological approaches (Liddament 2000).

On the one hand, the belief in positive and empirical findings on the inside of consciousness has found its way into research, even with Sartre; although he uses a structure of negativity to investigate the powers of the mind as it unrealizes and annihilates concrete objects in order to handle them within the mind, he offers a description of the inside of mind. Similarly, experimental psychology, cognitive science, and neurobiology and neuroaesthetics have been underpinned by a positivist perspective and engaged in an effort to gain insight into the empirical foundation of imagination and into the structures of creative processes (Howard, Culley, and Dekoninck 2008). However, these examinations increasingly embrace the reflective knowledge of the impossibility of revealing the full truth of the mind (Skov and Vartanian 2009). It is also important to integrate the critique of the simple deterministic models of the mind that are so prevalent in natural science into this discourse since all facts of nature are embedded in a space of cultural meaning and therefore require interpretation (Hörisch 2009; Seel 2006).[2]

Philosophy, however, has shown continuous interest in the topic, dating back to the epistemology of the English empiricists and the German philosopher Immanuel Kant as well as phenomenology and its focus on topics in experience and intentionality. Interestingly, Sartre, along with Merleau-Ponty, also belongs in this category. Sartre's method is empirical (experimental psychology in the form of introspection), although his interest is philosophical-phenomenological as he raises the question of how the imaginary can be experienced and how imagination comprises a structure of intentionality. In contrast to empirical approaches, this line of inquiry can be described as speculative and conceptual (Liddament 2000, 590); in avoiding presumptions of empirical essences, it works by establishing networks of hypotheses. My investigation too has a tendency toward philosophical ideas. My starting point for the discussion is establishing a framework for conceptualizing the imagination in a way that lets it be linked to design. Thus (and in order to be relevant to design theory, a theory that is relevant to designers in an augmentation of the knowledge about what happens when designers design), it is relevant to discuss the theoretical framework in connection to design epistemology—not with the assumption of entering designers' minds but in a dialogue between conceptual constructions and concrete matter.

The Coding of Imagination in Design

Thus, human imagination is per se inaccessible. In an important article, which has gained relatively little traction in design theory, Terry Liddament (2000) argues that not only can we not know what is going on in the inner space of consciousness with regard to imaging and picturing in connection with design; the very notion of a particular essence of creative imagination is problematic. Liddament criticizes the metaphysical assumption that in producing pictures, for example, we render explicit something that already exists inside us as a sort of essence. Similarly, he criticizes empirical approaches, for example, in cognitive science, in a similar pursuit of a particular mental substance:

"Imagination" and its "mental" cognates . . . are not "objects" with a place as such, in this particular empiricist ontological pantheon. Rather, they are important for the role they actually play in our conceptual framework; and to examine this role we need, not an empirical investigation into the "brain" or some sort of action, but a conceptual investigation, which here means: we look at how such concepts are employed. (598)

Liddament's (2000) point is that we need to deal with the myths of imagery precisely because concepts of imagination, imaging, and imagery are important in design discourse and design education and influence the ideology of designers' creative thinking. Following his argument, imaging and imagery are "not something intangible which takes place in a mysterious 'medium,'" that is, the mind; instead "imaging is a doing" that "alludes to the thinkable, and this means: to the do-able" (604). Basing his discussion on the role of picturing in design, he then reverts to the correlation of imagining and picturing: it is not on the basis of imagining that the creative dynamics of picturing is opened up; it is through the actual unfolding of a picturing that we are able, if at all, to get a "better grasp of the role that imagery actually plays in an activity such as designing" (605).

I will engage the discussion that Liddament points to but does not explore: the role of imagination for the conceptual framework in design. In his analysis, Liddament instead discusses the dichotomy of inward imagining and outward picturing in order subsequently to deconstruct it. The dialectic of inside and outside, of inward imagining and outward reaction, is at its heart the discussion of imagination from romanticism to the present day and will continue to contribute to the discussion. But I do not focus on the inaccessible inside of consciousness—the "inward sight," in Shelley's words.

In my view, imagination can be addressed as a structure that comes to itself in the dynamic interaction between inside and outside. It is a matter of their relation, not the inside of the mind. Just as cognition in design should not be regarded (only) as thinking but rather as an activity of inquiry and activity that is flexible in a context due to its specific function (Gedenryd 1998), I employ a concept of imagination that exceeds the closure of the mind. Furthermore, I agree with Liddament about the futility of trying to gain access to something that is constitutively inaccessible. In her pragmatist rethinking of the role of visuality in design, Kathryn Moore (2010) argues in favor of the importance of being critical to the implicit metaphysics that lurks in theories of creativity. She is especially critical of specific kinds of visual or sensory modes of thinking that are supposed to find their roots in elements of consciousness that precede perception and language. She states that there "is no need to look for anything hidden beyond or beneath what is already there in front of our eyes" (12), and in an attempt to "demystify the art of design," she advocates a noncircumventable and opaque role of the visual in design.[3]

I too think it is necessary to be critical of any metaphysical assumptions in the concepts we employ when speaking about design, imagination, and creativity. Nevertheless, it is important to avoid the positivist fallacy of implying that the only matter to be conceptualized is the graspable, the tangible, or the explicit and visual, something that Moore also acknowledges when she points to the formative role of emotions and feelings in design. My proposal is to be skeptical of hidden metaphysics but also to try to get behind the facade and surface of things.

In her informative study about imagination as knowledge, Sabine Wettig (2009) points to the importance of making the mechanisms of imagination explicit as it makes significant contributions to our understanding through its process of image production. With media studies as her starting point, she argues that we need to be informed about the tacit becoming of knowledge that is immanent in the image production within imagination in order not only to counter the overwhelming flow of images in media society but also to understand the larger picture of ourselves. Wettig seeks to enlighten imagination and its role in image creation and thinking processes, and without necessarily accepting her entire argument, one would nevertheless benefit by accepting the impossibility of gaining full access to consciousness, but by trying to get closer to the tacit knowledge evoked by the imagination and, according to my argument, see it in a dynamic interaction with concrete materialization. My proposal of the concept of schematization should be seen as an attempt at formulating operative structures of the imagination detectable in actual material manifestations, that is, design objects.

Thus, I will use the structure of dynamic interaction to look at the junction of internal, abstract conceptualization and outward, concrete materialization. My focus will be on this linking of concepts and concrete matter in terms of finished design objects. Conversely, my focus will not be on the designer's mental activity in an investigation of imagery processing in the form of image generation and transformation, that is, examining imagery as an equivalent of perception and interpreting imagined objects like physical objects (Kavakli and Gero 2001). True, a high "performance in cognitive activity may be dependent on the richness of representational structures and pattern goodness" (364); however, my aim, besides the concrete and different tools all designer use, is to look at the structural relationship of the activity of imagination and the becoming of concrete design solutions.

As a contribution to the discussion of specific ways for designers to approach the process of designing, the concept of imagination can be used to look at designers' mental settings toward their work that are expressed in a particular way of linking the conceptual framework with the material manifestation in the design objects. We cannot look into designers' minds, but we can indirectly detect what is going on by investigating ways of approaching their work. In this way, I aim to investigate some of the structural codes in the act of translation that takes place in design between a setting, an intention, or a wish to meet a need and the resulting physical artifacts. In analyzing these codes, I enter into a discussion of some of the factors that enable creativity in design. The methodological premise of this theoretical approach is that creativity in design can be indirectly enhanced by a better understanding of some of the mechanisms and processes in cognition that underlie design creativity, that practice can "perhaps take advantage of an improved understanding of its underlying principles" (Gedenryd 1998, 3).

To look for design codes is an ambition that dates back to Christopher Alexander's attempt in *Notes on the Synthesis of Form* (1964) to investigate the structural patterns of design problems by demonstrating an "underlying structural correspondence" with the "process of designing a physical form which answers that problem" (132). My goal is not, however, to stabilize problems that are otherwise in flux[4] but, much in accordance with Peter Murphy's notion of imagination as a dynamic production of "patterned form" (Murphy, Peters, and Marginson 2010), to theorize the structural relationship of inner and outer creation of meaning and transformation of meaning in actual design objects.

As we approach samples of design, we may of course ask why designs look the way they do and what kind of mental setting in relation to the design problem and what refraction of inside and outside, known and unknown they reflect. FUCHS+FUNKE's oversize origami chair *Papton* (2004, figure 7.2), for example, like much of the other work from this firm, is not so much a finished and physically circumscribed product as the result of an ongoing negotiation of an inner, mental image or idea of how it might be possible to make the ultimate chair from a two-dimensional surface and constraints of a standard sheet of paperboard. Thus, the question is how the ideal inner idea comes up against limits, and more generally, how imagination meets materiality. Finally, it is also a question of how both imagination and materials are ultimately and mutually transformed in the process: The inner idea must adapt to the material constraints, but the material constraints also constantly affect the idea, refine it, and push it in new directions. In its materializations, the chair is on its way to meet its idea; vice versa, the idea is not only something unattainable (as in a classic Platonic reflection) but is altered according to the design process of folding ever new sheets of paperboard. Ultimately the idea displays itself as incarnated in the design.

Design Epistemology

Dealing with imagination in relation to design practice is a matter of design epistemology. As a general philosophical term, *epistemology* derives from the Greek *episteme* and *logos*, meaning order or doctrine of epistemes, that is, knowledge of the structures and systems of how we know. Consequently, *design epistemology* often functions as a technical term in practice-based design theory, where it refers to designers' ways of knowing or experiencing in order to see the world as they do, and it uses this epistemological base as a starting point for the design process. Hence, design epistemology deals with cognition and knowledge in design and, subsequently, their foundation. In this section, I discuss the concept of design epistemology, point out a series of important issues regarding knowledge and the designer's role that are raised within its framework, and relate it to the field of imagination.

Practices and Processes

In my view, a founding and productive dichotomy in the debates on design epistemology is produced by the tension of inner, and often irrational, mental activity in design cognition and the outer, often rationally conceived tools and methods often employed in design processes. This tension structures my discussion of design epistemology, where I ultimately will regard the conceptualization of imagination as a contribution to the discussion of the inner properties of the designer effective in the design process.

Since the 1960s, there have been attempts to theorize the immanent space of design practice; especially the early design methods movement, initiated in 1962,[5] attempted to construct design process models in order to match the increased complexity of design practice (Jones 1980). Because design lacked its own methodology (and design often still struggles to define itself as a discipline with an agreed epistemological foundation; Galle 2011), there has been a tendency to create models with a normative bias, showing how ideal design processes should proceed (Bürdek 2005).

The models, however, often stand in contrast to the "tacit knowledge" of designers (Schön 1983) and the more intuitive elements of designing. In focusing on the designer (i.e., with less emphasis on design and the design process) in a series of articles spanning back to the beginning of the 1980s, Nigel Cross (2007) has propagated the concept of design epistemology with the goal of being able to "understand how designers think, or the nature of design expertise." He has been "trying to establish its particular strengths and weaknesses, and giving it credit where it might be due for design cognition as an essential aspect of human intelligence" (11).[6] Accordingly, he speaks of specific "designerly ways of knowing"[7] and seeks to delimit and specify the nature of "design ability" as being, for example, founded on "the resolution of ill-defined problems by adopting a solution-focusing strategy and productive or appositional styles of thinking" (37).

The goal for Cross is to know in order to solve problems. In this way, he also points to one of the central starting points for the debate on design epistemology that more commonly has been the "instability of the *problem*," as Jones (1980) acknowledged in 1970, than the assumption that design problems were easy to state and solve. The acknowledgment of design problems as ill defined goes back to Horst Rittel, who in 1969 introduced the concept of "wicked problems," which, unlike simple or "tame" problems, are structurally nondefinable and in principle unsolvable but can lead to innovation in a process of reframing the wicked problem (Rith and Dubberly 2007).[8]

Thus, much debate on design epistemology has been focused on how to solve problems with more or less sophisticated tools and methods.[9] However, the designer is still a central part of the discussion of stating and handling design problems. As Alain Findeli (1994) has pointed out, the paradigm of design problems is carried by the idea of the designer's intervention and creation of equilibrium in the state of things. The designer is someone who should make things right. As a consequence, Findeli argues that the designer should be seen as a regulator who alters the existing state of a system in the direction of a new state. This makes the moment of decision making central as the "epistemological crux" of the design process (61); we cannot rationally or by technical means calculate the proper solution but have to interpret and make an ethically informed choice, as "designing an artifact is acting in the field of ethics, not of technology alone" (59). Hence, "Criteria for choice in design do not arise, as in science, from truth: a solution is never true or false; it is more or less appropriate, more or less acceptable, correct, satisfactory and thus depends on an evaluative judgment of an essentially qualitative or rhetorical type" (61). On this basis, the conception of design epistemology takes its starting point in the evaluative act of the designer.

Evaluation is also pivotal for Herbert Simon's seminal approach in *The Sciences of the Artificial* (1996), where he not only states that proposing a theory of design is both to characterize the "shape of design and the shape and organization of the design process," but also says that it essentially is a matter of psychology, that is, "man's relation to the complex outer environment in which he seeks to survive and achieve" (130, 136). Even with its rationalist and technically optimistic perspective in questions concerning the application of logics and computer-generated algorithms in the generation of design alternatives, Simon's theory is essentially about human beings dealing with uncertainty, decomposing the design problem, generating the best possible alternatives, and finding a satisfactory design. In Simon's view, design is about achieving a sort of concordance between the inner properties and the outer environment of the artificial artifact, as it constitutes a basic component in the human creation of and interference with the world. As Per Galle (2011) pointed out, Simon's theory is more foundational in its ambition of expression underlying conceptions of the nature and purpose of design than instrumental in specifying how it can "facilitate, accelerate, or improve design practice." The global scope is both the strength and the weakness of Simon's approach.

On the level of inner mental activity, there have been several attempts to define the core characteristics of what can be labeled "design ability." Thus, Bryan Lawson has sought to define the cognitive foundation of design processes in *How Designers Think: The Design Process Demystified* (2005), *What Designers Know* (2004b), and *Design Expertise* (2009, with Kees Dorst). In *How Designers Think* (2005), Lawson states that regardless of the characteristics of different design fields, it is "certain . . . that design is a distinctive mental activity," "a sophisticated mental process capable of manipulating many kinds of information, blending them all into a coherent set of ideas and finally generating some realisation of those ideas" (9, 14). Lawson's point is that the "design process, by definition, takes place inside our heads" (41), but that the process is then externalized by means of problem formulation and solution generation, often through sketches, computer programs, and prototyping. These approaches are all methods that are considered specific to the design process and should be nurtured and encouraged in design education. Design is, he concludes, a "highly personal and multi-dimensional process" (289).

Following Lawson's argument, design is both an individual activity with a base in the mental space of the mind and an activity that involves the use of various common and generally applicable concrete methods and devices. Hence, Lawson integrates the inner space of cognition with the outer field of systematic methods. In asking how the design profession (broadly seen) relates to knowledge, David Wang and Ali O. Ilhan (2009) suggest that rather than possessing a specific domain of knowledge (in an ontological clarification of "design knowledge"), the profession operates through a specific approach in relating to other, nondomain-specific discourses of knowledge. What in their view constitutes the core of knowledge in design and, hence, the profession is foremost the creative act that in its operation contains the potential to reconfigure and ultimately transfigure existing knowledge. Rather than unlock the inner space of this creative core, Wang and Ilhan point to its effects and "sociological wrapping" in the constitution of design as a profession.

Imagination as a Mental Setting

The point of design epistemology is that the aspects of internal and external activities are interdependent and mutually influential; what happens inside our heads or in the creative act is the product of education and other social, cultural, and personal influences, and the habitus of our doing is marked by our cognitive and individual abilities.

On the level of design epistemology, I aim to contribute to the understanding of the way in which designers approach the design process with a mental setting. I will not attempt to offer a comprehensive theory of what it actually is that designers do (that would be a complementary theoretical component of protocol analysis) or what sets designers' abilities apart.[10] The point, as I see it, is that designers have special tools regarding methods and processes thanks to their educational training that can help them prototype and visualize possible solutions, but they do not necessarily have extraordinary creative abilities. Instead, they express their general human, creative abilities in specific "designerly ways" as they seek to transform ideas and more or less clearly defined problem statements into solutions with a more or less physical extension.[11]

With the chosen focus on possibility and imagination, it might seem as if I were attempting to get into the minds of designers to uncover their secrets, striving to understand the logic of intuition, and delving into the subconscious. In fact, my approach is aimed at the structural level: I seek to examine the dynamics between processes of internalization and externalization; between the designers' mental settings, that is, their approach to the design process, and the outcome in design solutions; between possibilizing and actualizing. In this way, my focus is not psychological or neuroaesthetic in an investigation of mental processes. I do not discuss concrete, design-based techniques or practical models for promoting design work, such as sketching, visualizing, modeling, and prototyping by different means (e.g., rapid prototyping or digital rendering).[12] Instead, I explore the epistemological foundation of the operations of imagination in the design process. Accordingly, I am not primarily interested in techniques for achieving creativity and innovation through skills of imagining.

In creative activity, "purpose and commitment cannot be artificially instilled through a carefully planned program of progressive techniques"; nevertheless, it is productive to investigate the factors of the "intentional activity" in creativity (Ainsworth-Land 1992, 25). I offer a discussion of the structural foundation of imagination in design. The questions are how imagination operates as a projective act of schematizing meaning and how this unfolds in design. What makes designers special on this point is that they externalize structures and processes of imagination when they in an "act of figuration" (Murphy, Peters, and Marginson 2010) attempt to turn a creation of new meaning from an imaginative base of possibilities into physical, material objects aimed at an impact on human experience. What is special for design—objects, solutions, concepts—is that we can detect the formative process of materializing meaning when conceptual constructions and concrete matter meet and intersect. In design, the wish for the possible is converted into (mostly) purposeful solutions. Thus, the next chapter investigates the construction of meaning in design structurally through the notion of schematization as it unfolds at the interface of consciousness and the material world.

7 Schematization

In this chapter, I propose a structural approach for understanding an important part of creative processes in design: human imagination. I introduce the concept of schematization as a model of the cognitive framing of reality and thus as a means of enabling the conceptualization of the otherwise volatile imagination and its coding role in design. At its starting point, schematization describes an exchange of conceptual meaning and sensual material. Next, I present a series of dichotomies that are formative in the development of design and describe this as a prism for some of the central characteristics of the operation of imagination in design (figure 7.1). Toward the end of the chapter, I propose an approach to the design process that is based on some of the findings set out in this chapter seen in relation to the dynamics of searching for and engaging possibilities (figure 7.9).

I developed this conceptual framework in conjunction with interviews I held with a series of top furniture designers, most of them with an experimental bias, in Scandinavia and Germany; these designers enter the argumentation of the chapter through their comments and examples of their design. I chose furniture designers for two reasons. First, I can use them to offer comparative cases, and second, with its focus on parameters such as form and material, furniture design can be illustrative in my discussion of the structural mechanism in transposing a mental setting to an outward expression in the medium of design. A piece of furniture is a form struggling to come into being in the process of externalizing the internal space of imagination. As a contrast, I also discuss the design consultancy 3PART, which mainly works with complex solutions in the areas of industrial design and service design. I also draw on established concepts of design methodology such as multiperspectivism and idea generation, thus demonstrating the continuity of my discussion as a contribution to design methodology and design epistemology. I begin by introducing the concept of schematization and then fill out this frame by discussing a series of conceptual dichotomies that deal with knowledge, perspective, and focus in relation to it.

The Dynamics of Schematization

I introduce the concept of schema and its dynamic form, schematization, as a means of describing a model of the cognitive, imaginatively framing a reality that is relevant for designers. Schematization is changeable, not fixed. Because all designers in looking at the world through the "design they are working on" are looking through a "set of lenses, and cannot help but do so" (Harfield 2007, 171), an awareness of the mode of operation of these lenses for perceiving and understanding the world and thus configuring experience is useful. When we see how we see and realize that we always see through one set of lenses or another, and when we reflect on our reflective frames (Agid 2012), we acquire reflective knowledge of our constructive perspective and avoid getting entangled in experience. The concept of schema is not unknown in design discourse; for example, in a context of actual design practice, the term *schemata* has been used to describe dominant ways of addressing problem solving in the "development of a growing pool of precedent" (Lawson 2004a, 456). Furthermore, the notion of image schemata from contemporary cognitive science (Hampe and Grady 2005) and its focus on conceptual frameworks has found its way into design research and design discourse, directed at users' responses to technological artifacts, which requires a reorganization of given knowledge structures to generate a new construction of meaning in a process of embodied interaction (Markussen 2010).

I focus on the process in schematizing linking concepts and materiality, as this process can be detected in design objects and traced back to the designer's mental setting in relation to the design process. In two steps, I argue for Immanuel Kant's role as an important philosophical source, in part because he connects imagination to epistemology and aesthetics and offers a foundation for the process of linking concepts and materiality through the concept of schematization and in part because he points to the dynamic nature of this process.

Kantian Schematization

In his seminal epistemology in *Kritik der reinen Vernunft* (1781/1787), Kant establishes a basis for a release of the productive powers of imagination that in English empiricism had been too tightly linked to the sensual.[1] The basic—and revolutionary— premise in Kant's epistemology is his shift away from a belief in gaining access to things as they are to focusing on human cognition as the entrance to knowledge, "our way of perceiving and recognizing objects" (Kant 1990, B25). That might enable the sort of free constructivism where the world is as we conceive it with our minds. However, Kant combines his investigation of the filtering of reality in the human mind with a search for intersubjective and, hence, nonarbitrary factors of human experience. Still, Kant operates with flexibility in cognition and relates this to imagination. To him, experience takes place at the intersection of sensual appearances (importantly, "appearances" and not the things-in-themselves) and inescapable structures, such as time and space, and the conceptual constructions of cognition.

The crux of the matter is that he proposes the scheme as a matrix for the apperceptive and synthesizing linking of concepts and sensual, sensory, and perceptually given appearances and thus for the human production of meaning (Kant 1990, B177).[2] The scheme therefore conditions our ability to construct meaning through synthesis. The key point is that the scheme is itself a product of imagination; it is not given once and for all but is a structure of the human mind that is open to alteration and new configurations. This kind of reflection is transcendental in the sense that it reveals the conditions of knowing and construing meaning and leaves it open to analysis. We see that meaning is not simply given but created in a complex interaction of constructive factors. Sabine Wettig (2009) has also pointed to the role of imagination in the active creation of patterns for understanding:

The imagination holds . . . a profound dimension of possibility for cognitive development. If this is to be experienced, it requires of human beings an active, present attention that perceives according to the patterns in our construction and subsequent dissolution of inner images/imaginings. (180)

Within her context of media studies, Wettig bases reflection on image creation. Similar to Kant, however, is Wettig's autoreflective attention to the constructive capacities of the mind: In understanding our own seeing and understanding, we learn about their nature and structure. The methodological and epistemological question is, however, how far the implication of the constructive aspect of schematization can be taken.[3] The question is epistemological because it is about cognition and methodological as it enables a reflection on the possible applications of the schematization of imagination.

In his work on aesthetic experience, *Kritik der Urtheilskraft* (1790), Kant uses the flexibility of schematization in relation to judgments of taste (Kant 1995). The judgment of taste operates without concepts; through the imagination, it may schematize openly without given concepts. It operates in a search for concepts that fit the appearances that seek to be comprehended through the judgment of taste. The point is that aesthetically, imagination can perform the operation of linking sensual matter with conceptual meaning in an open, nonteleological construction of the concepts involved. Thus, cognition can entail an open search of concepts to fit a given appearance.

This is what Kant aims at when he talks about "aesthetic ideas," which he sees as "that kind of apprehension of the imagination that entails much to think at, without some definite thought, that is, *concept*, can be adequate to it, and which, consequently, cannot be comprehended or made comprehensible by any language" (Kant 1995, 198).[4] The aesthetic ideas relate to the concept of added quality in aesthetic objects discussed in chapter 3. Through the imagination, aesthetic ideas exceed any given concepts; they produce a surplus and a multitude of ideas, conceptions, and apprehensions that may engage in new combinations and connections that paradoxically let "much unnameable [*Unnennbares*] be thought of in relation to a concept" (201). To Kant, aesthetic ideas have a double function. First, they do not have a concept as their starting point. Kant speaks of "reflective judgment" in opposition to "determining judgment"; the latter functions to make sensual appearances and concepts symmetrically fit, whereas the former describes an asymmetrical relation and open reflection of the sensual without the determination of a pregiven concept. Then, aesthetic ideas can be a means of relating to meaning beyond the given, to *Vernunftideen*, by which he means transsensual ideas of reason. In this way, the sensual is reflected in concepts that exceed normal comprehension. In Kant's example, the "poet dares to make sensual the ideas of reason of invisible creatures, the kingdom of the blessed, hell, eternity, genesis, and such" (199). With the aesthetic ideas we can, in Kant's view, see an open-ended constitution of sensual appearance and reach beyond the given. In the context of design and schematization, however, it is important to focus on exceeding given concepts and searching for new ones to fit the unknown.

Schematization beyond Kant

Concepts develop in parallel with the process of comprehension. This open and mutual dialogue of concepts and appearances is clearly evident in the special design feature of anticipation and prediction in grasping for the possible in something not yet existing and presumably preferable to what is already there (Simon 1996; Zamenopoulos and Alexiou 2007; Galle 2008), where the method of development (i.e., the concepts) is not given in advance but evolves during the process. In the words of Christopher Alexander (1964), designers, in contrast to scientists who "try to identify the components of existing structures," "try to shape the components of new structures" (130). In this sense, design can be said to be defined in a schematizing span of an existing reality that delivers the conditions for the act of designing and the imagination of a new condition, as John Chris Jones discussed in the 1980 book, *Design Methods*: "Designers . . . are forever bound to treat as real that which exists only in an imagined *future* and have to specify ways in which the *foreseen* thing can be made to exist" (10–11).

Hence, a central part of Jones's argument revolves around questions of prediction, of imaginatively projecting from a present to a future state of being, and of the complexity of designing when "designers are obliged to use current information to predict a future state that will not come about unless their prediction are correct" (1980, 9). Here he discusses the "mixture of both rationality and intuition . . . needed in the solving of any design problem" (62–63). In this analysis, he employs models of the designer as a black box that delivers an intuitive, creative leap and of the designer as employing rational methods and then, widening the search for a solution to a design problem, allows these two approaches to integrate in the notion of the designer as a "self-organizing system," where the designer reflectively establishes a meta-language to describe the "relationship between a strategy and the design situation" (55). Thus, Jones's aim is not to disentangle the internal capacities of the human mind but rather to describe methods of entering creativity by being aware of its outer workings.

This kind of open schematization can entail a new kind of perception relating to something not yet known. In this way, theories of art in particular have adopted notions closely related to schematization in claiming that works of art can operate as media for an estranging and prolonged perception (Shklovsky 1993) or an "imaginative perception" (Scruton 1974, 150; Seel 2000) that, in transcending everyday perception, enables a new kind of seeing and in this process contributes to an ongoing expansion of the field of perception (Iser 2003). Following Roger Scruton, this kind of seeing through a work of art is a controlled "seeing as" that focuses on specific aspects of seeing, consciously reflects this seeing, and points to an "unasserted thought" that is otherwise impossible outside the medium of art (see chapter 3). Thus, Scruton says that "the 'unasserted' nature of 'seeing as' dictates the structure of aesthetic experience" (120). The point is that schematization in different aesthetic media can be employed to grasp meaning that is otherwise difficult to handle—with Kant's notion of schematization without concept, we may say that schematization does not know the concept in advance—and that this operation can be activated in a variety of aesthetic media. Every aesthetic form performs in a specific way and with a power of seeing, a *Sehkraft* in the words of the German romanticist Novalis (1965, 125). In extension of Kant's notion of schematization without concept and of works of art as a way of imagining (*Vorstellungsart*) that indicates purposefulness but lacks determinate purpose (Kant 1995), in his theory of aesthetics, *Ästhetische Theorie* (1970), Theodor W. Adorno (1970) pointed to the ability of works of art to contain aspects of certainty and determination as well as aspects of the opposite, the indeterminate and thus enigmatic. In pointing to a truth that can never be directly expressed, to a surplus of meaning, the works of art in his conception act as a "question mark" that indicates a direction as well as a disruption. According to Adorno, the works of art may describe a figure that indicates a "passage in that direction . . . where the work of art breaks off" (188; see chapter 3). If they did not break off before directly presenting some kind of truth that they wish to reveal but must conceal, they would be testimonies of religion, mysteries, or direct transcendence. This is evident. Any medium of representation mediates and cannot then give access to the presence of truth. Any truth per se (whatever it might be) remains inaccessible, relating to Adorno's implicit critique of every metaphysical assumption of transcendent meaning. Far more interesting for the context of reflecting design as a medium and designers' mental settings is the ability of the aesthetic medium (for Adorno the work of art, *das Kunstwerk*) to point in the direction of where it must break off. This ability indicates that the process of schematization clearly still needs to be employed and performed with a sense of direction, even though the end target cannot be known or presented directly but only indirectly in the search process.[5]

My goal in this context is to go behind the dynamic mechanisms that create the imaginative structure of "seeing as" and pointing in a direction as well as their operation in the design process. My hypothesis is that designers can connect abstract conception and concrete views, and in this respect the design process can be considered one of schematization. This process produces new meaning through designers' intentions concerning the interaction of the design with its surroundings, including its cultural and societal contexts and its way of organizing meaning in a way that ultimately lets the design affect perception and understanding (on a small scale). Herein lies the way in which schematization can be activated as a dynamic and flexible operation that transgresses the individual and subject-bound perspective otherwise implied in traditional thinking of imagination and creativity. The insight into the structuring of experience through actual artifacts can be directed toward the creative process, where it can be made an asset of aesthetic production. Thus, in focusing on the general structures and patterns of ideas (and not on idiosyncratic-personal ideas of creation) and using the concept of schematization, we may be able to achieve valuable insights into designers' mental settings in relation to the outcome of the design process: the design objects.

Structures of Ideas

In this section, I present three dichotomies that offer a basic foundation for a design-specific schematization of experience, that is, the active use of the capability of imagination to create meaningful connections of material manifestations and conceptual structures in the mental setting. The three dichotomies together describe a prism for the process of transformation that takes place in the refraction of inside and outside and is part of designers' experience. I discuss this prism and model of schematization in relation to examples from designers I have worked with in my research: primarily 3PART Design and Ditte Hammerstrøm, both in Denmark, and secondarily FUCHS+FUNKE in Germany and Anna von Schewen in Sweden. Theory and practice should complement each other; the theoretical is important for my ability to make general statements about the processes of schematization, while the use of empirical material validates the general model and illustrates how analytical insights can be relevant in a practical context.

The focus of an investigation of the formative powers of schematization must be aimed at a metaconceptual level that analyzes the structures of this linking. What is of interest is not the actual and specific concepts that designers use in the design process, normally as part of the design brief and design requirements (e.g., concepts of efficiency, functionality, user friendliness), even if they are important in the design process. Instead, the analysis focuses on general factors in the transformation of an internal mental setting into an outward physical manifestation.

I identify three general metaconceptual concepts or settings that are effective in the designer's process of turning inner imaginings into products. The three settings are all theoretical findings related to the overall framework of schematization, that is, the process of linking concepts and materiality. These settings can be defined within a span of dichotomies that deal with knowledge, perspective, and focus in the search for a fundamental taxonomy of mental settings toward design.[6] These settings are not exhaustive for the discussion of schematization in design but indicate a structure for it:

These are the three mental settings in the design process:

1. Amount of presupposed knowledge: known versus unknown

2. Imaginative perspective: whole versus detail

3. Degree of focus: focusing versus defocusing

In combination, these settings define the structure of the prism of schematization in imagination that I propose as a model for design creativity (figure 7.1). The metaphor of the prism indicates that it is a filter that design can be seen or conceived through. The three dichotomies can be used to offer theoretically informed insights into the underlying structures and structural codes in the design process. The proposed prism of imagination can be used to challenge designers on their own conception of imagination and creativity, and the overall framework of schematization can be employed in analyzing actual design solutions and as a starting point for questioning designers about their mental setting in the design process. Thus, the combination of the three dichotomies should not be seen as a rigid taxonomy of possible mental settings in

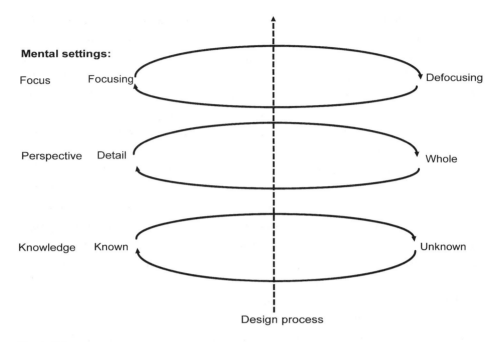

Figure 7.1
Model for structural coding of imagination in design.

design but rather as a flexible framework with many entry points that is capable of raising many types of questions and can be honed to match the work process of individual designers. Thus, the prism of imagination may have general descriptive potential in the analysis of design solutions and working practice, as well as a specific descriptive potential in informing designers about their mental settings.

Even if the figure suggests a starting point for the design process in the mental setting of the known and the unknown, none of the settings should be seen as prior to the others. They all contribute to the mental setting in the design process and approaches to design tasks as inner imaginings are turned into objects. The poles in the dichotomies should not be seen as mutually exclusive extremes but as dimensions that coexist in the design process: Elements of knowledge and nonknowledge can contribute to each other, and strategies of focusing and defocusing may simultaneously be applied.

Approach to Knowledge

First, it is important to address knowledge in relation to the design process because it may describe the way concepts are created and how well defined they are in order to meet and link with sensual matter. The question of what is known and what is not, how known and unknown are related, is a matter of how meaning is created in design. The amount of knowledge that designers have at the outset of a design process is crucial but can be difficult to determine.

In design theory, the question of knowledge is reflected in the debate about the relationship and interaction of analysis (gaining knowledge), synthesis (stipulating possible solutions), and evaluation (assessing whether more knowledge or new solutions are required). Positions here range from the linear and, hence, mostly one-way approach of analysis leading to synthesis and further to evaluation and then possibly to a feedback loop back to new analysis and synthesis, over John Chris Jones's (1980) notion of the design process as a dynamic succession of divergence (opening up problems), transformation (creating new patterns of the problem), and convergence (the creation of a solution) to Bryan Lawson's (2005) circular-dynamic models of the design process as an ongoing negotiation between problem view and solution view in the interchange of analytical, synthetic, and evaluative perspectives of design work. However, within design methodology, the point may not be to try to define the optimal type and amount of knowledge but to view most design problems as inherently wicked and ill defined, since it is the nature of the problem to evolve as the design process unfolds (Rittel and Webber 1973). In principle, one cannot know in advance what knowledge will be relevant for developing a design solution whose existence is emerging. Dorst (2006) proposed that design problems can be defined as paradoxical because the solution often requires reconciling conflicting discourses; therefore the designer, "in his/her paradoxical problematic situation, needs to construct a design that transcends or connects the different discourses" and create a new framework of discursive unity through the design: "Designers use their understanding of the ways of thinking within the different discourses to create a framework in which a solution is possible for the paradoxical situation" (15). In this perspective, handling design problems means describing the design situation.

From the perspective of imagination, however, the question is not so much how to gain information from the outer world (data about users, tests, market research) but rather what kind of knowledge is present in the designer's consciousness and how it is employed and transformed from the outset. This pushes the relationship of known versus unknown in another direction. Seen in relation to consciousness, the structure of known versus unknown can be regarded as a mental setting in relation to the design problem and thus as a method of filtering experience and schematizing meaning in connecting concepts and material matter. The question of what can be known or understood in design regarding the imagination is a question of what kind of knowledge can be produced in the imagination, how this product of consciousness interacts with the material world, and how it produces new kinds of schematization. In the design process, the process of schematization in relation to knowledge starts with the concepts employed in staging and formulating the design problem and how they are set in relation to engaging with materiality. On the one hand, the process can start with already formulated and known concepts of a brief, and on the other hand, an open schematization can start with the unknown, without having formulated any given concepts (this is discussed below as different imaginative starting points). Thus, the question is which concepts are employed and, more important, how these concepts are conceived and related to in the design process. In relation to an imaginative setting and the process of schematization, a concept that lacks clarity is not viewed as a deficit; rather, it can be explored as an asset.

The products of imagination do not fly free as they from their starting point relate to an empirical foundation. Most theories of imagination hold that the notion of creation from nothing, *creatio ex nihilo*, is by definition impossible, since all faculties of consciousness rely on experience:[7] All imaginings must be based on something factual and actual. From this starting point, they then undergo more or less profound transformation. This transformation may then, in a process of abstraction, point to potential or ideal meanings and with means of the given and known present "unasserted thoughts" (Scruton 1974) and suggest something that transcends the given but is still, paradoxically, present only through it.

In this sense, imaginings are located at the verge of the given and a possible transcendence that may be seen to resemble an immanent, non-Platonic "idea" in the sense of Merleau-Ponty's (1964) idea as a "transparency behind that which can be sensed" while it still is being part of the sensual (194). The point is that all imaginings must have a material base but in terms of meaning may produce an extra dimension that transforms meaning, that is, produces new entries to the linking of concepts and materiality. Potentially, the imaginings may perform operations of pointing to (in Adorno's sense of pointing to a passage in the direction where established meaning breaks off) or being open to a transparence of (but not directly presenting) dimensions of meaning that transcend the material while still remaining inextricably bound to it.

Alexander discusses the mechanism of the limitation of imaginings in his problematic but nevertheless important *Notes on the Synthesis of Form* (1964), where he asks how the design process, whose elements are "defined by the designer from things already present in his mind, can possibly have any outcome which is not also already present in the designer's mind" (110). As a way out of the closed space of consciousness, Alexander points to structure as an operation through which "a coherent and therefore new whole [can be produced] out of incoherent pieces." He also states that "form" can be defined when different physical implications of the requirement in the design "coalesce in [the designer's] mind, and take on organized shape." Thus, Alexander's main principle for conceptual construction is organization as a way of creating a unity that as a whole surmounts the component elements. Alexander's approach to organization is optimistic-positivist, relying on the belief that it is possible to construct ideal structures for design problems. Instead, I point to the inner dynamic of knowing that not everything is knowable or can be deduced to ideal structures of organization.

I focus on the inner interface of known versus unknown within consciousness and, as a structure of schematization generating meaning in linking concepts and material matter, localize it as a mental setting that determines how meaning is being produced. This is a shift from regarding nonknowledge as a lack of knowledge to be compensated for to regarding it as a resource in the process of generating new knowledge (Stephan 2010). As a linking of concepts and sensual appearances in the structure of schematization, the interface of known versus unknown filters the construction of experience and meaning. Awareness of this structure of knowledge can be an asset in the design process. For those who are aware of its tacit workings in consciousness, it may shed light on the inner dynamics of the design process and its material envisioning of something that not only was not there before but was also not previously knowable.

Models for exploring the potential and dynamics in the relationship of knowing versus not knowing can be found outside design and serve as a source of inspiration for design. It is an integral part of romantic discourse with its interest in exploring the darker and unenlightened parts of reality, the borderline of knowing/not knowing. Instead of seeing the knowable as the base of a sort of remainder of the not knowable, Novalis (1968) reverses this polarity and states the primacy of the unknown: "The unknown, the secrecy is the result and the beginning of everything. . . . The recognition is a means of obtaining non-recognition again" (302).[8] Novalis's point is not only that it is in the active search for the unknown that the biggest findings lie but further that it is more productive for creativity to use the unknown rather than the known as a basis for investigating human experience.[9] With clear inspiration from romantic thinking, the idea of exploring the unknown has made its way into management theory, as in C. Otto Scharmer's ideas about seeking self-transcending knowledge organized around emerging opportunities (Scharmer 2001) and developing a management culture based on the perspective of an open and becoming future, where a connection to the roots of human existence in a movement of "presencing" enables a "letting come" of the future and its not-yet-to-be-known paradigm of knowledge (Scharmer 2007).

To sum up Novalis's and Scharmer's points, there are strategic assets in seeking and being in the unknown and actively using it within a temporal setting in anticipating the future that is in the process of becoming. Thus, in combination with insights into design as an exploratory, emergent activity that uses the nonlogical logic of abduction—that is, the term in Peircian logics for the proposing or guessing of hypothesis on the basis of given data without claiming total validity, in generating a design proposal that may seem to be the result of a creative leap that may be hard to explain—the interface of known versus unknown not only designates an important feature of design work but can also be actively and consciously used as a tool by designers. It may explain why the starting point of the design process cannot be exclusively the acquisition of knowledge as part of a more or less structured process plan but must also involve an integration of unknown, emerging, and becoming layers of meaning. Thus, a mental setting that embraces the openness of the interface between known and unknown may make it possible to let the inner space of imagining develop into something new in the design process. This insight can hardly be converted into a cognitive tool that can help designers (and people in general) be more creative when they are on the verge of the known and the unknown; however, a first step toward a didactics of creativity would involve obtaining a higher degree of awareness of its processes and structures.

The interface between the known and the unknown is pivotal for most design work. I discuss it first with regard to 3PART, a medium-sized design consultancy located in Aarhus, Denmark,[10] and then with regard to some features in the working strategy of the German design firm FUCHS+FUNKE.

With its goal of creating growth through design for its clients, 3PART operates on a multidisciplinary basis and with a high degree of user involvement to create mostly technically advanced design solutions or service design concepts. Thus, 3PART does not see its task primarily as designing products or objects but rather as offering consultancy where the product or service design is a part of the solution. In this shift from product to concept, 3PART follows an overall trend in the development of design consultancies. The consultancy is ambitious in its approach to design and designing and curious in challenging given conceptions and methodologies of design. In this way, it resembles many contemporary design firms and consultancies that base their work on an open-minded and unprejudiced understanding of design, and it can thus be seen as an example of a reflective, well-informed, and methods-oriented approach to design. 3PART operates in an intense dialogue with contemporary design methods such as user involvement, design thinking, and strategic planning, which enable a double perspective on designing. In the employment of design tools, 3PART operates inside design methodologies, while at the same time taking an outside perspective on the role of design in, for example, the client's perspective.

The relation to the unknown plays a central role in several aspects and phases of the work of 3PART; these are all elements to be found in many design practices. The focus of the discussion here is to point to the role of the unknown and the setting of conceptual meaning as something that is staged at the outset of a design process (in the client's brief) and explored during the design process in a search for new solutions in new schematizing constructs of the design solutions where the conceptual meaning of the design problem may be reformulated.

Multidisciplinary teamwork: From a designer's point of view, to integrate many disciplinary approaches in the process of designing is to let in something new and transgress the known methodological perspective of the designer. This is seen as a moment in a self-transcending process of the designer. 3PART is conscious of the progressive dynamics that can evolve in the interaction of the imagining and "creative black box" of the individual and the externalizing discursive setting that is produced by open discussions in the group. Simon Skafdrup, the CEO and an industrial designer, points to the dynamic and productive interaction of individual mental setting and collective collaboration as enhancing the exchange of known and not-yet-known perspectives on the task.[11]

Acknowledgment of the user: The user has always played a central role in design, and the past thirty years of development in design methods have witnessed ever new ways to integrate the user's perspective in the design process: participatory design, user-centered design, and codesign, to mention just a few of the paradigms informing the discourse on design methods. 3PART is also oriented toward the user and methodologies of acknowledging the user and her or his requirements and needs in the design process. It is stated in the name of consultancy where the "third part" is the part beside the designer and the client. In 3PART's approach, the user's perspective is strategically positioned as something unknown; Skafdrup speaks of forcing oneself into the unknown by integrating the perspective of others and then trying to look at things through the eyes of others. Here, the conceptual framing of the design process is something to be searched for. Hence, for 3PART, integrating the user implies a strategy of constantly shifting perspectives and trying different models of seeing.

Employment of interpretation: To operate at the intersection of known and unknown and to be projective in the becoming of the not-yet-existing requires strategies of interpretation as the new perspectives are transformed and implemented in the design process. Often the design process for 3PART starts with a vague overall conception of the wholeness of the design solution that, in combination with the input from the users, needs to be integrated as a knowledge component in the design process but often without any knowledge or interpretive method of how to do this. Instead, the strategy is experimental and open-ended in the sense of Kant's reflective judgment of open reflection of the sensual without pregiven concepts: What is to be known is not known in advance, so what the designers do is turn to their methodological tool box in order to evoke an interpretative process. In this way, 3PART works with a dialectics of framing and unframing the problem, a shifting in perspectives, an attempt to steer and evenly distribute new knowledge content in the design process, and, central to design work, a formulation and testing of possible approaches and solutions through prototypes: all methods are used to get the process to move from unknown to known. But in the end, the road to the solution cannot be prescribed. As Skafdrup says: "To start with, you don't know what you get out of the input and how it can be transformed into a design, but our experience as designers is that we will always get there!"

Relation to methodological setting: Like other design consultancies in general, 3PART is very aware of the need to sell its product on a market. This means that it is not enough for 3PART to refer to its creative offerings; it must also control and steer the creative process. The phases and progression of the design process need to be made transparent to clients. This element of a methodological setting (e.g., in process models structured in phases of delivery that prove to be effective in communicating with clients) can be seen in relation to a tension in design epistemology between the outer tools or methods of design and the inner mental activity in design cognition (see chapter 6). 3PART views the methodological setting not as an outward, communicative tool that might gloss over the creative chaos and unstructured procedures of the actual designing. As a tool for structuring and steering the design process, the methodological setting helps drive forward the process of formulating a design solution, turning the unknown, or not-yet-known, into the known.

The German design firm FUCHS+FUNKE provides another example of a conscious approach toward imaginative creativity. Often in their experimental design in the dichotomy of known versus unknown, FUCHS+FUNKE employ an inward meditation in an attempt to position the design process as a search for the unknown. In an interview about imagination, Wilm Fuchs, one of the two associates of FUCHS+FUNKE, talks about the process of enabling imagination in order to transform and implement (*umsetzen*) it as design (*Entwurf*).[12] In this creative zone, he points to an "ability of sensitizing [*sensibilisieren*] oneself" by focusing on mental images in the first stages of the design process. Furthermore, he speaks of both negative and positive aspects of imagination at the border of possibilities and nonpossibilities of design; the positive side of imagination can activate "passive knowledge" and evoke cross-links (*Querverbindungen*) at the intersection of known and unknown, thus enabling something hitherto not possible.

This is reflected, for example, in *Papton* (from 2004 and on; figures 7.2 and 7.3), an origami chair that is still underway to discovering its form. In many ways, *Papton* is a design in progress; based on the material constraint of the standard sheet of paperboard, the design can be understood as an ongoing search for the ultimate and minimalist form by using origami techniques for a chair. According to Fuchs, the design came from a basic idea that operates as the principle for development by setting the direction for taking the idea to new levels. One way of conceiving this search might be to see it in relation to an implicit assumption of the possibility of creating a perfect expression of form, where the inside properties of the paperboard contain an "ideal" chair that simply needs to be discovered and carried out in the design. This conception has neo-Platonic, Plotinian traits in positing an ideal substance that flows through the design and ultimately would lead to the perfect, one-and-only expression of form. Traits of this are present in contemporary design discourse (Brix 2008).

Another approach would be to see it as an example of Kantian aesthetic schematization where the concepts for the design (the principle of folding in the right way) are continually explored in a process of infinite approximation. In this perspective, the ways of folding of the paperboard all contribute to the open process of the non-teleological construction of the concepts involved. On the level of discourse, Fuchs deliberately employs and works with imagination, and his testimony can be seen as

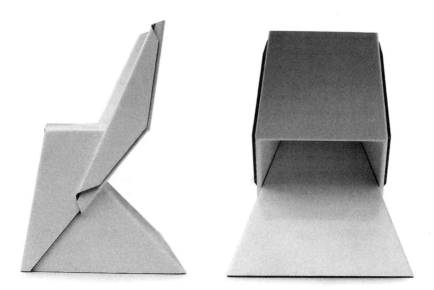

Figure 7.2
Folding of *Papton. Design:* FUCHS+FUNKE.

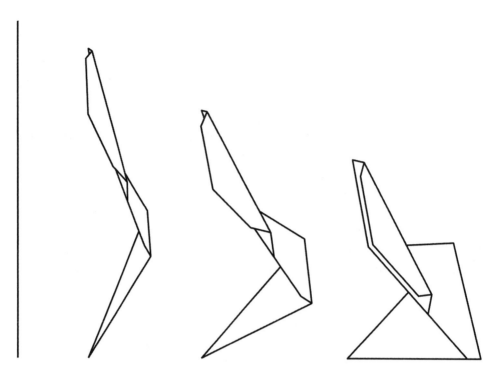

Figure 7.3
Papton. Design: FUCHS+FUNKE.

an expression of the ideology of imagination as a creative power in setting and transforming meaning. More important in this context is his employment of a mental
setting in the process of immersion where he and Kai Funke, the other associate of
FUCHS+FUNKE, seek sensitization as a specific way of relating to the character, structure, and challenges of the design process. In the case of *Papton*, the mental setting is
one of openness toward the relationship between known and unknown. By taking
into account the fact that the solution to the problem (how to make the ultimate
origami chair out of a standard sheet of paperboard) is developed in a process of infinite approximation (the folding may always change slightly), the design process takes
on the character of a negotiation of the known and given in the material matter of
the chair and the unknown in the conceptual construction of its form.

Imaginative Starting Point
The mental setting of the starting point for the design process in either an overall (typically ideational) conception of the design as a whole or a more experimental exploration
of details plays an important role in the way in which concepts and materiality meet

and produce meaning through schematization. In the first case, a stated conceptual meaning dominates, and the material expression is to be searched for; in the latter case, the materiality is the starting point and the concepts are to be searched for.

Within design theory, the relation of whole and detail is suggested by Simon (1996) with regard to the question of whether "possible subsystems will be carried before the over-all coordinating design is developed in detail, or vice-versa, how far the over-all design should be carried before various components, or possible components, are developed" (129). With regard to the ongoing development of concepts in design, these two positions describe the extremes of a span between a top-down and a bottom-up process.

If the starting point is the conception of the whole, key concepts are often clearly stated, or—considering the imaginative framework of developing design between known and unknown—as clearly stated as possible, typically in the form of stated criteria for success or requirements in the design brief. This is often the approach in goal-oriented industrial or engineering design, for example, at 3PART, where the client and the client's expectations form an integral part of the overall setting of the design process, even if experimental strategies also are employed in the actual design process.

The strategy of beginning from an exploration of a detail is often at the heart of experimental design where new forms, new combinations of materials, and new design principles can be openly tested without regard for a set of requirements in a design brief. This is clearly the case in Ditte Hammerstrøm's work, where the design process is often initiated and guided by an exploration of a dimension of materiality (e.g., the tactility of upholstery as in the chair *Bistro Light*, 2005,[13] which turns upholstery inside out; figure 7.4) or a question of tectonics, as in the assembly of furniture. I will turn to Hammerstrøm's work in this section because she experiments with design at the intersection of material expression and the conceptual meaning of design. Since 2000, she has been exploring furniture design, not within the framework of critical design in investigating design objects as critical statements about and interaction with contemporary culture, but rather as a sensual-phenomenological and, in this sense, aesthetic (see chapter 3), meditation on the impact and effects of elements (e.g., in details) and structures (e.g., in crossing different types of furniture) in design. Her work reflects an ontological questioning of design: what its being and constitutive elements are, and what happens if these are challenged or combined in new ways. This investigation makes her work and working strategies illustrative for discussing mental settings in design.

The duality of different starting points is usually not so rigid in real life; concrete design situations are often defined and situated in between—in fact, both starting points may coexist in the same design process. Thus, 3PART may employ a top-down

Figure 7.4
Bistro Light, 2005. Design: Ditte Hammerstrøm. Made by: Källemo AB for Thorsen Møbler. *Photo:* Ole Akhøj.

approach in initiating the design process (due to the requirements of the design brief), but over the course of designing, it often uses experimental, bottom-up strategies in the search for new ideas. The point is that whole and detail are ontologically linked. Every detail is structurally and hermeneutically bound to a totality or a whole that can perhaps hardly be fully stated. Thus, details can be developed and understood only as fragments in the light of a totality that may be only on the verge of becoming through fragmented details.[14] And a whole would be empty but for the richness of details. The distinction is which perspective the designer mentally chooses as his or her starting point.

The span between whole and detail is related to a span between abstract and concrete. Abstract reasoning is part of all design processes when the overall requirements of the design are stated, that is, in the metadesign, or the design of the design. Designing is also always an operation of making the abstract concrete, that is, designing (more or less) material matter in a way that contains and condenses specific immaterial knowledge (Brix 2008).

With reference to the artistic object, the relationship between abstract and concrete, or general and particular, has been widely debated within traditional aesthetic theory. The romantic philosopher Schelling (1991) had an optimistic focus on the general and claimed that the special feature of artistic creation is its ability to connect "the absolute" with "the specific" and let the "divineness of the general" be created through "the particular" (177).[15] Later aesthetic theory, however, has illustrated the dangers of letting the general perspective take over; it contains an element of power because it subsumes and thus levels the particular (Adorno 1970). Hence, this line of aesthetic theory has emphasized the importance of maintaining the perspective of the singular in the aesthetic experience of the work (Bubner 1989). The general, however, always plays a role in artistic creations; it must not be allowed to take over but should nevertheless be acknowledged for its constitutive and formative role in aesthetics. Thus, aesthetic experience can be seen as a process that starts in a sensual experience that at the same time leads to the "search for the totality in the detail" (65). A noteworthy point is that the general and the abstract play a constitutive role for aesthetic objects, as their wider implication of meaning lies in the abstract-conceptual constructions of the aesthetic work, while the specificity of the aesthetic creation lies in the extension and implication of the singularity of the aesthetic creation: The concentration of meaning is constructed from the bottom up with a base in sensual matter.

In a discussion on expert designers, Nigel Cross (2007) implies that these can embody aspects of both abstract and concrete at different levels of their design process: On the level of metadesign, creative experts often define a broad framework for the problem, defining "the given task so that it is problematic, *i.e.* deliberatively treat it as ill-defined," while simultaneously, on the level of the actual design development, these creative experts "do not 'reason' towards a design concept in an abstract way, but rely more on their experience and on visual information" (113). In an endeavor to clarify design cognition, Cross seeks to describe the difference between novice and expert designers and at the same time explores the epistemological theme and dimension (i.e., schematization) in design of relating abstract concepts and concrete matter. He also describes how the design process can be accessed from two angles, the abstract and the concrete, and that these two aspects can coexist in a design strategy.

By examining aspects of the design strategies of Anna von Schewen and Ditte Hammerstrøm, we can see how the meaning of design solutions is created at the intersection of overall abstract considerations and concrete matter.

As an architect and interior designer, von Schewen often works with the design of spaces, for example, in exhibition design, that is, the overall frame for design. At the same time, she often focuses on the detail out of a desire to "explore something,"[16] in the same open manner as Ditte Hammerstrøm, and her work as a designer often develops in the explicitly stated tension between an overall and rather abstract concept of the idea and the space for the design along with a desire to transform design and the space that it interacts with by exploring possibilities in the material and the technology. By looking more closely at the chair *Hug* (2002) for the Swedish furniture manufacturer Gärsnäs (figure 7.5), we can approach an understanding of the actual piece of furniture by seeing how these perspectives of abstract overall reasoning and concrete detailing meet and impose structure on the design.

According to von Schewen, two different intentions meet in the chair: the chair should appear massive and organic while at the same time making the user feel embraced by it. This marks an experiment with pure form and experiments with material and technology: the open shell of the chair is made of solid wood that is shaped in a computerized CNC router. In a top-down process the chair should fulfill the intention of its concept by performing an embracing gesture, and in a bottom-up perspective, this operation should be invigorated by the detailing of the design through its form. Thus, the chair can be comprehended as a physical structure that through its detailing and work with form reaches out for a totality of meaning implied by its use and its placement in space. The point is that in its design, the chair contains this pointing; through its embracing gesture, it posits itself as a fragment of a whole that

Figure 7.5
Hug, 2002. *Design:* Anna von Schewen. *Manufacturer:* Gärsnäs (opposite page).

cannot, however, be fully realized in and through the chair. The point regarding the process of schematization is that the chair is conceived in a way that lets abstract conceptualization and concrete matter meet in a way where the meaning of the object is under ongoing construction in a span of detailing and grasping of space. The chair is an expression of a design process that developed its concepts as the process unfolded. Like Kant's aesthetic concepts, it can be seen as the result of a schematization without given concepts in an open search for concepts that fit the appearance as well as an appearance that fits the concept of letting the chair reach out for the space and letting the space pervade the chair.

Hammerstrøm deliberately takes her starting point in the exploration of details of material, texture, form or structures—for example, decoration:

When I work with details such as decoration, it's like working with the necessary unnecessary. What interests me is that decoration isn't just a minor aspect of the design; it intervenes in the whole. I therefore use different scales in the design when I explore the impact of the detail on the whole. Models in 1:10 can provide an idea of the overall appearance of the design, whereas working with models in 1:1 gives an impression of how, for example, materials, surfaces and shapes can meet in the design. I always test different kinds of material, as materials also contain a certain cultural memory or frame of reference within which they operate.[17]

The last point is important for our discussion. Hammerstrøm might embark on the design process in an open, experiential exploration of details and materials, but this open search for opportunities, possibilities and new paths is also motivated by the relationship to and embeddedness in specific frames of reference. Hammerstrøm in fact works deliberately with the connotative and culturally framed nature of different materials and strategies of detailing, as illustrated, for example, by her mental setting toward decoration, which contains a comprehensive cultural repertoire. This is evident, for example, in the seven-part sofa *Loungescape* (2005, figure 7.6), where brightly colored plastic wire, otherwise used in outdoor furniture from the 1970s and as clotheslines, is used nonfunctionally as an element of decoration. Hammerstrøm thus operates within the productive tension of culturally established frames of reference that simultaneously represent a factor of the known in the design process and the unforeseen operations of testing different types of detailing or exploring materiality, texture, and structure, that is, the new and, hence, unknown. In balancing the design between what appeals to common understanding through known parameters and what is unknown (due to a surprising use of details), at least until its introduction in the design, Hammerstrøm challenges cultural and formal design conventions.

Like designers in general, she does not frame this challenge as a strictly intellectual-formalistic endeavor but also takes her starting point in a sensuous and emotionally charged quality. Not only does she turn her conceptual conceptions into actual form;

Figure 7.6
Loungescape, 2005. *Design:* Ditte Hammerstrøm.

her painstaking work with details and decoration demonstrates the sensual appeal of the design and its goal of engaging directly with its users or audience. In and through the detailing, her design performs an aesthetic function. With its high degree of detailing, the design has a tactile and sensual quality that exceeds the ordinary and thus calls for extraordinary perception. This can be described as an aesthetic effect of letting the actual appearance be reflected and marked as appearance, as the design puts forward a presence that stands out from everyday experience. We want to sit on and use Hammerstrøm's furniture and are intrigued by its character and texture, so that we do not see through it but notice how it interacts with us. Thus, the design encourages the formalistic feature of prolonging the perception. Furthermore, the design challenges our conceptual meaning of what design is about. It sets its sensual appeal in connection with its conceptual meaning (the sensual-phenomenological and the conceptual-hermeneutical platforms of aesthetics addressed in chapter 3); they relate to and consolidate each other. The sensual means of prolonging the perception is engaged in order to challenge the concept of design, and the conceptualization of design points back to the role of the material devices in the design.

In this vein, Hans Ulrich Gumbrecht (2003) has pointed to aesthetic experience as being constituted by a duality or, rather, an oscillation of the effects of material presence and those of conceptual meaning. On the one hand, all artifacts are circumscribed by cultural contextual meaning: as our everyday world is historically and culturally specific, "the objects of aesthetic experience [are] likewise culturally specific" (206). Cultural meaning is, so the general argument goes, unavoidable as the frame for all types of artifacts. Aesthetic artifacts can, in moments of intensity, offer a presence that is evoked in experience on a phenomenological basis as soon as perception has occurred but before interpretation has distributed cultural meaning to the artifacts in a process of signification.[18] To fix this argument on behalf of the aesthetic artifacts, something in the objects must encourage the production of intensity or an epiphanic presence, and the pressing question then is what it is exactly. Gumbrecht does not enter into a specific discussion of the nature of the aesthetic object[19] but offers a hint regarding the general characteristics for encouraging intensities in experience: "When aesthetic experience is always related to moments of intensity that are not part of the everyday worlds respective of these moments, it is implied that aesthetic experience is necessarily performed at a certain distance from these everyday worlds" (207).

What is interesting about design in relation to this kind of aesthetic reflection that examines the distance to the everyday and the ordinary is that design is in many ways a medium of everyday life and the ordinary. This makes the question of the means of aesthetic communication available to design even more urgent. Hammerstrøm's proposal is not to allow features external to the design language to invade or supersede the design but instead to use design-specific means such as detailing and decoration to achieve a distance from the ordinary within the design itself. Thus, the detailing evokes a presence that traverses the basic everyday functional frame of the design.

As in the case of von Schewen, concrete exploration and the abstract perspective of cultural reference are closely connected and interrelated. The detailing gains value by virtue of pointing to or relating to the overall structure of meaning within the cultural frame of reference, and the frame of reference is relevant only insofar as it is actualized by the operations of detailing. Hammerstrøm's deliberate incorporation of the frame of reference in her work is in part motivated by a deep wish to challenge the cultural tradition of Danish modern and its design dogmas, as she sees them, of simplicity, rationality, and claimed timelessness[20] and in part by a desire to engage in dialogue with the inherent ontological factors of design, such as frames of reference concerning types of furniture design through the elements they consist of and the kinds of proportions that structure the furniture (e.g., What is a dining table or a desk like?).[21] On a conceptual level, it is important for Hammerstrøm to maintain that the frames of reference are unavoidable, as it is impossible to design outside culture, but that these frames can be employed to enhance the clash, for example, of opposite structures or strategies of detailing, as it is exactly through the meeting of opposites in a clash that the frames of reference that are normally implicit and in the background can move to the forefront.

In this way, Hammerstrøm actively engages elements of the contextual-discursive level of aesthetics in its questioning of how and at what aesthetic meaning is produced and the stages in which this happens. Her design relates itself to the cultural frame of reference that attributes aesthetic meaning to objects like hers. Thus, by challenging the ideology of Danish modern, Hammerstrøm produces clashes in order to question the frames of references that are tacitly but effectively at work in the design. These clashes can produce a new kind of intensity or epiphanic presence that operates through her design. In the clash of abstract references, principles, and concepts and concrete detailing, matter, and material in the design, Hammerstrøm seems to go in a different "designerly" direction from Kant's concept of schematization, which aims at letting abstract and concrete be mediated, exchanged, and connected. What characterizes Hammerstrøm's design is creation of new meaning that might be based on a clash (the negative-destructive aspect of her design) yet still seeks new ways of relating the abstract and concrete (the positive-constructive aspect), where both polarities undergo changes during the process of meaning creation.

This point is evident and performed as a principle in the simultaneously heterogeneous and homogeneous *Sofa set* (2004, figure 7.7). The elements in this sofa set are designed to be as archetypal as possible. According to Hammerstrøm, they should "look like an experiment in the furniture laboratory." At the same time, they play with the culturally shaped expectation of combining furniture in groups. Hammerstrøm has taken the ongoing fusion of furniture in contemporary culture literally and created a set where the different pieces are built into each other. Thus, instead of grouping and arranging discrete and separate pieces of furniture, she has created a brutal clash of disparate elements of different kinds of furniture: sofa, sofa table, shelves, and lamp. In this way, she has tried to push the design of the sofa set, and thus the content and meaning of the design, in a new direction. By using known elements of furniture, *Sofa set* applies to a level of given signification where we can understand what it is made of; in its structural clash, it simultaneously seeks to explore a dimension of design that was not given before its actual design. *Sofa set* displays an open schematization of meaning without concepts given in advance. Furthermore, this way of operating can be conceptualized as an asymmetric relationship between the comprehensible meaning of the design as based on existing elements and a dimension of yet-to-be-grasped but

Figure 7.7
Sofa set, 2004. *Design:* Ditte Hammerstrøm. Made by: Erik Jørgensen. *Photo:* Jeppe Gudmundsen-Holmgreen.

still incomprehensible meaning of the new type of object that can be sensed and detected as something that shimmers through the design but has not yet come into being. This position of being on the verge of an established meaning of the known and a dimension of still unknown meaning can also be considered in light of the Adornian reflection on the aesthetic structure of the work of art that simultaneously breaks off and points in the direction of a truth that can never be fully spoken.

Degree of Focus

The aspect of focusing versus defocusing deals with the question of the mental setting toward a design problem and how the problem is formulated in relation to the concepts employed. This is again a question of schematization: how clear—or consciously unclear—the concepts are stated during the design process.

Within design theory, a stated axiom is that it may be impossible to state and define the full scope of the problem directly or take it as given in a way that leads to an ideal solution in a generic and linear fashion. Instead, theories of design methods view the relationship between problem and solution as on ongoing process of "negotiation" in the "tension between a problem view and a solution view of the situation" (Lawson 2005, 271), in a structure of a "co-evolution of solution *and* problem spaces" (Cross 2007, 102), where the problem remains continuously open to investigation, as "creative design is not a matter of first fixing the problem (through objective analysis or the imposition of a frame) and then searching for a satisfactory solution concept" (Dorst 2006, 10). When the span of problem and solution is open to investigation and continuous reformulations, the process of framing the problem, that is, the context for approaching and naming the problem and its components (Schön 1983, 40), takes on importance along with the actual generation of solutions, since it is often through the strategy of proposing "satisfactory" solutions that the requirements of "ill-defined problems" can be met, as these can rarely be converted into "well-defined problems" in an analytical phase (Cross 2007, 103). Conversely, it may even be productive for the design process to treat all design problems as ill-defined, or "wicked," which may produce new and unforeseen insights during the process.

Seen in the context of imagination, the relationship between problem statement and solution generation defines the path from inner imagining as an adaptation of the problem statement to outward manifestation in a design solution. Thus, the attention shifts from framing as a discursive activity of naming to focusing as in the process of schematizing a way of structuring the transfer of meaning between inner imaginings in possible ideas or concepts and outer physical manifestations. Like framing, the process of focusing is open to ongoing reformulation in the concepts employed, even if its functional position in the interface between inner consciousness and outer world lies in the span between clear and rational discourse and the inaccessible mental space. The concepts employed and stated in a design process may be more or less clear or vague; they may, if clearly stated, entail a top-down process to meet materiality, or they may produce an open schematization without given concepts. The case is that strategies of focusing or defocusing can be evoked as strategies for choosing different entries to the process of schematization.

As a filtering of inner meaning that is transformed into form, the activity of focusing is closely connected to the methodological complex of idea generation described within the field of design method theories. Here, idea generation can be seen in the dual perspective of keeping the mind open to new and unforeseen turns in the development process and leaving the field of opportunity open "as long as possible" while acknowledging the power of the initial proposal in guiding the design process: "The very first conceptualizations and representations of problem and solution are . . . critical to the procedures that will follow" (Cross 2007, 54, 34).[22] The emphasis is often on many focal points rather than any single point, as they become part of the dynamics of the design process. Thus, in *How Designers Think* (2005), which deals with design cognition and "design thinking as a skill," Bryan Lawson speaks of design as a "multi-dimensional process" and points to designers' "ability to think along parallel lines, deliberately maintain a sense of ambiguity and uncertainty and not to get too concerned to get a single answer too quickly" (289, 298). He points out that in working with multiple frames, the designer can achieve a position of metaframing and metaperspectivism by reflecting on the fact that although adopting a certain perspective is a constitutive condition, awareness of this fact may alter the frame: "The skill to create and manipulate frames is a central one in determining how the process will unfold" (292). Nigel Cross (2007) speaks of designers' ability, through sketches, to "handle different levels of abstraction simultaneously" (57). In industrial designers' actual working processes it can be observed how multiperspectivism and multiabstraction are integral parts of designing. As a methodologically informed design agency, 3PART, for example, is aware of the emergence and shifting of perspectives within the idea generation phase and of the productive power of operating with different levels of framing at the same time or, to be more precise, the continuous oscillation between specifying a frame for the design work (i.e., sticking to the client's brief) and, in an operation of unframing, "driving the process forward" (Simon Skafdrup, industrial designer and CEO, 3PART) by asking new and unexpected questions, something that often is expected by the client who wants the designer to create solutions that "exceed the brief" (Harfield 2007, 164).

An integral factor in the generation of multiple and parallel ideas and solution proposals is the relational proportion of focusing and defocusing in each proposal. The multiple ideas and the kind and degree of focusing in each proposal interact in a structural network of constructing new meaning that is crucial to design: While the presence of multiple ideas enables a dynamic design process (more approaches and concepts are being tested, although the openness eventually has to come a halt and be narrowed to form the basis of the final design), the kind of focusing in each proposal points directly to the structure of schematization and its process of meaning construction in the intersection of sensual materiality and conceptual construction.

Thus, the discussion of the structure of focusing and defocusing explains how meaning is not just given as something to be found in the design process but is developed as a result of the designer's mental setting with regard to meaning. It further underlines that this meaning contains definite as well as more elusive elements. In a philosophical context of epistemology, the determinate and the indeterminate can be said to be eternally intertwined in the sense that the indeterminate can be regarded as the conceptual background of the determinate, as within conceptual knowledge there will always exist a constitutive difference "between what from the given perspective is determinate and what is indeterminate" (Seel 2006, 188). On the one hand, all ways of addressing meaning in the world are seen from a specific perspective and bound to see only aspects; on the other hand, we cannot presume that any specific, given concepts fully circumscribe the process of determining since indeterminism is always lurking in the background.

Reflecting on the actual phenomenology of the mental setting in design, the types of focus and defocus gain importance as active devices of not presuming any given components in the process of actively creating form and meaning in design but instead obtaining an awareness of the implied process and its internal demarcation of determinate and indeterminate concepts. A sharp and conceptually determined focus will often be associated with a goal-oriented process that is close to the client's stated requirements (as well as the conceptual limitations and constraints imposed by the client). Through a complementary strategy of defocusing, the goal loses prominence, while the broader background with more or less directly related ideas and concepts becomes more important. This widens the conceptual scope. Thus, Kavakli and Gero (2001) speak of "defocussed attention" or "remote association" as a method of "divergent thinking which refers to the general process of thinking of unusual associations"; thus it may be "important to deliberately defocus one's attention when attempting to discover creative solutions to a problem" (358–359). Absolute focusing and defocusing cannot, however, be attained simultaneously, a principle illustrated by picture puzzles such as Wittgenstein's famous duck-rabbit, where either the duck or the rabbit is seen but not the two at the same time: The outer picture (or design situation) may be the same, but the internal cognitive modes can vary. Focusing and defocusing can be present in various degrees at the same time, or a design process may involve variations in focusing strategies.

This doubling of focusing and defocusing is often internalized within design practice and tacitly employed by designers, not least in the dialectical dynamics in creative processes between modes of concentration and relaxation, of conscious and nonconscious work.[23] In an apparent homology with the dual process of framing and unframing, strategies of focusing and defocusing are evident in the work of 3PART. 3PART design works especially with the dichotomy of focusing versus defocusing as a means of challenging the borderline between known and unknown in their search for new design solutions.

While the operation of framing and unframing characterizes the overall setting (and unsetting) of the design situation in defining the context for the problem to be solved—library or postal services in the overall context of the whole cycle of relevant operations and the theoretical framework of service design (3PART 2010)—the dialectic of focusing and defocusing is employed as a device for shifting perspective during the design process and as a strategy for interpreting different aspects and sequences of the design situation. In this way, 3PART deliberately plays with shifts in perspective and focusing by using not only sketches to test how ideas can be transformed and implemented but also linguistic devices such as metaphors, similes, and analogies and by addressing and interpreting parts of the problem in new ways. Metaphors can be seen as devices for posing virtual meaning ("as if") and turning "the possible into the impossible" whereby "new meanings emerge" (Murphy, Peters, and Marginson 2010, 6). Thus, designers employ a strategy of "seeing as" when they use metaphors to highlight certain aspects of the design. When designating a wheelchair for teenagers

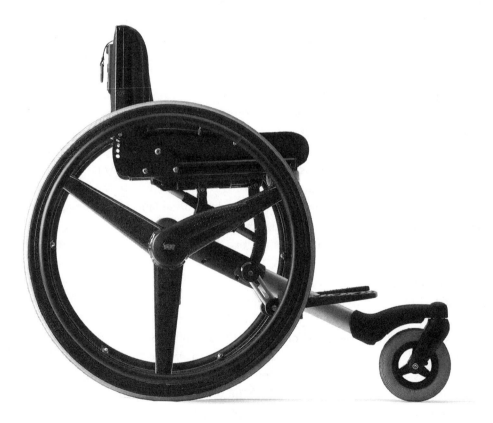

Figure 7.8
Cheetah, 2003. *Design:* 3PART. *Manufacturer:* R82.

as a "Transformer wheelchair" (figure 7.8), they used a method of metaphorical defocusing to draw attention to the design features that would make the chair desirable to its users: that it should be flexible and adapt to many kinds of uses and situations:[24] "We often add little twists and turns to the way we see and address the design problem, and this heightens the qualitative standards of the design," noted Simon Skafdrup. In general, the point of reflective multiperspectivism can be said to obtain several perspectives of focus and defocus, be conscious about the devices of obtaining them, be reflective about the role and function of the different perspectives, and exchange and compare them with perspectives generated in the design process, whether individually or within the team.

Searching for the Possible

After having proposed the dichotomies of known versus unknown, whole versus detail, and focusing versus defocusing as parts of an overall conceptual framework of schematization, the next step is to ask for practical application.

The big question is how to combine the three dichotomies in design practice. The general and easy, but valid, answer would be that they all help to inform a design-relevant and design-specific discourse about the formative powers behind creative processes in design. In this way, the proposed theoretical framework can contribute to our knowledge about design processes that normally have the character of tacit knowledge. Exploring imagination also means exploring productive factors of creativity. A greater awareness of the mechanisms of imagination helps us understand how imagination contributes to our ways of constructing meaning and lets us create and use design as a medium for this process.[25] In addition to this kind of methodological reflection that considers the general benefits of conceptualizing means and procedures of practice and tacit knowledge, the three dichotomies can be used to offer theoretically informed insights into the underlying structures and structural codes in the design process.

A concrete proposal for employing the structural coding of imagination in relation to the design process may be to connect it to the search for possibilities and see this as a conscious approach to the work with concepts through the prism of schematization. This can be visualized in a model (figure 7.9) that can contribute to both understanding and describing the dynamic workings of an imaginative creation of new possibilities. The aim of the model is not only to state the opening of new possibilities in design but also to indicate a succession of stages of mental settings in the creative act of "possibilizing," that is, the act of actively searching for new possibilities. The

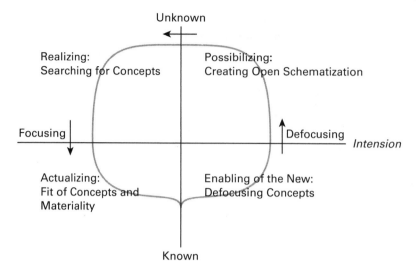

Figure 7.9
Model for exploring the possible: The development of imagination in design in the span of possibilizing and actualizing.

model is not meant as a prescriptive tool for all processes of imaginative designing and searching for new possibilities, but it may serve as inspiration for ways in which imagination can be employed and engaged in the search for the possible in design. In the same way, it may be productive to state all design problems as "wicked problems" as that may produce new insights, a reflective grasp of possibilities, and a conscious venture into the unknown that may also set the design process in a new light. The model describes a process in the polarity of actualizing and possibilizing, with phases involving the enabling of meaning and realization of design.

Constructing a coordinate system with the dichotomy of amount of presupposed knowledge, known versus unknown, on the y-axis, and the dichotomy of degree of focus, focusing versus defocusing, on the x-axis (and setting aside the dichotomy of imaginative perspective, whole versus detail as the models aims at describing phases of setting toward new knowledge) produces four quadrants, each of which designates a phase in the design process. Starting in the lower left quadrant, the process is based on focusing and the known. This is the element of the existing and the given. Moving in the direction of defocusing, the next phase is an enabling of new meaning (the lower right quadrant). The strategy of a mental setting of defocusing pushes the meaning in new direction. This may take the form of formulating new metaphors in stating and staging the design problem in new ways, that is, in reframing and reformulating the problem. Within the setting of defocusing, the challenging moment arrives in the effort to push the frame of knowledge across the border of the known into the realm of the unknown. This phase represents the act of letting go (in Scharmer's understanding) of the previously known and pushing the knowable to its border, reverting it. Thus, the concepts are consciously positioned as not yet given. This is the critical moment in design where it may enter, in the reversal of the known and the embracing of the unknown, the phase of possibilizing (upper right quadrant in figure 7.9), rendering the design process open to the open space of the possible and the search for new concepts. At this stage, however, it is easy to lose hold of the unknown because it is also a state of insecurity and relapse to known properties. Thus, design is a risky process of actively attending to and imagining the unknown in a search for concepts. On a practical level, the combination of defocusing and entering into the realm of the unknown can be facilitated in a number of ways: by an experimentally set, explorative process that begins in the details, as in Hammerstrøm's simultaneously rational and intuitive approach to design, or by constantly questioning the framing of the design problem, as 3PART does. In the phase of the purely possible, anything can happen, at least in principle; the premises of the design and its problem (if there is a problem) can be altered and seen from new perspectives.

Next, the challenge is not to let the phase of possibilizing be simply imagined but to also incorporate it in the further design process. Within the realm of the unknown, the design process may shift from defocusing to focusing. Thus, the possible enters a phase of realization, in the sense of becoming real (obtaining reality) and, even more, of being recognized as a possibility that is productive of a process of designing (the upper left quadrant of figure 7.9). Thus, possibility is not just "pure" possibility but is experienced as such, enters cognition, and can be employed in the design process. Where possibilizing describes a phase of imaginative internalization (of the imagining subject but also of the meaning in a turning away from reality), the phase of realization is part of the start of the externalization of imagined possibility as it gains in relevance and importance outside the pure imaginative process itself. Here, new concepts emerge. Thus, the next and final phase is the phase of actualization, where the unknown, through the device of focusing and by the use of design tools, enters the realm of the known. In terms of schematization, concepts are to be found to fit materiality. In being made actual, the possible goes from being imagined and pure openness of meaning to be a part of the design when the design process becomes the sort of conclusion that might be the draft for a product or a solution. This brings us back to the state of the given but with new knowledge and new material for the design.

Thus, according to this proposal, the design process follows a trajectory from the known into the unknown and from here back to the known: The known is possibilized, and the unknown is actualized. This movement may be revisited repeatedly; thus, imaginative design not only takes place as a single passing from the given to possibilizing and back to actualizing; it may oscillate back and forward dialectically by reaching out to the unknown and the integration of the hitherto unknown in the realm of the known. Thus, reaching out for the unknown in actualizing it, integrating it, and making it a part of what we do know is a never-ending process and an integrated and constitutive element of the process of designing: Designing is, among other things, expanding the realm of knowable by constantly bringing it to the edge of what can be imagined.

8   The Imaginary in Design

I now turn to the objects of design as containers for meaning. Taking up the line of reflection in chapter 5, the argument of this chapter is that the imaginary is a productive category for conceptualizing the creation and circulation of meaning in and through designed objects. Through this entry into the discussion of meaning in design, the prevalent materiality of objects can be questioned and opened to a dimension of the possible that is attached to the imaginary. Formed on the basis of an act of negation, the imaginary is at a distance from the present, the actual, and the materially given, and it is this distance that can make it a productive asset for understanding the formation of meaning in design. Thus, the imaginary is part of a movement of unrealization that not only negates the actual but negates it in order to let the imaginary meaning relate in new ways to the actual, which then can be led in new directions. At the same time, goes the argument, this concept of the imaginary is best seen from the perspective of the actual design object.

A core argument in my approach is that the imaginary is an integrated part of design; the imaginary is not, then, a kind of immaterial substance that moves into the previously inanimate design object or an element that can emanate through or be subtracted from the design object. Instead, the imaginary should be understood as an inherent part of the design object. This may offer new insights into the nature and constitution of design objects. Thus, I propose a foundation for design that takes into account that being is always permeated by structures of nonbeing that are difficult to grasp firmly but leave traces that are important to understand in relation to the creation of meaning in design. Furthermore, this can lead to a discussion of the ways in which open possibilities and cultural potentialities are enabled and produced by design objects. This entails a phenomenological description of the character of the imaginary in relation to design.

First, I describe the methodological perspective of using the ontology of the design object as the starting point. My aim is to question what design objects are—how they contain imaginary meaning of possibility and thus produce meaning that in a next step, in chapter 9, can be labeled symbolic.

Design Ontology: Meaning Through Objects

The question of meaning in design objects deals with the interdependence of objects and their various cultural contexts. As design objects carry, convey, and structure meaning, they engage in a variety of contexts. The discussion can be entered from the side of either the context or the objects.

Analysis of context is important to understand the role of design. The discipline of design history examines how design in its many manifestations in products, graphics, and Web design, as well as service and concept design, has coevolved with modern society in a manner where design both mirrors its surroundings and cultural conditions and contributes to them (Raizman 2010; Sparke 2009).[1] Thus, it is vital to consider the cultural framing of design, just as the sociologically informed field of cultural studies has demonstrated how design can be analyzed within a dynamic "circuit of culture" where production, the representation of products in media, consumption, consumer identity, and the regulation of habits interdependently contribute to the cultural dynamics of a designed product (du Gay et al. 1997). Thus, we can speak of a "design culture" (Julier 2008) since, essentially, "design history is cultural history" (Fallan 2010, 54), that is, design is always and constitutively embedded in the context of culture.

It is also important to consider the specific nature and being of the design objects when they engage with culture. Herein lies, as I see it, a discussion of design ontology, that is, the theory of being of design objects—how design objects are constituted when they enter, become a part of, interact with, and ultimately change cultural patterns of social action, meaning, and understanding. As such and as a term, design ontology is not a topic of debate within design theory; it does, however, pervade a range of positions within the fields of culture, sociology, and design history that have all reflected on the ontological status of the object in relation to culture. This is my starting point for reflecting on how design creates meaning. Indeed, when we look at more theoretical approaches, I think it is possible to discern an object turn in the overall acknowledgment of the role of the object.

In *The Culture of Design* (2008), Guy Julier argues that design culture, "as an object of study," includes both "material and immaterial aspects of everyday life." On one level, it is concretely "articulated through images, words, forms and spaces," and on another level, it "engages discourses, actions, beliefs, structures and relationships" (7). Moreover, studies in material culture place the emphasis directly on the specific kind and nature of material things as the starting point of cultural analysis and the investigation of patterns of consumption and on the "artifacts as objects" that not only have "a major role in the development of cognitive abilities" but also in "the ways in which the world is perceived, understood and lived in" (Miller 1987, 85–86). In *Wild Things* (2000), Judy Attfield conceives of design as "things" that, in a "practice of making meaning material" (42), investigate how design operates within a social and cultural context. Thus, although Attfield keeps her main focus on the material object, her project is "not really about *things* in themselves but about how people make sense of the world through physical objects" (1). She refuses to speak about design as a category of material sublimity—as in lifestyle magazines—but regards design as "things with attitude" that are "created with a specific end in view—whether to fulfill a particular task, make a statement, objectify moral values, or express individual or group identity, to denote status or demonstrate technological prowess, to exercise social control or to flaunt political power" (12). To study material culture, Attfield states, is to study "the social meaning of the physical world" as it revolves around the interpretive relationship of object and subject—of the "thing" itself on the one hand and the cultural process of understanding, distribution, and attribution of meaning on the other (15–16).

Contemporary sociology has attempted to analyze meaning as socially constructed around objects (of technology, e.g., Bijker and Law 1992), and to investigate how a "sociality with objects" creates the self and mediates social relationships and social integration (Knorr-Cetina 1997). In the study *Global Culture Industry* (2007), sociologists Scott Lash and Celia Lury employ a "sociology of objects" where the analyzed object is tracked "as it moves and transforms through a media environment" that is characteristic of culture in the age of globalization where the movement of the object produces a sort of "sense making" through its specific "orientation or navigation" (31). Thus, Lash and Lury regard "culture as a *system of objects*" that does not work through a structure of representation (what the object "means") but through an active generation of new meaning; the object "constitutes itself as a system: a system whose virtual or deep structure generates a series of actual forms" (181). In this way, Lash and Lury challenge the notion of a fixed ontology of the object, as it does not contain a static kernel that might serve as the starting point for a process of representation (hence the critique of representation) but is instead changed by the uses and the media-based environments it is a part of. Thus, a concept of objects as "unfinished" and as parts of open-ended series or systems (Julier 2009; Knorr-Cetina 1997) may prove productive to an understanding of the founding powers of cultural dynamics in and through the objects. From this perspective, "objects of global culture industry may come to act as life-forms, give faces to and animate the markets of the global culture industry" (Lash and Lury 2007, 19).

In addition, approaches within science and technology studies, the social construction of technology, and actor-network theory (ANT) have focused on various aspects of the social construction of meaning in networks of objects, subjects, and contexts (Fallan 2010). In particular, ANT has proposed the object of research as active. ANT (Callon 1987; Law 2004; Latour 2005), whose methodology has entered design analysis (Yaneva 2009; Petersen 2010), has demonstrated a reversal of paradigms from excluding the objects in the analysis of social forces to acknowledging the role of the object as an active actor in a relational network with human subjects. As Latour (2005) states, "*Any thing* that does modify a state of affairs by making a difference is an actor . . . things might authorize, allow, afford, encourage, permit, suggest, influence, block, render possible, forbid, and so on" (71–72). In an ANT perspective, the social is not a preexisting substance that guarantees a stable context for meaning, but is constructed from within and through the relations of groups, actions, and objects. A central element is to "register the links between unstable and shifting frames of reference" (24) in the social texture.

What design objects can do, like other types of objects, in this context is not to stabilize social meaning but to create a new frame of reference within instability. Thus, design objects partake in the construction of the social. Reflected by ANT, they are in a "a process of enacting the social" and a way of making "scripts" for the "vision of the world incorporated in the object and the program of action it is supposed to accomplish" (Yaneva 2009, 283–284). The analysis of how design structures experience points to design phenomenology (see chapter 10) but also to an exploration of how design objects in a postphenomenological reflection (Verbeek 2005) or as "concrete phenomenology" (Oldemeyer 2008) can operate as agents in this process of imposing structure on experience and, even better, transform the conditions of experience.

A further argument for discussing design ontology is the prevalent immaterialization of design. As a vehicle for transmitting meaning, design has always also been a medium of the immaterial; today, however, the immaterial dimension is more upfront in products, as more and more products are not just objects with a physical extension (e.g., a chair) but also products that incorporate elements such as electronics that introduce a physical radiance as well as cultural resonance beyond the actual being in space. Thus, debating design ontology and the immaterial scope of design is important because design objects are not only objects with a finite physical extension but always contain levels of meaning beyond this limitation. I approach this discussion through the concepts of the imaginary as a means of conceptualizing meaning in design as open toward the possible and as a way of giving structure to this meaning in a balance to the actual.

Imaginary Meaning in Design

As I stated in chapter 5, the imaginary can be seen as the resulting process of a double process of applying negation and opening up to a new dimension of possibility. This is the process of unrealization where the imaginary enables a complex relationship of negation and positioning, of absence and presence. Negation can allow something new to come into being. But because it is imaginary, this "new" emergence is founded on the opposite of an ontology that is the result of a scientific or rationalistic thought where "true knowledge is conditioned by the existence of physical objects that are identifiable in space and time," even as this imaginary is founded on and thus attached to "a perceived and thought reality" (Wunenburger 2003, 71, 85).

With the imaginary, the relation to physical present reality changes, even as the imaginary—by virtue of the starting point in reality that it is based on—remains connected to reality. Thus, the process of unrealization alters the ontological status of the real. This is a loss—but also a gain: what the imaginary loses in physical presence, it gains in freedom to create new, possible transversal connections to other aspects and dimensions of meaning. To illustrate, this crossing of meanings can be seen as a metaphoric act, from the Old Greek *meta* (over, beyond) and *phero* (carrying, convey), where the process of negating abstraction in the imaginary enables meanings to be carried over from one domain to another or several other domains and thus to cross-fertilize.[2] As an example, this comes into being in linguistic metaphors such as "love is a rose," where the floral domain of the rose extends the meaning of love, or in a paradoxical description of the beloved as "a lovely sun of the night" (Novalis). In design, a similar effect occurs when products have the likeness of objects of forms from other domains, for example, the Anna G. corkscrew by Alessandro Mendini for Alessi[3] or Anna von Schewen's floor-lying loudspeaker, which resembles an onion-like object (figure 8.1).[4] What is special, indeed crucial, in this context is the ability and potential of the imaginary to render meaning open and have it point in new directions.

As the imaginary loosens the ties to reality and—in consequence of Wunenburger's reflection—evokes an ontology of elusive nonbeing, a counterworld, dealing with the imaginary, becomes problematic. In describing the nature of the imaginary in design as a central entry for discussing how possibility is enabled in design, I will focus on three aspects: how the imaginary comes into being and alters meaning as *presence*, as *representation*, and as *possibility*. These aspects deal with the imaginary—and preceding this, the imagination—as a process of signification, of giving and exploring dimensions of signification. This will not be evident in the context of design semantics (Steffen 2000; Krippendorff 2006) with its focus on product language and contexts of

Figure 8.1
Sound objects, 1999. *Design:* Anna von Schewen.

meaning or of design semiotics with its attention to the construction of meaning and value of signs in design (Vihma 1995); rather, it will be evident in the phenomenological aspect of changes in meaning when the visible becomes invisible in the process of imagination and, as imaginary meaning, takes on a new role in design objects, when material and immaterial meet and intersect.

The Imaginary as Presence

The imaginary is in itself invisible and nonpresent. Its presence is structured by the negation that makes it come into being. Or, rather, it puts at stake what visibility is. When the imagination is said to produce images and, conversely, ordinary perceptions are based on implicit and ongoing comparisons with our inner images, these images are characteristically unclear and out of reach: They cannot be projected on a one-to-one scale in order to be evaluated by others and thus enter into an intersubjective dialogue on the specific images. Sartre dedicates a large part of the book *L'imaginaire* (1940) to investigating the extension and nature of this inner image, which can only be less than ordinary perception, because its material derives from perception, but acts differently: It has fewer dimensions, it is flatter, it is often blurred, and we cannot get to the back of objects or look behind objects blocking our view of other objects; for example, we cannot see behind an imagined chair (to use one of Sartre's examples).[5] The imaginary is constitutively on the verge of the visible and the invisible (Merleau-Ponty 1964, as referred in chapter 5): it points to something to be seen, as an image, but as a mental image, it remains strictly unseen. Furthermore, its contours will always be unclear and bound to a subjective perspective. Only when it is externalized—as a drawing, a prototype, or a design—may it begin (possibly) to clarify what the mental image was in the first place, but only in retrospect. Importantly, through the interconnectedness of the visible and the invisible in the ways that phenomena and idea are entwined in each other, as in the phenomenology of Merleau-Ponty, we also see that the imaginary is not entirely to be viewed as a secondary, invisible product to a primary and originating materiality in the visible, but that this duality can be reversed, and the visible can be viewed as something that is embedded in the structures of invisible, imaginary meaning.[6]

To link the ontology of the imaginary to the dichotomies investigated in chapter 7 on the designer's imagination as a schematization of meaning at the intersection of concepts and sensual material, the imaginary can be said to be situated in a span of focus and defocus. The imaginary can be detected as something with a relationship to the real that it is imagined on the basis of, and hence the focus, but it loses the definite contours, materiality, and structure, and hence the aspect of defocusing. By definition, this is a characteristic of the imaginary that is not necessarily linked to the constitution of imaginary meaning through the act of design-oriented imagination. However, a relation pointing back to the initial act of this imagination can be seen in the constitution of a mental setting for enabling meaning in design that is not solely connected to a clear focus and the definite visualization of design solutions but also seeks the blurred in an attempt at a different "seeing as" in its starting point.

In its constitution, this kind of mental setting of focusing and defocusing evokes a double, simultaneous perspective of the real and the imaginary: the real—the quality of the design task—is kept in focus, but at the same time the "defocused attention" (to quote Kavakli and Gero 2001 again) places the meaning in the realm of the imaginary, at a distance from distinct characteristics. The approach of defocusing implies an active search for the possible in the sense of new perspectives that transcend the focus on the actual. The defocusing enables possibilities that at the same time are connected to the actual: the double approach of focusing and defocusing leads to a double perspective and, hence, a duplicity of actuality and possibility. In its detachment from the real, the imaginary can lead in the direction of the possible, a basic characteristic of the imaginary. But this process of loosening the link between imaginary image and referential object can be nurtured and promoted by establishing the object that the imagined is based on in a mode of defocusing from the outset. In the phase of imagination, the defocused object is partly positioned in the imaginary and thus open to possibility regarding the character of the object and the attribution of meaning to it. Thus, as imagined, the defocused object already carries traces of possibility.

Next, the question of control is essential. When objects turn imaginary, they get out of control, or, rather, they can be seen in a complex relationship of control and noncontrol. This depends on the constitution of the imaginary as both related to and detached from the material world. On the one hand, the imagined objects are, as a consequence of negation and the mental space they inhabit, always out of reach and thus uncontrollable; as mirrored in our emotions, the objects can lose importance as specific objects because the imaginary is also a matter of exciting inner sensations of pleasure and nonpleasure within us (Wunenburger 2003). Thus, we can even be controlled by imaginary meaning if we fail to distinguish it from the nonimaginary, as is the case in a delusion or psychosis.[7] On the other hand, the imagined objects are marked by their connection to and hence their dependence on their origin in something real; this relationship lends a sense of physical contact to the imaginary. Furthermore, the imaginary can be altered and manipulated to some degree; when we imagine something, we can easily use our cognitive abilities to conceive of it in new way. We may, for example, add wings to horses or to cars and houses (or why not conceive of flying houses in line with Matti Suuronen's 1968 UFO-shaped *Futuro House*?). These examples are, however, constructed by coalescing known entities (horse/car/house and wings; or not wings, specifically, just the ability to fly as in the space-age–inspired *Futuro House*) in new combinations.

The interesting question is what happens when we, generally in cognitive functions and specifically in the process of designing, attempt to reach for something not yet imagined that more or less radically transcends the given entities we imagine from: Then the imaginary as a presence is pushed to its limits, and the question arises as to how it is related to something real prior to the process of imagination.

The Imaginary as Representation

The questions of visible-invisible, focusing-defocusing, and the degree of control point to the constitution of the imaginary not only as a type of presence on the basis of negation but as a practice of representation based on unrealization: the imaginary always stands in a relationship to the entity, be it an object or a structure of meaning, that it is imagined from. This is, however, a special kind of representation. In short, the imaginary forms a kind of blurred, distorted, or simulated representation. Seen as a signifier, the imaginary points to a signified in the real; this relationship is not only problematic (How does the imaginary represent the real?). The signified in the real is also not left unmarked but is ultimately altered or influenced by the signifier in the imaginary (as when we also understand the real through the ways we imagine it, i.e., the mirroring of the real in the imaginary).[8] The ability—or inability—of the imaginary to represent the real is central in relation to the change of extension and content of meaning from the real to the imaginary and thus to the degree of liberty in the imaginary. Thus, the latter is both tied to the real and attributed with the ability to transcend the real. The relationship of the imaginary to the real can be illuminated by examining the imaginary as simulation and through the schematization prism of known and unknown, that is, how the imaginary in relation to the real not only contains known elements but also reaches out to the realm of the unknown.

As a form of representation, the imaginary operates as a simulation of the real: it points to the real while it simultaneously instantiates a structure of meaning that erases the relation to the real. In this turn, the real loses its prevalence as the origin of meaning, and the imaginary takes over. In this reversal of meaning and erasure of the importance of origin in the real, the imaginary approaches the role of simulation described in the context of semiotic-cultural analysis by French sociologist Jean Baudrillard. He develops a theory of the perceptual organization of meaning in late modern societies where the image, in his assessment, dominates the distribution of meaning. The images no longer simply reflect reality; they take over and create reality, and in this movement they produce simulated simulacra. Thus, Baudrillard (2009) states, "Simulation is no longer that of a territory, a referential being or a substance. It is the generation by models of a real without origin or reality: a hyperreal" (166).

Strictly speaking, the simulation cannot live without a link to the real (hence the references of the Luxor hotel and casino in Las Vegas to the Egyptian pyramids), but what is interesting in Baudrillard's conception of simulation is that in its act of performing its own hyperreality, it evokes a break with the ontology of the real. Simulation has a starting point in reality, but simultaneously it has, in its own act of simulating, the power to create its own kind of ontology with new and open possibilities. Thus, the Luxor can attempt to not only improve but even supersede the pyramids in terms of function, structure, and aesthetics: it can place hotel rooms in the wall, employ a multitude of materials in the creation of a variety of tactually and visually engaging surfaces to promote ambience, and it can be a temple of mundane pleasure for the masses (as it is intended) instead of simply being a monument for a single dead person.

When the imaginary simulates representation, it performs the same act: it creates its own space of representation. Interestingly, that is already a heritage of the romantic conception of the imaginary. In theory, the romantics knew that imagination "dissolves, diffuses, dissipates, in order to re-create" (Coleridge 1984, 304) and that this is an act within the constraints of reality (for a discussion of this in the romantic context, see chapter 4). But in practice, the romantics experienced the imaginary, the external-ized product of imagination, not as out of control but as something producing its own meaning. An example is Coleridge's poem *Kubla Khan* (1798, published in 1816) which in its transposition of inner (narcotic) vision to poetic description of an almost sur-realistic landscape projects a surplus of meaning, a *Mehr* in Adorno's sense (see chapter 3), which is hard to grasp in understanding and interpretation. Hence, poetic language is often attributed the ability to create an abundance or overflow of meaning. Imagi-nation in this romantic context produces a language that is capable of containing and representing the poetic mind (Engell 1980), and in its externalization in poetic lan-guage, the imaginary acquires a power of its own.[9]

Thus, by virtue of being simulation, the imaginary is capable of pointing to and even creating new spaces of meaning. It may be instantiated in its relationship with reality (as representation), but as a virtually new being and as a presence in its own right, it is saturated with the ability to transcend reality. Before connecting this aspect directly to the ability of evoking possibility through the imaginary and containing possibility in the imaginary, I will relate this to the polarity in schematization of the known versus the unknown. Establishing a relationship with the unknown is much in line with obtaining a defocus in the design process: It has to do not only with focusing too sharply on what is given and known and what knowledge can be acquired in order to inform the design process (this is, of course, also important); it also has to do with a mental setting that is capable of acknowledging and integrating emergent and becoming layers of meaning that we are not yet known. A mental setting, accord-ing to the argument in chapter 7, that embraces an interface between known and unknown may make it possible to let the inner space of imagining develop into something new in the design process. Thus, when the formative phase of imagination itself is structured in the schematizing polarity of known and unknown, and the process of imagination is, to a certain degree, being liberated from its fixed bond with given knowledge, the product of the act of imagination, the imaginary, also acquires greater openness. That is, the same mechanism that was applied to the constitution of the imaginary regarding the degree of (de)focusing is in operation here: the process of imagining in the intersection of known and unknown reaches out for a constitution of the imagined object or meaning where the transformative power of the imaginary is central. As marked by the unknown, the imagined object gains by being open-ended and operating as a catalyst for emergent meaning that was not known in advance. When it is less rigidly tied to representing something given, the imaginary is free to go in new directions.

The possible directions of the imaginary do not mean that the changes are random or arbitrary in direction. At the intersection of known and unknown, the imaginary at one and the same time blurs the borders to the known by entering the realm of the unknown and tied, bound, to the known. In this context, the imaginary can be seen to apply to different kinds of logic that can be expressed in dualities. First, it has the double structure of applying to both a logical structure in the representation of the real and a simulating, nonlogical meaning that transcends the constraints of reality. Thus, the imaginary is logical representation and nonlogical simulation at the same time.[10] Next, the imaginary may be a closed structure of fixed meaning, or it may contain an open principle of self-generating meaning. This is formulated by Jean-Jacques Wunenburger in his analysis of the products of the imaginary. On the one hand, he sees the imaginary as restrained, static content that is produced by the imagination. This would be in line with Sartre's limiting conception of the imaginary: the imaginary can never step beyond the content that is put into it by imagination as it is restrained by the limitations of perception. On the other hand, Wunenburger (2003) points to a sort of dynamic-expanding imagination that "in integrating all sorts of activities of imagination, designates systematic groups of images while at the same time carrying on some kind of auto-organizing, auto-generating principle that without halt permits the opening of the imaginary towards the innovation, transformation, the new creation" (12–13).[11] Thus, the imaginary may involve an openness in meaning and itself be a generative principle of meaning; it may give way to an autoorganization of ideas beyond its originating imagination.

Seen in this perspective, the imagination becomes less important as the origin of meaning. That also implies a challenge to the myth of original, creative intention as the force that drives and controls meaning.[12] This suggests that the designer loses control when her product leaves her sphere of intention, for example, when it hits the market. Ultimately that makes the design more interesting than the designer, even though the fetishist fascination with the designer is still part of the contemporary consumption circuit of design, probably due to the romanticized notion of the unique artistic qualities of the creative individual, the genius.[13]

Seen in the context of consumption, any product is always adapted by users who meet the product with their own horizon and expectations and thereby actualize certain parts of the meaning of the product while ignoring others, as well as sometimes actualizing layers of meaning that run counter to the intentions of the designer or the corporation behind a brand (as when Burberry was used by British soccer hooligans who thus adapted classic gentleman fashion in their own way).[14] This mechanism has been described in studies in culture and consumerism as a phenomenon of critical adaptation and consumer feedback (Gabriel and Lang 1995; du Gay et al. 1997). In principle, all objects are "fabricated in the mind" (Fry 1988, 56), that is, they can change in meaning according to different perceptions and understandings.

My point in this context is that the product itself also generates a meaning that is not under the intentional control of the designer or the corporation (or whoever else might be the sender of the design and its message). Paradoxically, however, this ability to generate meaning links back to the mental setting that initiated the imaginary meaning. With a degree of defocusing and a structural openness toward the new, unexpected, and unknown, the potential of an "opening of the imaginary toward the innovation, transformation, the new creation" (to repeat Wunenburger's words) is encouraged, although it is not a certainty. To follow this line of thought, designed products with an open-ended conception of incorporating the unknown, of entailing both "knowledge and not-knowledge in projecting" (see the title of Stephan 2010), may be more creative in the sense of evoking and enabling new meaning. But this can be difficult to trace back to the origin of a design. For instance, the conception of Burberry's designs can be difficult to disentangle, and if we were to go digging in history, such a study would produce only new myths of privileged moments of creative designers initiating new designs. If an origin proved difficult to detect, it could be constructed and subsequently repeated and thus rhetorically take on the status of truth. If there is a kind of original moment, this can be stabilized through narratives describing how this particular moment laid the ground for the success of the corporation. But conceptualizing the dimension and dialectic of known and unknown in design is not a question of tracing the imaginary back to an origin but of investigating on the constitution of the object.

Imaginary Meaning and Possibility

The imaginary can be regarded as a trace of meaning that affects the material product. This raises problems in two ways. First, it is constituted in a complex and entangled relationship with an origin in a process of creative imagining where meaning is constituted in the constructive and productive meeting of concepts and sensual material, while at the same time no causal relation between the imagination and its imaginary product can be discerned, and thus the imaginary places this origin in a position of erasure and establishes itself as pure origin.[15] In relation to the philosophical terms of this book, this is a question of how design epistemology influences design ontology and how—and if—the designer's conceptual and imaginative conceptions can be transferred from the phase of designing to the actual design.

Second, it raises the question of the role of the imaginary within the material product, that is, how it manifests itself and pervades the object, how materiality goes along with the moment of negation implied in the imaginary, and how materiality is affected by the imaginary. Plainly put, it can be difficult to see and feel the imaginary when confronted with a material object such as a chair. To detect the imaginary is not, however, to look behind the coded surfaces of materiality and learn, as the protagonist Neo learns in the movie *The Matrix* (1999), that all materiality is only a representation of structures of virtual meaning. In the context of *The Matrix*, Neo ultimately gains the ability to see behind the representation by applying a new kind of gaze to the unreal reality behind all things. He sees the reality of the code: that reality is just a representation of a digital code. To acknowledge the imaginary in design is instead to see and conceive materiality as permeated by a layer of meaning that promotes new perspectives on the structure of material but does not defy it.

Before embarking on an attempt to connect this layer of meaning to possibility, I will note that materiality can be difficult to maintain in the singular form in design; the solidity of materiality varies, as in the briefly discussed examples in chapter 5, where Campbell's chairs and the Web site Tilbygningen.dk involve different kinds of material ontology and, hence, different types of presences and structures of representations of the imaginary. The aesthetic coding in the spectrum of anonymous and self-reflective objects plays a role, as objects relate to their immaterial idea content in different ways (see figure 3.8). Thus, the specific features and characteristics of the different media of design are important to consider as they engage in various relations between material presence and immaterial structure, discussed in the next chapter in relation to the symbolic.

The possible is a product of the flexibility that results from the processes of negation and unrealization. First, the act of the imaginary—negation and unrealization—opens up the static closure of material objects; we see that all material objects are also always manifestations of a mental process that renders meaning dynamic. The approach used in the act of designing is often guided by explorative aesthetic ideas and an open-ended schematization that search for new combinations of sensually mediated material and structuring concepts. Second, the imaginary can contain and evoke an opening of the possible in the sense that the objects may be transparent in relation to their flexible foundation in the imaginary in its way of being presence and representation. The imaginary may entail an open idea content (springing from things that are not only known but also unknown, on a focus based on defocus). As a result of the foundation in the imaginary, the objects in question can put forward a simultaneously material and immaterial aesthetics. When they implicitly point to nonclosure in conception, idea content, and material structure, they can point in new directions. As examples, Campbell's chairs challenge the function of seating furniture, and inventive industrial products can prescribe or be potentially charged with new types of use, as when responsive, intelligent textiles or innovative materials can point to not-yet-known uses or when electronic devices (smart phones, tablet computers) contain a vast inner dimension of possible applications and information systems.

Thus, seen as presence and representation, the imaginary operates at the intersection of the material and the immaterial; or, rather, as a structural component of a phenomenology of the creation and ontology of meaning, the imaginary can be regarded as a vehicle of meaning that mediates material and immaterial; through it, material meaning becomes immaterial, even as the unrealized meaning remains connected to the material. The imaginary presents a productive challenge to design ontology: It does not promote an ontology based on solely negated meaning (thus the locus of Sartre's investigation); instead, it underpins a new ontology of design that combines materiality and immateriality, actuality, and possibility.

9 Symbolism

In this chapter, I turn to the background of the concept of the imaginary and discuss materiality and immateriality in design. A key concept in relation to this discussion is the symbolic, a term that is equally laden with imprecision and broad implications. With the term *symbolic meaning,* I refer to the aspects of meaning that transcend purely functional, denotative elements of design and thus open the space of meaning in design. This must be guided by an awareness that the functional and the symbolic in design are not easily separated and that the symbolic-communicative aspects of design can consciously include and employ functional aspects.[1]

In cultural theories, the symbolic has been associated with the effects and impacts of design, that is, how symbolic meaning is ascribed to objects and products. My perspective is to center the analysis on the design object while using the imaginary as an entry point. Having employed the imaginary as a concept to ask, "How, on the level of objects, is meaning made open? How are spaces of possibilities opened?" the question now is, "What is the structure of this space of possibility? How is the symbolism of design constituted in the balance between the actual and the possible?" I use the insights from this discussion to explore the material and immaterial dimensions of design in objects and systems. My aim is to investigate the demarcation of material and immaterial dimensions in design to challenge the notion of the material being of design and, at the same time, relate these reflections to the material objects of design.

To investigate how design objects create new meaning on the basis of this constitution, I discuss the symbolic dimension in design. In the section that follows on symbolic coding, I examine how design objects, in their flexible constitution on the basis of imaginary meaning, organize meaning in order to transform it and in the process actualize the potential of the possible in the objects. Thus, the imaginary gains in importance in relation to the structure, appearance, and effect of the design. The concept of the imaginary offers an entry into conceptualizing and understanding the flexibility of meaning in design objects, and the concept of the symbolic opens it to wider implications.[2]

Symbolic Coding

Any discussion of the symbolic in design must be careful to attach it to the constitution of the design object. In general, design objects are always reaching out to various cultural contexts, incorporating dimensions and resonances of meaning, and thus may engage with a wide variety of cultural contexts. When analyzed as part of culture, design can be seen as a practice of representation where every structure of sensually appealing materiality always has an immaterial double, engaged in a process of signifying meaning in a way that reflects or affects culture. This semiotic relation of representation may be called *symbolic*, where design in its use and circulation in culture has its basic function of operating on the level of symbolic meaning that is produced and articulated by people in their attachment and engagement with design.

Even in early consumer theory, the objects of consumption were seen as vehicles for the symbolic function of articulating and creating meaning and identities among consumers. Sidney Levy stated this in his 1959 article, "Symbols for Sale," where he pointed out that people buy things "not only for what they can do, but also for what they mean" (118). He pointed directly to the function of the symbolic and the ability of symbols to point to something outside the design object; to him, a "*symbol* is a general term for all instances where experience is mediated rather than direct" (119).[3]

Instead of examining the creation of meaning in a cultural dynamics, I focus on the design objects and their constitution of meaning and use the concept of symbolism in order to understand how and within which properties design objects themselves structure meaning. My focus is not on the consumption of symbolic meaning created by design but on how design objects constitute, produce, and encode symbolism and how design objects in the ontological question of materiality and immateriality evoke possibility.

Within design theory, there have been a number of attempts at approaching the ability of design to enable and encode symbolism and conceptualize the structure of a doubling of (symbolic) meaning within the contexts of culture. Mostly these attempts have scrutinized the effects of symbolism produced by design, not design itself. In early design semantics, Gert Selle opened the debate on the production of meaning in design in 1973 by pointing out that we can speak of a "language of products," "as design objects not only carry functions but also always information" (Selle 1997, 13).[4] This kind of reflection lies at the heart of later design semantics, for example, as articulated by Klaus Krippendorff, in its focus on how the designed object is embedded in various contexts of meaning[5] and how meaning must be regarded as the central feature of design, as it is the way in which people use and conceive design that defines how design works. Krippendorff (2006) says that only by making sense can "forms" be used and understood. Krippendorff's interest is with the meaning enabled by design, and in accordance with a human-centered perspective, he says that meaning through design functions as "*a structured space, a network of expected senses, a set of possibilities* that enables handling things, other people, even oneself" (56).[6] The cultural studies tradition has emphasized the role of design with regard to producing meaning. Within the comprehensive framework of a circuit of culture, the components of production, representation of products in different media, consumption, creation of consumer identity, and regulation of cultural habits have been studied; all are seen as contributing to the cultural dynamics of the designed product. The seminal case study *Doing Cultural Studies: The Story of the Sony Walkman* (du Gay et al. 1997) explains how, within the circuit of culture, design is not merely functional but is "inscribed with *meanings* as well as uses": "design produces meaning through encoding artefacts with symbolic significance; it gives functional artefacts a symbolic form" (62). Thus, a Walkman is not only a device for playing tapes; through its design, it also encourages certain modes of use and cultural patterns. Furthermore, the ability of the design object to enable, encode, and communicate a symbolic meaning is evident in the practical context of design studies, for example, in experimental, self-reflective design. Anthony Dunne and Fiona Raby's Nipple Chair from the Placebo project (2001) employs cultural resonance by vibrating when radiation from electronic products passes through the sitting person's body (see figure 9.1; Dunne and Raby 2001). An example of critical design, the Nipple Chair is explicitly a frame for cultural contextualization. The chair frames a symbolic meaning that points away from the chair itself but at the same time is clearly contained in and through the chair. The chair establishes a sphere of meaning at the intersection of the actual of the medium of the chair and the possible in its implications that goes beyond the chair and is made possible only by the strategy of design that the actual chair expresses.

So although every symbolic ecology of a network of objects (regardless whether they are marked as design) acquires its value through individual perception and sense-giving processes determined within the socially construed worldview of a given culture (Csikszentmihalyi 1995), and the symbolic function of a product can be fundamentally different to different persons (Schneider 2009), my contribution to this discussion goes in another direction. Based on the flexibility of meaning enabled by the imaginary, I examine the constitution of design objects in their process of enabling the attribution of symbolic meaning and examine how this opens a space of possibilities in and through the design objects. This process of meaning creation may be referred to as *symbolic coding*.

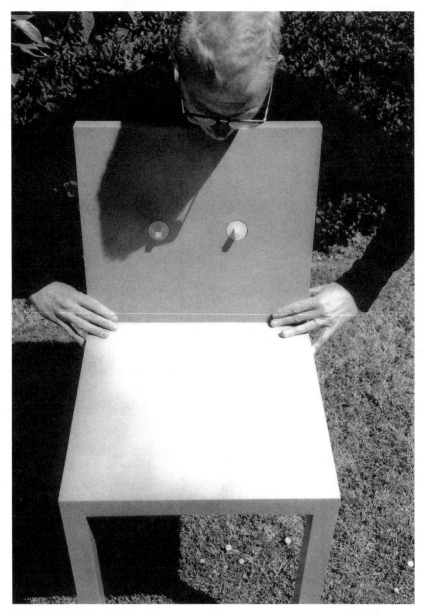

Figure 9.1
The Nipple Chair (2001) relates itself to the cultural context of modern technology: it vibrates when radiation from electronic products passes through the sitting person's body. *Design:* Anthony Dunne and Fiona Raby. *Photo:* Jason Evans.

Thus, symbolic meaning not only surrounds design in its cultural context but can be analyzed as specific, intrinsic properties of design.[7] My point is that the symbolic doubling of meaning is inherent in all designed products and can be attached to the level of the object, whether they deliberately show and reflect it in a direct display of the idea and with a high degree of aesthetic function (as is clearly the case in experimental design) or whether they mediate the idea indirectly with a lower degree of aesthetic expression (as in most design). Thus, I believe that the properties of design— at the intersection of materiality and immateriality, actuality and possibility—that form the basis of this creation of meaning can be opened to discussion.

The Symbolic

The concept of the symbolic is inherently imprecise. Not only is the commonsense content of "standing for something else," which is often "more" or has wider implications than the nonsymbolic meaning, rather unspecific, it designates a general process of signification, value attribution, and meaning making, for example, in sociological or psychological terms (Csikszentmihalyi 1995). Furthermore, in its history, dating back to antiquity as the Greek *symbolon* (to coalesce or to throw together), and to European classicism and romanticism, the concept has been defined in numerous and often contradictory ways (Sørensen 1963).

However, in the late eighteenth century, Goethe set a trend by speaking of symbolism as an operation that turns an appearance into an idea and, further, the idea into an image, so that "the idea in the image always remains infinitely operative and unattainable and, even when pronounced in any language, remains unsayable" (470).[8] Goethe does not make clear how the symbol's unsayable, unattainable and thus inexhaustible meaning can be grasped and comprehended, but on a metalevel he indicates the basic nature of the signifying process of the symbol: that it can ontologically transform an idea and somehow make it representable. He states that the symbol is not only a process of transforming meaning but also the structure of the transformation. This structure—stating the overall signification of the symbol, that it transforms meaning, while at the same time remaining unspecific about what meaning is transformed and how it is being transformed—has become typical of the rather loose everyday use of the term.

By contrast, other models exist that can be used to provide a more nuanced picture of the activity of the symbol. In this way, the German philosopher Ernst Cassirer proposed an epistemological model of the symbol. Cassirer developed a post-Kantian theory of symbolic forms where the symbolic serves as general schemata for human apprehension and being in the world. According to Cassirer (2009), the symbolic forms of images and signs serve to mediate between the "things" and a larger totality of the "spirit" that he aims at. Cassirer's important point is that we understand through the symbolic forms, which are human creations but at the same time also frame human cognition. This can prove productive for a theory of design as symbolically signifying objects: Seen as expressions of symbolic forms, design objects fundamentally contribute not only to shaping the world; they also give feedback to our understanding and perception of the world.[9] Reminiscent of Goethe's notion of the symbol, the ontological level of how objects are constituted and contain meaning is also important to Cassirer (1964). He says that the symbolic can be charged with meaning, so that an "experience of perception" can be sensual and at the same time "contain a definite non-comprehensible 'meaning' and bring it to immediate concrete representation" (235). But his major difference with Goethe lies in the openness toward the creation of symbolic meaning as an epistemological act.

Thus, in both the ontological and the epistemological comprehension of the symbol, the symbolic evokes a transformation of meaning. Goethe's conception of the ontological model leaves the symbol unattainable to understanding but is still important, as it points not only to the ontological status of the symbolized meaning but also to the operations of the medium devising the act of symbolization. In relation to design, it is the medium itself, design, that is ontologically affected by the process of symbolization; it draws attention to the question of how design objects are in their being as objects. By contrast, the symbol in the epistemological model is the result of the construction and organization of meaning. This point is touched on by Herbert Simon (1996), who states that part of the artificial environment "consists mostly of strings of artifacts called 'symbols'" whose laws "govern the occasion on which we emit and receive them" (2–3). Following this argument in relation to design, the strings of symbols to be contained within a "symbol system" (22) can be seen as a principle of organization as well as a contextual frame for design that determines how we may perceive and understand design. To sum up, then, we may ask,

• *Epistemologically* How the symbolic in design operates as a transformation of meaning through a productive structuring of the conditions of understanding and perception

• *Ontologically* How the symbolic in design functions as a vehicle for organizing meaning within a cultural frame of reference and how this operation affects the way in which design operates and is constituted as a medium

Thus, in my view, symbolism in design both transforms and organizes meaning, whereby a specific focus on the dimension of the symbolic can contribute to the ongoing discussion of the ways in which design stages experience and operate as a medium for symbolic cultural meaning and thus how design communicates and functions within culture. The important question here is the role that design plays, in its ontological being and in its giving of an epistemological structure, in defining and structuring the parameters of culture. "We swim in an ocean of design [*Gestaltete*]," Selle (2007, 9) poetically states, whereby design as the *Leitmedium* of modernity in its deliverance of the basic structure for our entrance to perception and understanding (Hörisch 2007; see chapter 2) positions itself as the point of interest. Design is a gateway to understanding culture; in understanding the concrete objects of design and how they are ontologically constituted, we have access to understanding the formation of meaning on a cultural level. Thus, in his book *The Culture of Design* (2008) Guy Julier attempts to analyze how concrete artifacts and systems of design create an image of and an understanding of culture. He says that design has to be "mobilized to develop a vocabulary of understanding" (200) and suggests that it may act as a facilitator, opening up new cultural possibilities that can "challenge the collective imagination and to help in the fashioning of new dispositions" (208). In the next chapter, I explore how design, on the level of experience, can evoke an effect of transformation. In this chapter, I discuss the constitution of design objects as the locus and vehicle for creating a symbolic layer of meaning.

Symbolism and Possibility

Design is a medium of symbolic meaning based on possibilities enabled by the flexible nature of imaginary: In the process of unrealization, meaning is activated and made dynamic. To structure the discussion of how symbolism and possibility connect, I propose a series of analytical spectra that can be combined in several ways:

• *The extension of design*   That is, what kind of design we are talking about in a range from products to systems and organizations

• *The intension of design*   By which I understand the content of the design in the span of material and immaterial being

• *The ontology of design*   In this context, defined as the span of the actual and the possible

I investigate the spectra of material-immaterial and the actual-possible in relation to the spectra of product-system to introduce discussion of the nature and character of, especially, the immaterial and possible in design objects. Finally, I combine the spectra of intension and its discussion of the material and the immaterial with the ontological spectrum of the actual and possible. I then summarize the discussion of the symbolic coding in design and link it back to the dimension of imaginary meaning in design.

The Material and Immaterial in Design

The spectrum of intension describes a span of materiality and immateriality in design. In the growing importance of design throughout the previous century, the materiality of design as objects and even as objects of desire (Forty 1986) was a basic feature, whereas immateriality as a concept is fairly new and primarily entered design thinking when computer technology had its rise in the 1970s and 1980s, although this kind of technological immateriality was—and still is—dependent on material hardware (Moles 1995). Although it is impossible to conceive of communication content without the materiality of the medium, where that which characterizes modernity is the use of highly "artificial channels of communication" (Moles 1972, 293), there is, in both communication and design, a complex interplay of material media and immaterial content. Materiality and immateriality thus reach into each other in an intricate complexity. Less tied to a reflection of media and communication, the immaterial as a concept has been associated with frameworks of meaning behind and around physical products such as the acts and processes of communication, the embeddedness in structures of service design or branding concepts or a way of structuring and affording a pattern of actions and activities through the material object.[10] Although the development of design from product to system and organization can be traced and four orders of design can be identified—communication (graphics), construction (physical products), strategic planning (activities, services, processes), and systemic integration (systems, environments, ideas, values) (Buchanan 1998)—the general point remains that every design is simultaneously material and immaterial. Because it always incorporates an idea in its process of signification, design has a dimension of immateriality, and, vice versa, regardless of how immaterial a design may be in its conception, it can be conceived only in its concrete manifestation. Thus, design is not only to be conceived as ever higher degrees of conceptual thinking, as implied in Krippendorff's (2006) model of a "trajectory of artificiality" that points from "products" in the ascending direction of "goods, services, identities," "interfaces," "multiuser systems/ networks," and "projects" in order to end at "discourses" (6). Rather it is to be conceived in a dialogue between the concrete/material and the conceptual/immaterial, as Stephan (2010) suggested in his critique of the one-way direction of Krippendorff's model, which in his view should be supplemented by a feedback mechanism from the discursive to the product.[11]

Seen as a span, then, we can determine different ways for design to be material and immaterial, and with regard to the extension of design as products or systems and to the symbolic, coding can vary in the same manner. In placing the intension of design on the *x*-axis and the extension on the *y*-axis, it is possible to visualize the different types of symbolic coding and obtain a theoretical framework for analyzing materiality and immateriality in design (figure 9.2). Singular products as well as comprehensive systems have immaterial resonances that point to the production of potential symbolic meaning; on a small scale, connotation may be regarded as immaterial communication isolated to the singular product and thus with limited extension.[12] By contrast, culturally determined and determining contexts signify on the level of the system, which can be designated as a system of signification. The signifying process of the product, then, should not be limited to singular connotation because it is also embedded in context and even, as demonstrated by product semantics, in a variety of differently scaled contexts. The point is, however, to look into the different ways in which the material product points to its immaterial and, hence, potential symbolic dimension.

Based on the analytical distinctions of the model, the different scaling of the symbolic dimension in design can be illustrated by two designs that, in a search for radical innovation, have challenged or challenge the state of things and, in Guy Julier's expression, "the collective imagination" (Julier 2008, 208). The Ford Model T, manufactured from 1908 to 1927, is an early and now classic example of innovative product

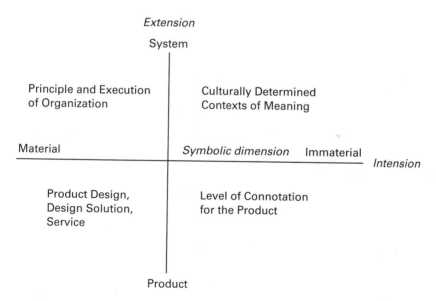

Figure 9.2
Model of symbolic coding in the span of materiality and immateriality in design.

design that set new standards for personal transportation in its leap from the horse carriage. By contrast, abstract service, system, and organization design are evident in contemporary electrical car systems, which presuppose not only the design of cars but also of energy distribution, infrastructure, service logistics, and potential for mass customization, since the most urgent task for electrical car systems is to make it easy and possible for people to alter their driving habits. That is evident, for example, in the system of the U.S.-based company Better Place, with its holistic approach to creating a principle and a transportation system and aims at changing cultural habits concerning the use of electric cars.[13] Interestingly, however, the success of the Model T stemmed not only from its product design, which was the result of a mass-production system with workers on a moving assembly line (Heskett 1980), but also from the innovative conception of the establishment of a large network of sales outlets to make it easy to purchase a car. The Model T Ford was itself part of an early system design. In this way, many successful product designs are inevitably intertwined in systems, as it is often the systems that carry the products and support them on their way into culture and consumption.

The point is that the differentiation and scaling of the immaterial dimensions in design and thus its symbolic coding can help us understand the ways in which design conveys layers of symbolic meaning and, further, that it is important to be aware of the full scale of the symbolic coding and communication in design from singular connotations to the broader product context. Apart from their hundred-year time span, both the Model T and Better Places signify singular products with a certain range of connotation and should also be inscribed within the frame of a cultural context.

To be more precise, connotation and cultural context refer interdependently to one another, because connotation is always culturally circumscribed, as contexts are supported by the specific products and their means of communication. In the two examples of innovative transportation design, it is possible (but perhaps not necessary) to see the historical development of design from focusing on the product to being oriented toward complex systems. The Model T had its historical impact mainly because its standing as a singular product was able to employ a culturally laden connotation that was in step with or even ahead of its time, signifying "innovative modernity," "status attainable for the rising middle class," "the promise of a better future," and so on, although it had many similarities with a horse carriage (Heskett 1980, 67) and in that respect was not that innovative on the level of denotation, it became a powerful symbol of its age and of modernization due to its culturally circumscribed operation at the level of connotation. It had the quality of being conceived and imagined in an open-ended perspective and with an initial integration of the unknown in possible new uses and new applications of the emerging technology that enabled its leap in invention from the horse carriage to the mass-produced automobile.

In design theory, the term *affordance* has been proposed to describe the constrained possibilities for specific actions inherent in an object (Gibson 1977; Norman 2002), that is, as a way in which the product, through denotation, might designate an objectively graspable framing of its use. The concept of affordance is problematic, as it aims mainly at design with self-explicative functionality, but my point in discussing immateriality in design is that every product contains a symbolic-connotative affordance that is hard to grasp but important in scope and implication. In its conception and execution, that is, its design, the product contains a certain value taxonomy, an idea, that it wants to communicate in and to culture; implicitly or more explicitly, the design wants to have an impact or an effect on culture and society and the way in which people comprehend and engage in culture and society. Thus, the Model T held a promise of modernity, just as the electrical car system of Better Place invests itself directly in contemporary, late modern culture.

Better Place is not just a material system in the sense of being a principle and execution of organization; it intervenes directly in the formulation and thus the symbolic immaterial organization of the cultural context that it is a part of. This symbolic organization of cultural context is underlined by image campaigns of the company. For example, a TV ad from 2008 claims that Better Place offers "the best car in the world" and uses a visual rhetoric of abstract white, clear surfaces and sketches of the process of charging the cars to evoke a sense of efficiency, functionality, and green technology.[14] The focus is on the system, the principle of organization, and, ultimately, at the end of the advertisement, a change of scenario and color as the neutrally appealing car drives from the abstract white surroundings into a green environment of rich texture as if to say, "This is the look of our green future and the change in perspective."[15]

At the functional level, Better Place affords a way of handling transportation. At the same time, it is coded with symbolic-connotative affordance that points to values such as sustainability and innovation. On the basis of its symbolic coding, Better Place attempts to augur a cultural shift in worldview.

Thus, a double reflection of the material and the immaterial can indicate how we might approach symbolic meaning in design. If design is to transform meaning by simultaneously reorganizing meaning, which in turn augurs a new worldview, this has to occur through the coding of the symbolic value system with which it engages. Design not only has to solve or imagine solutions to more or less well-defined or ill-structured problems; it must actively, consciously, and constructively reach back to the phase of exploring the dynamics of imaginary meaning and its negotiating of known and unknown while at the same time in this process reaching forward and defining its place within the specific cultural contexts that it seeks to effect. Both the Model T and Better Place make reference to large-scale cultural trends, respectively, the search for modernity and a wish to improve the environment. One major difference is that the Model T was not born with a wish to transform meaning, while Better Place deliberately attempts to change the paradigm of transportation. By intervening on the level of culture, this system seeks to be a vehicle for organizing meaning within a cultural frame of reference and thus, on an ontological level, enhancing the extension of design and its symbolic impact, which may affect the way we experience the cultural landscape of the modern world on an epistemological level.

The challenge for contemporary design is to grasp this epistemological-ontological dialectic of transformation and organization on the level of culture and incorporate it—or a conscience about how it affects the encoding of meaning in objects—in design practice. Looking at the ability of design objects to act as vehicles of cultural transformation and the organization of meaning brings us back to the question of the role and impact of the imaginary in this process: how the imaginary can be seen as a constitutive factor by enabling the evolution of new, open-ended meaning in design. More specifically, design objects may be seen as the locus for negotiating meaning at the intersection of the formative dynamics of the imaginary and the cultural logic of engaging meaning in design objects in various contexts.

Possibility in Design

The next spectrum describes a span of actuality and possibility in design. This is a span that touches directly on design ontology, the nature and structure of design objects.

In their physical and material intension, design objects are actual entities that give character and structure to the world of phenomena. At the same time, design, in its different extensions as products and systems, may be seen as a concrete manifestation and expression that designate new patterns of action or new ways of doing things. In design theory, this epistemological structure, which is based on the ontology of design objects, is often linked to the notion of possibility. To be more precise, what can be regarded as special about design is its ability not to mirror the world as it is, reflecting the given, but to "stress what is *possible* in the conception and planning of products" (Buchanan 1995, 19), while at the same time not letting this sphere of the possible remain in the abstract but seeking to implement it in the physical medium of design. How the actual and the possible are ultimately interrelated is complicated. My point is, as I noted in chapter 2, that the possible should not be seen merely as something that exists before the actualization of the design but rather as an inherent structure of design. As a tool for actively organizing the mode and appearance of reality in the modern world, design indicates what is possible and what is not. As a complex manifestation that mediates ontologically between the material and the immaterial, design provides models of how to perceive and filter reality in its epistemological effect.

Accordingly, two lines of reflection regarding the possible are important to a discussion of the symbolic in design. The first is the ontological relation of the actual and possible and the question of whether the possible can be an integral part of the finalized product. The second is the question of possibility regarding the extension of design, as most conceptions of the possible are focused on products, not on the wider and more extensive types of design (i.e., systems). Considering design as spans and visualizing it in the framework of a coordinate system lets us differentiate how it may, on an ontological level, be actual or possible in different ways, depending, again, on the extension of design as products or systems (see figure 9.3). The point here is that the interesting discoveries regarding the symbolic lie on the right side of the model, within the sphere of possibility.

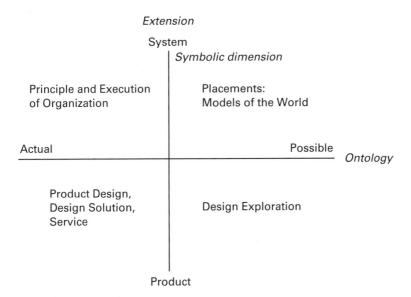

Figure 9.3
Model of symbolic coding in the span of actuality and possibility in design.

Another key point is that the possible in relation to the singular product to a high degree covers design exploration as a practice of showing design alternatives (see chapter 2). It is a method that explores the possible before converting the acquired knowledge into an asset for the actual product, where the "splendor of the possible" serves as an invitation to "create something *not-yet-existing*," which in the end must be the "ultimate particular" (Stolterman and Nelson 2003, 125). The possible on the level of design exploration can be seen as a concrete design research methodology where "alternative scenarios can be visualized, and the significance and use of products can be investigated in a critical or exploratory fashion" (Hjelm 2007, 121). This is, for example, evident at a concrete level in the Swedish project *Static!* and the design of a "power aware cord" that lights up in varying degrees of brightness depending on the amount of power surging through it, thus exploring how energy can be used as an actual design material (figure 9.4). This is in line with the critical design ideology, which states that design critically could, and should, project possible productive counterimages of a given reality, thereby functioning as a critique of everyday habits and practices of creating and using design. The power aware cord illustrates how design can turn the otherwise immaterial or invisible into tangible materiality, displaying its symbolic implications.[16]

The possible on the level of systems can be seen in a more direct intertwined dialogue with the actual. I will argue further that it is on this level of design that the ontological complexity of actual or possible proves productive for the discussion of the symbolic with its perspective of transforming and organizing meaning. This is a level of design where paradigms of design are at stake and where the broad conceptions of what design could be are brought into play while reaching out for an attempted realization. To qualify this discussion of the possible on the level of the system, I point to two different concepts within design theory: the concept of placement and the model.

Richard Buchanan (1995) coined the term *placement*, which refers to the general framing of a design problem or design situation. He defines placements in opposition to the categories that he says have fixed meanings and serve the purpose of forming a basis of analyzing what already exists. Instead:

Placements have boundaries to shape and constrain meaning, but are not rigidly fixed and determinate. The boundary of a placement gives a context or orientation for thinking, but the application to a specific situation can generate a new perception of that situation and, hence, a new possibility can be tested. Therefore, placements are sources of new ideas and possibilities when applied to problems in concrete circumstances. (10–11)

Placement, according to Buchanan, is an "ordered or systematic approach to the invention of possibilities" (11) and thus applies to the level of context while at the

Figure 9.4
Energy as design material. The power aware cord lights up according to the amount of energy surging through it. The cord is one of the results from the research project Static! which was led by the Interactive Institute in Sweden. *Design:* Sara Ilstedt Hjelm.

same time pointing to a specific application. Design is, he states, in concordance with Nelson and Stolterman, "fundamentally concerned with the particular" (16) yet at the same time embedded in a framework of not only solving problems but also implicating worldviews. Thus, the "designer forms an idea or working hypothesis about the nature of products or the nature of the humanmade in the world . . . and holds a broad view of the nature of design and the proper scope of its application" (15). Implicitly referring to Simon, Buchanan claims that designers "explore the essence of what the artificial may be in human experience" (17).

With this kind of openness in the concept of placement we can see, from the perspective of general possibility, that every design object always contains a specific and open-ended, broadly conceived framing. In its concrete being, the object transmits the flexible, open-ended structure of the imaginary while simultaneously giving it direction. The imaginary is materialized but works through the object as a structure of its possible meanings. By virtue of its way of being in the world, every design object—from anonymous design like a white sheet of paper or a paper clip[17] to self-conscious lifestyle design—has epistemological implications of the staging of experience and thus the creation of symbolic meaning. And from the perspective of the specific design, we may note that there is always a doubling regarding the space of possibility that performs the process of framing. Rather, the design and its double in this imaginary possible are present at the same time, the one always implicating the other and mutually co-originating each other. In this notion of placement, which extends Buchanan's original concept, the process of framing has wide-reaching implications, going beyond the more goal-oriented concepts of framing in practical design methodology. It points to the whole dimension of the symbolic, ideological setting that design can be a part of and which can be a more conscious—with this kind of reflection—and integrated part of the design process, whether it deals with concrete, practical objects that structure experience or with more complex and only partly object-based designs such as service design or organization design. The focus of the general perspective of design, that is, its implicating worldview in the sphere of possibilities, brings us closer to the logic of formatting transformation in design and thus has epistemological implications. With its potential for indicating new directions, design transforms meaning on the level of the ideological setting of how to act within and be a part of culture. By this, design proves itself a formative power of culture.

The model may function as another way of staging the relationship of design to a space of possibility, as it also implies an ideological setting while reaching out to a concrete application. This dialectic of the concrete and the abstract in the model was sharply debated by the German graphic designer and cofounder of the Ulm School of Design, Otl Aicher. Within his modernist ideology, design must be concrete; it must be made for concrete use in a specific context where it is stripped of all external means and intentions. But design also should always be recognized as part of a larger whole and a progressive phenomenology (see chapter 10) where human beings through design not only seek to experience the world but also to create and project the world and—to follow Cassirer's reflection—create a sphere of symbolic forms that, as human creations, also frame human cognition in a feedback to our understanding and perception of the world. Thus, in Aicher's (1991a) view, the model may prove productive in shaping a new possible world on the verge of realization:

The access to reality, to the world, emerges through a model, a construction of statements, concepts and conceptual operations. The jump into the future, into a new, possible world, also
requires speculation, reworkings of the model. Cognition is congruence within the model, and
the future is a development within the model. Projecting means constructing models. (195)[18]

Through the model, "new spaces of thinking" are opened, and a hypothesis is stated
whereby we, according to Aicher (1991b), "transgress the limits of the given world in
order to reach new possibilities" (29).

   This kind of reflection is, of course, abstract, even though it is aimed at concrete
entities such as design objects or solutions. The model and the placement have the
shared feature that both make a dialectic of the actual-concrete and the general-
abstract possible. They are ways of opening up the space of possibility that surrounds
every design and pointing to the symbolic creation of worldviews that is part of all
design.

Condensed Graphic Meaning

To anchor my point about the creation of worldviews by symbolism through design,
I discuss an excellent piece of industrial graphic design: the series of pictograms that
Aicher designed for the 1972 Olympics in Munich, where Aicher had the overall
responsibility for the graphics and visual identity (Figure 9.5). The original system of
sports pictograms consisted of 21 elements, each signifying an Olympic sport; it was
expanded with pictograms to designate services, restrooms, and so on and came to
include 180 elements (Rathgeb 2007, 107). Despite this apparent simplicity, the task
in designing the pictograms was complex: Each pictogram had to function as a clear
sign of the sport it was to represent, and it should be universally comprehensible:
anyone should be able to read what may now be called an "Esperanto of globalization"
(Heilig 2008).

   The major point in relation to my discussion of the symbolic is that it is a design
solution that is effective on the level of the concrete while also remaining open to
the abstract. It should be effective in actual use; the pictograms should be easily identifiable, which was supported by the fact that they were based on a common grid with
standardized graphic elements that made the pictograms part of a "larger aesthetic
pattern" (Rathgeb 2007, 107), even if some of them might seem rather cryptic. Thus,
they should function as transparent media for their communicative task.[19] They are
also an example of a design that in its abstract character points to a wider frame of
meaning—an ideological setting where it mediates the polarity of reality and possibility. The pictograms are not simply symbols that stand for something; they are also
symbolic in the sense that they transform meaning and in their final and fixed graphic

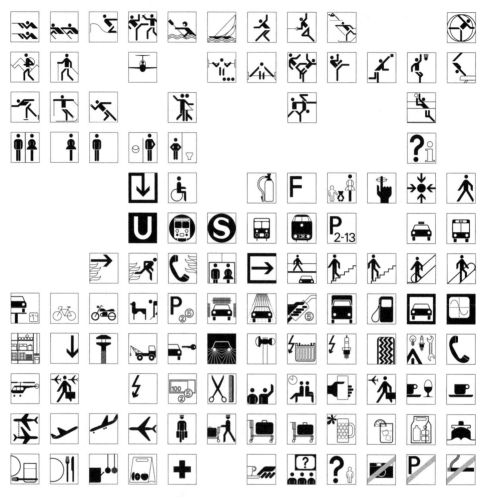

Figure 9.5
System design: Otl Aicher's pictograms were meant not only to mirror the universe of sports (and other meanings) but also to create a comprehensive and universal image of it. Copyright, D-58509 Lüdenscheid, © 1976 by ERCO.

expression condense and organize this meaning. It is exactly by virtue of their condensed operation that their original broad framing coexists within them. This should not be seen as a reflection of what Aicher might have been thinking when he and his team conceived the graphics. Instead, as the pictograms both condense and organize meaning, they imply a wider context of meaning. In and through the graphic elements, meaning is transformed, simultaneously expressing (the graphic elements) yet also hiding behind visual appearance as a symbolic structure of potentiality.

One of the most famous elements in the system, a man with the ball by his leg and his head pushed slightly toward his shoulder, signifies and symbolically stands for soccer (football), thus representing reality (figure 9.6). At the same time, in its reduced, abstract character, the element is a medium for the open space of cultural possibility in a game such as soccer where the struggle between opposing teams (soccer clubs; cities—in Spain, for example, the Catalan city and regional capital Barcelona versus the Castilian and national capital Madrid; or, on a national level, the World Cup 2010 final between the Netherlands and Spain) is symbolized within the framework of the game. Soccer is a game imbued with latent, potential symbolic meaning and is often an object of people's projections of cultural, regional or national identity. Paradoxically, in the graphic elements of reduction that point to soccer, aimed at limiting the interpretation to make the pictogram clearly comprehensible, the opposite task is performed as well. Through its reduced form, which is open to cultural interpretation, the pictogram affords an open space of symbolic connotation. In its highly reduced graphic performance, the pictogram epistemologically sets the stage for a way of approaching and experiencing the specific domain of culture that is at stake. In this process, the idea of soccer is symbolized in the pictogram (to follow Goethe's reflection), and so not only the symbolically laden notion of soccer is ontologically altered. The medium of this operation, the actual pictogram, draws attention to itself as the locus of this operation. And as a stage for our meeting with the world (see Seel's concept in chapter 3), the pictogram is not only a more or less casual singular object struggling to be heard through the overload of information in contemporary society, it is also a device for proposing a model (in Aicher's sense) of the world or a process of cultural framing entailing a worldview that reaches into the symbolic sphere of possibilities.

Thus, the pictograms create a symbolic model of the world. They have transformed our understanding through graphic elements just as they organize meaning in a new way. They frame human cognition and point to an openness in interpretation. The generic challenge for designers is to look critically at their own work to see how it might perform the same task and point to a wider context of cultural possibility that may be contained and expressed in the design.

Through the analysis of the objects obtained through the theoretical framework of the two models above, we find the culturally determined context of design and the models of the world that are always implied in any design object or solution and, importantly, articulated in and through the design objects. With their design, designers propose an interpretation of culture while offering a way of approaching the world.

Figure 9.6
Condensed symbolism. The soccer player in Otl Aicher's series of pictograms for the 1972 Olympics in Munich is a graphically reduced sign that at the same time represents the open cultural possibilities of soccer. Copyright, D-58509 Lüdenscheid, © 1976 by ERCO.

The Immaterial and the Possible

To summarize the discussion on the symbolic in design, in this last section, I combine the axes of the intension and the ontology of design. That is, I examine the dichotomies of material and immaterial in design in relation to the question of the actual and possible and place this general discussion within the overall framework of symbolic communication and coding in design. With symbolism as the overall matrix for the discussion, possibility can be directly connected with the span of materiality and immateriality in design. Even if all design is simultaneously material and immaterial and contains elements of both the actual and the possible, as an experiment to explore the symbolism of design, I will state them as polarities in a combined coordinate system (figure 9.7). In this way, the model will visualize how different types of products and systems, in their different constitution and entangled structures of both material presence and immaterial structures of meaning, and, beyond this discussion, their particular specific contexts of use, evoke possibility and symbolism in different ways. Because all design is both material and immaterial, actual and possible, the ends of each axes of the dichotomies should be seen as tendencies; for example, the tendency of a specific type of design toward the possible and material.

Here, the polarity of the actual and the possible will be interpreted as a polarity within a closed structure of known properties and an open structure of the unknown where the properties of meaning are to be found. This concept points back to the ability of the imaginary to contain, negotiate, and transform the relational structure of known and unknown.

Closed-Structure Design

On the side of the material with a tendency toward the actual, we find design that takes its starting point in having a material intension and a closed internal extension. Typical examples are traditional product design such as chairs, bottles, or tooth-brushes. The point is, however, that this type of design always draws on the structures of meaning of the immaterial while also containing and evoking possibility. We simply have a certain kind of thing with a rather closed material being as design type.

An interesting example that also demonstrates the wide implications regarding the engagement in immaterial systems of meaning and the ability to create possibilities is the physical medium of money. Money is not only a far-reaching medium for exchange of value that comprehends and concentrates symbolic meaning at the highest level and thus, through this structure of exchange, becomes a purpose in its own right, as stated in Georg Simmel's *Philosophie des Geldes* (1900), the basis of "modern equality" (Miller 2010). It may also be regarded as a *Leitmedium* and a scheme (Hörisch 2007) of the modern world because it has been structuring exchanges of value and meaning since the Middle Ages.[20]

Money is also an object of specific design endeavors where graphics and tactile structures contribute to the construction of the perception of the inherent, possible, and symbolic meaning of money, whether the coins are heavy or light, silver or gold colored, and whether the notes are colorful and large or small and plain. U.S. bills imply a feeling of special value through their system design: they are green and all the same size regardless of their value and the historical references of the images on the bills, reaching far beyond the American history in the reference to, for example, the Egyptian pyramids. The symbolic perception of a special value in American bills

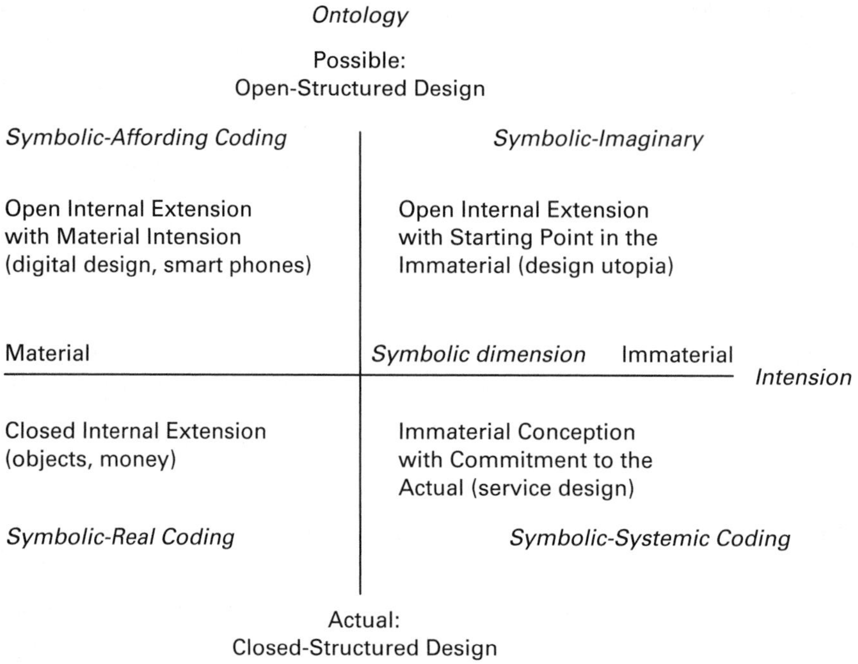

Ontology

Possible:
Open-Structured Design

Symbolic-Affording Coding	*Symbolic-Imaginary*
Open Internal Extension with Material Intension (digital design, smart phones)	Open Internal Extension with Starting Point in the Immaterial (design utopia)
Material	*Symbolic dimension* Immaterial
	Intension
Closed Internal Extension (objects, money)	Immaterial Conception with Commitment to the Actual (service design)
Symbolic-Real Coding	*Symbolic-Systemic Coding*

Actual:
Closed-Structured Design

Figure 9.7
Framework for different kinds of symbolic coding

is widely supported by the status of the dollar as the most important world market currency as well as the role that this currency plays in popular culture, especially film. Andy Warhol's experiments with using dollar notes as a motif in *One Dollar Bills* (1962) epitomizes this. The point is simply that the metaphysics of money, which is a central part of the American dollar, is also enabled by the specific design of, in particular, the notes: *Green is the color of money.*

A contrasting yet still Western example is the money of the European currency. The euro was introduced in 2002 and is being used by seventeen countries in the so-called eurozone within the confederation of the European Union (EU) (figure 9.8).[21] From the outset and before the financial crises of the late 2000s, the euro has been a tool for political and economic development in the ongoing and indeed symbolic Europe building within the EU. Thus, the currency has been strongly laden with a variety of purposes on behalf of the EU, which lends importance to the symbolic level of communication: euro coins and notes should be an integrated part of people's lives and something they should be able to identify with while at the same time acknowledging the currency and themselves as part of the larger entity of the EU. The coins reflect the double identity of the nation and the confederation; on one side, they carry a common motif of the currency value, and on the other side, each nation has been allowed to create its own design line. Because the currency is transnational, the coins are used across borders, and Portuguese coins can be found in Finland, for example, and vice versa.

Of particular interest are the notes, which in their series (5, 10, 20, 50, 100, 200, and 500 euros) are clearly distinguishable. The different values have different colors and different sizes, and each of them portrays a motif from a period in the history of art and architecture (classicism, Roman and Gothic styles, Renaissance, baroque, Art Nouveau, postmodernism). Because the images on the notes could not favor specific buildings in the eurozone countries, they are not images of actual buildings but of virtual, possible, and simulated abstract models of the style in question. Thus, the motifs on the notes are hyperreal in Baudrillard's sense, as they do not represent anything real but stipulate an imaginary simulation that bears a resemblance to something real but is in fact an idealized image of a type of building or construction. In this way, the images follow the idealizing strategy of Blanchot's imaginary, as discussed in chapter 4. Their distance of imaginary manipulation is itself a matter of design, as are, in general, all graphic abstractions. Importantly, the notes are not conceived to show existing buildings and do not conceal the fact that they do not, an embedded feature in the design of the notes. It may, however, be hard to detect, and a user has to be quite knowledgeable in either art history or the history of the common European currency to be able to dissect the motives. Still, the notes openly display and reflect

Figure 9.8:
System design with wide implication. The notes of the euro, the common currency for seventeen European countries, operate through means of graphic abstraction and hyperreal representation: None of the buildings on the notes exist in real life. *Design:* European Central Bank.

the virtual nature of the nonreal character of the buildings and constructions on the notes. In this way, they include the act of cultural construction that they perform through their design: through the element of symbolic simulation in the design, euro notes reflectively display money as a means of creating culture and construing and exchanging value in culture.

On the side of the immaterial but with a tendency toward the actual, the type of design takes its starting point in immaterial conception and is situated within a specific frame of commitment to the actual. An example of this type of design is service design, which is characterized by asking questions on the level of the system in order to solve a task, for example, the organization of a postal service, the delivery of books to libraries or the provision of water in areas with limited or poor water supply. By taking an immaterial starting point, the conception of a system requires a high level of cognitive skills (Romero-Tejedor 2007), but the point of reflecting on the material and the immaterial is that even service design solutions require material manifestation in products, for example, in information graphics for the postal service, delivery devices for the library, or pumps and distribution pipes for the water supply. Even so, possibilities can be stipulated in the design process of searching for the unknown in new types of solutions; the tendency toward the actual is based on framing the design problem that in the coevolution with the proposal of solutions leads to a result that is applicable in actual production and use.

Open-Structured Design

In the upper part of the model in figure 9.7, we find types of products with an open structure, engaging in a search for possibilities. As examples of products and systems with a tendency toward the material, we find design with an open internal extension bound within the frame of material intension. More broadly, this type of ontological constitution can be applied particularly to objects based on or using digital technology. With its digitally generated interface design, the Internet exemplifies the technologically enabled possibilities in this type of design. As a medium, it contains the open structure of being able to link structures of content in a variety of layers and contexts; as Lev Manovich (2001) put it in a now classic statement, the Internet is a "soft medium" due to its open boundaries with other media and types of representation in image, text, and sound. The medium of the Internet, which comes into being in the design of Web sites,[22] thus blurs the boundaries with other media in order to allow them to be part of the conglomerate structure of the Internet. The Internet is an open structure, and it attributes open structures to the elements that are circulated within it. At best, this open structure is used and reflected in the design, as evident in the experimental Web design of the 1990s (Engholm 2007) or, in a contemporary example, in the interactive play of opening and closing layers of meaning that is explored by the design group Oncotype, for example, in its Web site platform for Thorvaldsen's Museum, Tilbygningen.dk (figure 5.1).

With clear material boundaries, the open, technologically enabled structure of meaning can be found in pervasive or ubiquitous computing.[23] Here, the relationship between user and computer technology is not mediated through a screen in some sort of desktop device but takes its starting point the seemingly invisible integration of digital technology in ordinary objects. This is made possible by the miniaturizing of electronic microchips.[24] Typically the objects performing ubiquitous computing rely on a wireless exchange of data in the processing of information; they create a network of meaning that operates invisibly because they do not necessarily display their interface of interaction. In this way, ubiquitous computing entails a change in perception, as our interactions with our surroundings become increasingly digitally mediated (see Wershler 2010), though it often still bears a visible visual sign as in QR codes, which then contain a meta-reflective designation of being a transmitter of digital communication. In a media reflection, we might say that ubiquitous computing responds to our growing need to consume not only products but also information (Flusser 1999). In a reflection on the intension of design, pervasive and ubiquitous computing puts the relation of the material and the immaterial at stake as open-ended and open-structured phenomena, thus representing a frontier in the development of new design and new design concepts: the material as a medium of the immaterial and the immaterial as defining the parameters of the material.

Products employing ubiquitous computing are still far from reaching their market potential. In many ways, it is being explored and investigated at design schools and in mainly artistic projects (Troika 2008). But as a contemporary example of immaterially networked structures of meaning combined in an Internet-like interface, all compressed in a product with popular appeal and wide distribution, I will point to the smart phone (figure 9.9).[25] The smart phone is an example of a material product with an open structure of engaging in possibilities. Smart phones are a combination of a cell phone and a pocket-sized computer. They combine the use of the wireless network of cell phones and an accessible and visible interface through a touch screen. Apple contributed to the popularity of smart phones with the introduction and design of its iPhone in 2007, which has been a trailblazer with a culturally and symbolically trend-setting impact.

The structural openness of smart phones concerns several levels of its functionality but is mostly related to computer functions such as browsing the Internet and bookmarking news and weather pages. A special feature in this context is the app (short for "application"), small programs that can be downloaded and used to widen the spectrum of functions and possibilities on the device: games, maps, search functions (e.g., for best places to eat, using GPS), fixed browser platforms with specific targets (e.g., the nearest recreational space, where to buy train tickets): the possibilities are endless. A special meta-app on a smart phone is the one that directs the user to the app store of the app market (depending on the platform—for example Blackberry OS, iPhone's iOS, or Google's Linux-based Android system), where the variety of apps can be downloaded for free or purchased.

A smart phone is a material device that provides access to a potentially ever-expanding space of possibility. As open-structured in internal extension, its success as a design depends on the nonclosure of the material entity toward the possible and the conveyance of the possible to the material. Thus, the interface design of a smart phone, which often places apps in grids on a vertically or horizontally movable menu, is intended as a transmitter between device and functions, the material and the possible, and has to perform a double process. In an outward, centrifugal movement, it should act through its open structure or, rather, its structure of opening up new meanings; and in an inward, centripetal movement, it should contract and contain the centrifugal aspect of the device within its design. Thus, we can see the design from the perspective of the specific design in an emphasis on a design that reaches out to the space of possibility that it potentially engages. It may, of course, be poorly designed, and in that case it does not achieve this kind of framing of possibility. And from the perspective of possibility, we have a perspective on the means of the design to contain and transmit possibility: how the smart phone, in its concrete being, conveys the open-ended structure of the possible while at the same time defining a direction and a scope of operation.

Here, then, the possible displays itself as founded on the process of unrealization in the imaginary—meaning is detached from the static closure of material objects, and the object, the smart phone, is transparent to its open-ended constitution—and at the same time, this mental aspect of its operation is drawn into the operating system, the interface design, and the interaction and navigation structures of the design. The mental aspect of imaginary meaning is made tangible. A formula that is applicable in the world of competing smart phones is, "the more the mental structures and cognitive behavior are made tangible and present in the design, the easier is the user's access to the world of possibilities and, further, the more intuitive in use is the design." Manufacturers of smart phones are of course aware of this aspect of the design, and the competing and differentiating factor is not only the advanced technology (in a continuous flow of constantly upgraded software and operating systems). It is also, and even more emphatically, the aspect of intuitive interaction that makes technology accessible and performs a task on the level of symbolic communication: Through their

Figure 9.9
Smart phone, manufactured by HTC.

design of intuitive interaction—signaled through the often discreet cabinets of the devices with only a few bottoms outside the screen and marketed, for example, as "HTC Sense" by the Taiwanese manufacturer HCT—smart phones enter the circuit of attribution and consumption of symbolic meaning, as it is the easy adaptation by users that enable them to ascribe symbolic meaning to the product.

Plainly put, a smart phone not only has the potential of looking good; it also easily becomes an integrated part of the user's basic structuring of experience and cognition, as it has the potential to become an extension of the primary sensory, tactile, and mental interface through which the user meets the world. Thus, on a phenomenological level, smart phones have the potential ability to define new ways of experiencing and "living everyday mobility and relating to information" (Vial 2010, 63).[26] Furthermore, on a symbolic level, this experiential aspect, together with its integration in the imaginarily constituted search for the new and unknown—every new app widens the scope of possibility—facilitates a type of product design that is easily attributed with symbolic meaning.

Thus, the methodological point of this chapter, the attribution of symbolic meaning in and through possibility, is not only a matter of people in different cultural contexts investigating meaning and value in a more or less casual object of design, but even more of design objects encouraging this attribution of meaning through their constitution.

Finally, in the upper right quadrant of the model, we find a category that is rather hard to grasp: design with an open internal extension that takes its starting point in the immaterial. In essence, this designates the most open space of possibility in and through design. This is a matter of transfiguration through design and will be addressed in the next chapter. Here, I briefly mention that this immaterial-possible dimension of design has a conceptual and often utopian element in that it points in a direction where nothing exists yet—hence the etymological reference to *u-topos*, a nonplace.

The point is that the immaterial intension does not stand alone; it will reach out to the sphere of material artifacts. Thus, all kinds of conceptual design—ranging from the generation of ideas in a design process that eventually leads to the generation of a concrete solution and further to abstract, explicitly noncommercial proposals of design ideas and visions as in the Italian antidesign movement of the 1960s—have to be mirrored in something concrete with a physical extension in order to be comprehensible. Thus, the antidesign movement manifested itself, for example, through sketches and exhibition projects, none of them aimed at practical application but stipulating new possibilities of using, thinking, and engaging with design.

An illustrative example is the object for sitting and lying called *Pratone* (Italian for giant meadow, 1971) by the Italian art/design group Strum (figure 9.10). As an oversized section of a meadow or lawn, *Pratone* plays with a series of dichotomies that constitute design but are seldom made visible or reflectively present in the design.[27] To employ the different platforms of approaches to aesthetics (see chapter 3): sensually-phenomenologically, *Pratone* plays with the visual and tactile aspect of interaction; it seems hard but is in fact soft. Conceptually-hermeneutically, it operates at the intersection of display and use, of conceptual exhibition piece and functional object; *Pratone* may serve as a seating object but does not demonstrate how. It challenges the concepts of an object to sit on and of what design is. And, discursively-contextually, that is, on the level of cultural meaning, it plays with the structuring notion of nature versus culture, reality versus simulation; it imitates a fragment of nature but does this with polyurethane and overtly artificial simulation. Thus, according to Misselhorn's (2010) analysis, it plays with our conception and ways of experiencing nature and displays to us the unavoidable and fundamental "illusion of perception" (93).

Pratone is an exemplary case study of the materialization of the mechanisms of conceptual design; it is indeed tactually and visually overwhelming; even more, it is an open exploration of the conditions of conceptual framing. In this sense, it evokes an open search for its constituting concepts, that is, the concepts that would define it in meaning and extension in much the same way as Kant's (1995) aesthetic ideas offer us "much to think at, without some definite thought, that is, *concept*, can be adequate to it" (199). Thus, as a material, sensually communicating artifact, *Pratone* is in search of defining concepts that would comprehend and fixate its meaning, and it is exactly this search process that opens the sphere of the possible.

Figure 9.10
Pratone—Ceretti/Derossi/Rosso, 1971. Gufram. Experimental furniture design; Pratone seems hard but is soft. It is a conceptual design but can work as a sitting object, even though it does not display itself as such. Giant blades of grass form an artificial comfortable seating zone. Made of cold-polyurethane foam painted with green washable Guflac paint. 140 × 140 × 95 cm.

Thus, the material dimension is important as the sensual means of design appeal and communication. In the engagement with possibility, however, the immaterial is central, as it gives way to an open exploration of what is possible without regard for material constraints. In the sphere of the immaterial, aesthetic ideas can be explored that as yet have no (or only the vaguest) anchoring in material manifestation, while also exceeding any given concepts. Here we have open and unspecific ideas that in the process of searching come into sensual and conceptual being but still designate the pure possible and utopian design of the not-yet-existing.

Dimensions of Symbolic Coding

In conclusion, I point to four different ways of questioning the dimensions of symbolic coding in design. These may be designated in relation to the four quadrants of the model of materiality/immateriality combined with actuality/possibility. The different dimensions of symbolic coding can, of course, coexist; however, different designs may have tendencies or an emphasis in one or the other direction.

From the lower left quadrant of the material-actual to the upper right quadrant of the immaterial-possible runs a line that reaches from the real to the imaginary, and from the lower right quadrant of the immaterial-actual to the upper left quadrant of the material-possible runs a line from abstract closure to concrete nonclosure. Focusing, then, on the four quadrants, beginning in the lower right quadrant and moving clockwise, we can ask four types of questions regarding symbolic coding in design:

• *Symbolic-systemic coding* (immaterial-actual)   With the focus on abstract system defined within certain restraints, how can systems be attributed to and afford symbolic meaning?

• *Symbolic-real coding* (material-actual)   What are the conditions of the material-actual that promote and enhance symbolic meaning?

• *Symbolic-affording coding* (material-possible)   How can design objects in their open inner extension be coded to afford symbolic meaning? How are objects in their design open to integrating symbolic meaning in their structure and performance? Hence, how does this open-structured affordance of symbolic meaning affect the ontology of the objects?

• *Symbolic-imaginary* (immaterial-possible)   What is the inherent potential of the conception of design for the possible and how, in this process, does it reach out to a formulation of symbolic meaning?

The exploration of symbolic meaning in design is a never-ending venture. People attribute symbolic meaning in different ways, and design objects afford symbolic meaning in a variety of dimensions. In detecting a line from the opening up and destabilizing of meaning through the imaginary to the affording of symbolic meaning that also enables a space of possibilities, I have focused this discussion on the process of making meaning in the objects of design. My claim has been that objects of design are not closed entities—dull materiality, to use Sartre's expression—but carry with them in their constitution layers of meaning that render them open to the imaginary, the symbolic, and the possible.

10 Transfiguration

In this chapter, I enter the discussion of how design affects and transforms experience. On the contextual level of implication, this is a discussion from the starting point of the kind of aestheticization where design operates as entry points for our ways of accessing the world and on a large scale creates new schemata for perceiving and understanding the surroundings.

As artificial constructs of human beings, design objects and solutions can serve the purpose of realizing a stated goal, for example, of improving existing conditions in the directions of preferred ones, to paraphrase Herbert Simon's dictum of design.[1] Thus, on a large scale, design can be a tool of optimization in a more or less clearly stated and more or less ideologically laden ambition of improving human life and creating the best of all worlds. This is indeed something worth striving for; it is, at the same time, part of the historical concept of modernism with its almost unlimited belief in the improvement of all human conditions with the help of artistic endeavors and a strategic and well-informed approach to form giving, that is, designing, as epitomized, for example, by the progressive Bauhaus movement (1919–1933) in Germany with its many programs and promising concepts of design and its equal lack of fulfillment. However, all design objects and solutions have an impact on the level at which they engage with human experience. Thus, design is never "just" material presence; it also always operates on the level of the immaterial and the imaginary. Design is a medium for sensually and conceptually influencing and—potentially—challenging human experience.

That the devil is in the details certainly applies to the field of design. With design, human beings have entered the world; reciprocally, the artificial creations of design on the level of the smallest detail also make their influence on how human beings approach, perceive, and experience the world. Hence, two different entries into the discussion of the impact of design on experience can be identified: whether one looks at general statements of intention or at the actual effects of objects. In my view, the latter entry is the most productive, as it focuses on the actual and concrete in the structuring of experience by design, that is, on the design itself. Design can be a tool of imaginatively envisioning possible interactions between us and our surroundings, and it can make these possibilities physically manifest and tangible and evoke a new space of possibilities in the responses and reactions required of us. Because all designs are the result of choices and hence also of not choosing, they open possibilities by indicating direction: a specific design thus points in this—and not that—direction in the way it frames and designates of experiential meaning.

In this chapter, my aim is to raise structural questions regarding how design affects, challenges, or even prescribes experience.[2] The starting point is to position the discussion methodologically within the framework of design phenomenology. Next, the argument focuses on the imaginative opening of possibilities in design, that is, how strategies of imagination operate as a force for transformation through design. Here, the terminology of figuration and transfiguration of experience will be introduced and set in connection with the schematization of experience. Next, I discuss the creation and (trans-)figuration of experience in relation to the logic of projection in design (i.e., which direction the intended process of figuring or transfiguring experience is attributed with) and to the question of scaling in design, that is the level of impact and scope of the design in question.

Design Phenomenology

Whereas epistemology deals with the conditions for knowing and ontology with the state of being of things, phenomenology is a branch of philosophy that concerns itself with the importance of experience and its basic conditions. But phenomenology also contains an inherent paradox in that it aims at getting to the objects but only seldom takes the actual objects into account. Even in the later phenomenological philosophy of Maurice Merleau-Ponty, which with its corporeal starting point gets a step closer to actual experience, the reflection often remains transcendental in the sense of being oriented toward the basic conditions of experience. Merleau-Ponty does, however, speak of access to the world of objects when the "unity of the world, before being posed by consciousness and in a strict act of identification, is experienced [literally *lived, vécue*] as something already done or already there"; thus, Merleau-Ponty (1945) sees the possibility of "getting back to the objects in themselves, that is, getting back to this world before consciousness becomes the constantly speaking consciousness" (iii). Consequently, it is impossible to separate the experiencing subject from the experienced world; subject and object are thus reciprocally intertwined, whereby consciousness, as the locus of experience, is always incarnated in a body, in a concrete world of things, and in intersubjective relations. The point is, however, that although Merleau-Ponty (1964) states that the sensing subject cannot be separated from the sensed material and the viewer cannot be separated from the viewed but participates in it and is influenced by it, he still takes his starting point in consciousness.

What is interesting about design in this context is that it—in its many appearances—designates the specific appearances of the world of objects. In observing and sensing the modern world through its tactile and visual surfaces, it becomes clear that these affect and structure experience. The challenge of the actual objects to phenomenology has been concisely conceptualized by the philosopher Peter-Paul Verbeek in his book *What Things Do* (2005), where he investigates the "thinking from the perspective of things" in relation to subjects and labels it *postphenomenological*. His point is that human beings act and perceive through artifacts, which therefore take on a fundamental mediating role. This brings the relationship of subject and object beyond the traditional phenomenological focus on the conditions of experience in the subjects; the acknowledgment of the role of the actual "things" produces a shift in focus to the objects as conditioning experience: "Things—and in our current culture especially technological artifacts—mediate how human beings are present in their world and how the world is present to them; they shape both subjectivity and objectivity" (Verbeek 2005, 235). Like Merleau-Ponty, Verbeek sees subject and object in a reciprocal relation, but whereas Merleau-Ponty sees it from the perspective of consciousness, the starting point for a postphenomenological reflection is, just as in actor-network theory,[3] the being of things and the fact that things are entities inherent in the world. Consequently postphenomenological reflection is in part an attempt at deconstructing the dichotomy of subject and object in experience and thus not accepting human subjectivity as the origin of the structure of experience.[4]

A design phenomenology from this perspective of postphenomenological reflection has not yet been developed in an investigation of the mediation of experience through design objects, even though the theoretical outline has been stated in relation to design and proposals have been offered from various approaches to design. Verbeek initiated the debate by proposing the concept of "material aesthetics," which focuses on the material effects of the objects (see chapter 3). From the perspective of a cultural analysis of design, Prasad Boradkar has followed the line of reflection in order to investigate the cultural effects of design objects. In his book, *Designing Things* (2010), Boradkar points to two interpretations of the title of the book: it aims both at looking at the process of designing things, that is, the human-based creation of new artifacts imbued with meaning, and at the "network of *designing things*" (4), things designing their possible interactions with human beings. Boradkar's principal point is the following:

Designing Things, therefore, refers to a *reciprocity of agency* and an ambiguity of design's locus of action. *People and things configure each other*. . . . Indeed, this relationship directly influences how we produce our social structures and cultural forms. And it is this relationship that design seeks to "civilize" in all that is does. (4-5)

In the course of the book, Boradkar employs this approach productively to address how meaning emerges on both sides of the design process (in envisioning and creating the new) and the effects of design objects (in people's consumption of them), in "processes of production *and* consumption" that are seen "as contiguous courses of action responsible for the creation of the meaning of things" (10).

In addition, an important contribution to design phenomenology has been made by the philosopher Stéphane Vial, who proposes a focus on the different layers of effects produced and entailed by design. In his book *Court traité du design* (2010),[5] Vial differentiates three types of effects in design: a "calli-morphious" (56) effect regarding the formal beauty and outer, aesthetic appeal of design in shape, volume, tactility, graphics and interactive expression; a socioplastic effect dealing with shapes "capable of acting in society and remodeling it" (60); and an effect of experience aiming at the ability of design to configure new modes of experience:

Design is nothing but a generator of human experience that proposes experiences-to-live to people; this goes for products of consumption, urban settings or a digital service. It is not about use value, which is a simple, preliminarily required condition, but about what I will call an *empiricism of use*, that is, the quality of the lived experience of use. (64)[6]

Vial (2010) makes two points. The first is that design in the context of experience is more an event than a being, more an impact than a thing, and more an incidence than a property (55–56).[7] In his view, design produces effects that can then be contained and mediated by different objects. Second, the effect of experience is the central and uniting factor for the two other effects; these contribute to the creation of the space of experience, which is simultaneously mediated and structured by the design. Hence, the form (the calli-morphious effect) and the social impact (the socioplastic effect) of a design object contribute to its framing of experience. This is a point that I also touched on in chapter 3 in relation to aesthetics in design. Sensuous form delivers the setting for our way of meeting and experiencing objects and surroundings, and in line with this reflection, all forms have ethical implications as they contain an attitude or an ideology about how we meet the world and how we ought to meet the world. With his three different effects of design, Vial pinpoints the mutual relationship of outer form, social impact and context, and the reflective setting of experience.

While Boradkar focuses explicitly on the cultural processes of attributing meaning to design in the various and multilayered contexts of producing and consuming design, and Vial turns his philosophical attention to the system of interrelated form and experience in design, my aim is a structured attention to the imaginative and imaginary aspects of the constitution of meaning by the design object.

Still, it is productive to use the postphenomenological frame as it keeps the attention on the effects of the objects. Thus, I believe that it is important to focus on the specific character of the design objects—how they produce meaning and condition experience—and to use this reflection as a frame for the interaction of subjects with design (in a kind of post-postphenomenological reflection that goes beyond the principal distance to the subject in the position of postphenomenology). Furthermore, design not only has the character of "things," "objects," or "effects" but also of meaning incorporated and contained in material entities. Design is material as well as immaterial and as such requires a phenomenological framework capable of encompassing both. This is why Merleau-Ponty's phenomenology is still relevant today. Besides the reciprocal structure of subject and object, Merleau-Ponty speaks of an interlaced structure of experience where every concrete, visible manifestation carries with it an invisible idea or meaning (see chapter 3). This "idea" is not the opposite of the sensual but its double and its depth. According to Merleau-Ponty, the idea may be difficult to grasp, but it is always inherent in the sensual as a structure of immanent transcendence.

Thus, we may ask how design objects stage certain modes of experience on the level of material presence and also how—inextricably bound to the material manifestations—they can be media for invisible structures of meaning, value, and power and how, on a level of ideology, they can be and perform as containers of value systems with effects on people's behavior and mentality. With the concept of ideology (Selle 1997; Petersen 2010), it becomes clear that objects of design are never innocent as transparent vehicles for the way that the modern world appears (even though much design is made to remain anonymous and invisible and thus not to claim any importance for its own appearance); instead, design is always ideological in the sense that it carries with it value systems and directions of use. Seen within the context of design phenomenology, design always carries with it assumptions, and hence ideological structures, of how it frames experience.[8]

The concept of the possible and the aesthetics of imagination in design provide a new contribution to design phenomenology. The analytical focus on the role of the inherent imaginary in the design objects, that is, imagination on the level of design ontology, offers us a device for addressing the discussion of how design objects condition experience on the level of their material presence as well as on the level of their immaterial layers of communication. In this way, various mixtures of materiality and immateriality in design can be investigated, ranging from traditional objects (e.g., chairs) that contain and structure meaning, to conceptually conceived solutions of service design, concept design, and strategic design that must ultimately be materialized in concrete and physically present objects and proposed solutions. In its doubling of material and immaterial, of physical-visual presence and imaginary meaning, design can effect major shifts of paradigm in how we see, perceive, and understand the world. In this way, design has the potential to transfigure experience; it can contain and perform "matrices of ideas" that can be altered and thus impose "coherent deformations" (Merleau-Ponty 1960) on the appearance of the world and the way that imaginary meaning is contained in the world and mediated in order to be present in the world.

Figuration/Transfiguration

In its structuring of experience, design has the ability to alter the frame for how human beings engage with the world. In relation to the future of design and in proclaiming the twenty-first century a design century, Wolfgang Welsch (1990) states that "the matter is . . . to alter the *frame* of condition for our circumstances of living" (218). It may be that the basic structures of how we perceive and experience remain the same in an unaltered state regardless what outer surroundings we meet (hence the discussion in phenomenology and beyond it in Kantian epistemology about the basic, "transcendental" conditions of human experience), but of course surroundings contribute to experience by framing it.

In this section, I discuss how design can point in the direction of inaugurating new modes of experience, operating as a filter for our meeting with the world. After focusing on the setting of imagination in design processes in chapter 7 and the imaginary as being a founding factor for meaning in design in chapter 8, I now turn back to one of the central features of the imagination: the ability to abstract from the material foundation of existing entities and, using the vehicle of the imaginary, create new meaning that is bound to the existing while at the same time transcending its starting point in a reach for the possible.

In order to discuss this vital matter of the relation of design to experience as it is mediated through forces of imagination and structures of imaginary meaning, I employ the concept of transfiguration. Basically, design can be said to create figurations, that is, shapes (from the Latin root of *figura*) of experience; in a dialectical interrelationship with experience, these figurations can be remodeled and reworked in order to create configuration and reconfigurations of experience. That is, this process may occur when new design (new objects, new types of design, new concepts of what design is and how far it can reach within the realm of human existence) attempts to impose on us new ways of entering, conceiving, and engaging with experience: when design tries to frame experience differently. Pushed even further, this process may transcend the figuration that is then brought on the other side of itself and thus becoming a transfiguration. The prefix *trans-*, to bring to the other side, underlines the inherent and potential aspect of transgression in the process. But in that case, why not simply speak about design objects with the ability and impact to alter experience, that is, why use the concepts of figuration and transfiguration in this discussion? The reason is twofold. First, it is an analytical construct employed in order to speak about the structural relationship between design and experience. The concept of figuration displays and makes visible the ongoing mediation of actual design and experience; design configures and reconfigures experience, and experience influences the figurative ability of design. Second, the notion of a figuration that can transcend itself is linked to imagination and the imaginary, central concepts in the context of this book. While figurations have their root in the actual, the moment of transfiguration relates to the freedom of imagination to create and recreate (according to Coleridge; see chapter 4) and aligns with the search for the possible and not-yet-existing on the verge of actuality and possibility.

Thus, the discussion of the transfiguring potential of design also raises the question of the limits of the possible, of which aspects of the possible can be made actual and hence incorporated in the domain of the existing, as design is a matter of the mundane world of things and actions and not of the religious sphere where "transfiguration" means a radical, supernatural, and often miraculous transformation of entities (water into wine) or beings (the dove as symbolizing the Christian Holy Spirit). Design also does not employ the same devices as the culture of "naturalized supernaturalism" in romanticism (Abrams 1973) which within the frame of the given world of the here-and-now conjures up an often eschatological renewal and reversal of things.[9] Friedrich Schlegel (1988) speaks prophetically in 1799 about a "lightning at the horizon of poetry" where "there cannot be spoken of a single tempest, but the whole sky will burn in one flame" in a new beginning of a new age, that of the nineteenth century (2:240).[10]

Transfiguration in design does not make everything virtually possible, verging on an impossible utopia; rather it reveals an ability in design to point in new directions of experience and explore the potential of design—as an aesthetic medium that operates on the level of the sensual-phenomenological, the conceptual-hermeneutical, and the discursive-contextual—to interfere with and imaginatively alter the conditions of experience. Thus, to put transfiguration on the agenda of design is to state its ability of possibilizing (Casey 1976; chapter 7) and render this ability open to reflection.

In its freedom, the human imagination can create new figurations of meaning with few boundaries. One central condition is to employ given material; any new creation has to be based on something. The imagination has the freedom to push the creation of meaning in any possible direction, even to the boundaries of comprehensible meaning, whereby the comprehensibility of meaning is challenged. Perhaps the new imaginative creation (a cubistic painting, for example) simply requires a different setting of perception and understanding on our behalf. Still, it is a key question how imagined meaning, which originates in human subjects, that is, in singular human beings, can have an impact on a level beyond the subject.

An important contribution to the concept of imaginary meaning transcending the individual subject was made by the philosopher Cornelius Castoriadis in his 1975 work on the imaginary institution of society, *L'institution imaginaire de la société*.[11] Castoriadis employs the concept of imagination as an origin of creative meaning on the level of the subject and links this with a concept of the social imaginary where the imagination has an effect on the level of the social and collective. Furthermore, the imaginary can be radical in the sense that it creates out of nothing, a *creatio ex nihilo*, with an impact that goes beyond the singular subject; as "sociohistorical," the radical imaginary is like "an open river of the anonymous collective" (493). A central premise of Castoriadis's (1994) approach is the dismissal of the difference between the real and the nonreal; or rather, as a formative power for the creation of meaning, the imagination exists prior to our categories of meaning and creates meaning by us and for us: "this imagination is *before* the distinction between the 'real' and the 'fictitious.' To put it bluntly, it is because radical imagination exists that 'reality' exists *for us*— exists *tout court*—and exists *as* it exists" (138). Castoriadis's arguments orbit around this primary origin of meaning and are employed to explain how language and other "primordial institutions" circumscribing social life have been able to evolve beyond human reason:

Inasfar as they are neither causally producible nor rationally deducible, the institutions and social imaginary significations of each society are free creations of the anonymous collective concerned. They are creations *ex nihilo*, but not *in nihilo*, nor *cum nihilo*. (149)

With this statement, Castoriadis contributes to the discussion of the origin of creation, as he says that while these institutions may be creations out of nothing (thus contradicting my premise in following Coleridge), they are not creations in nothing or when there is nothing: They do not develop in a void but into a context of being. Therefore, to follow Castoriadis, they are subject to constraints. He mentions four types of constraints: external constraints of the physical stratum of the world of things; internal constraints, which the human psyche imposes on itself when it enters a "public time and a public world" (150); historical constraints of institutions and meaning as always embedded in relation to a past and a tradition;[12] and intrinsic constraints of the social imaginary significations of being coherent and complete.

In relation to seeing design as an imaginative figuration with a massive potential impact, Castoriadis's approach has several implications. Along one axis of thought, design is enveloped by the same complexity as the social imaginary; it takes the starting point in imaginative creation, which then, in a social process (of designing, of reaching the market), gains in meaning. What starts out as an immaterially operating imagination is materialized while remaining imbued with imaginary meaning. Along another axis of thought, design can be seen as the materialized crossing point of the external conditions of the physical world and the internal constitution of the imaginative mind. This is close to Herbert Simon's (1996) view of design or, rather, artifacts: as interfaces "between an 'inner' environment, the substance and organization of the artifact itself, and an 'outer' environment, the surroundings in which it operates" (6). In Simon's view, the interface of the artifact can be employed in a functional and descriptive analysis of the artifact and used as an entry into the principal discussion of the characteristics of a science of the artificial, Simon's main claim.[13] Hence, to Simon, the interface of the artifact is a focal point for scrutinizing the operations of the artifact *as* artificial, that is, how human beings enter the world with synthetic objects which in having "desired properties" deals with "how things *ought* to be—how they ought to be in order to *attain goals*, and to *function*" (4–5), and, consequently, how the artifact is then embedded in the context of an outer environment and submitted to certain inner requirements and constraints. In this sense, Simon uses the interface of the artifact to investigate the ontology of the artificial in its challenging of the natural world.

Following the train of thought in Castoriadis and seeing the design object as an intermediary entity at the crossing of the physical world and the inner world of the imaginative mind, the view on the role of the interface or the mediation of the intermediary entity is slightly different. It raises the question of how the design object can perform this role and both link back to some sort of origin in the imaginative mind and, with this as its starting point, be materialized with an impact in the real world of things. Furthermore, the question is not just how the object operates, but also what effects its operation has on both sides of its mediation, that is, how it affects the constitution of the imagining mind and what consequences it has for the real world of things when the design object is also a mediation of imaginary meaning.

To summarize, in relation to design, this discussion can lead to three insights. First, design objects play a structural role in translating and mediating between imagining and the world of things, between the imaginary and the real, between the polarities of possibilizing and actualizing (to use the terms employed in chapter 7). Second, design objects can carry elements of the imaginary and the possible into the sphere of the real and actual (as the argument goes in chapter 8). And, third, design objects will always play a dynamic role in this process; that is, they are not static in creating a structure of mediation; the structure is flexible and variable depending on the role, function, and type of design. To illustrate, when Otl Aicher's pictograms for the 1972 Olympics (see figure 9.6) mediate possibility and actuality in the form of condensed graphic symbolism, they perform the task of mediating between the imaginary and the actual in a reflective and openly communicative manner (we can clearly see that the pictograms condense the expression in order to obtain a new kind of representation).[14] Their structure of mediation is limited in extension (as a small-scale graphic pictogram), and even as condensed it is in expression, it is still broad in its openness of cultural implication. By contrast, electric cars mediate on the larger scale of the system but in many respects less imaginatively; in the rational systemic approach, the cars carry a large amount of functional possibility with them but achieve only a relatively small amount of the cultural level of possibilizing.

The key point here is that this mediation between the imagining and the realities of material presence is a subject for different perspectives, for change, and for designing: The mediation of meaning by design from its imaginative starting point to its phase of actualization is in itself a matter of design.

Schematization of Experience

The interface of imagining and materiality touches on the process of schematization. Thus, schematization is not only an aspect of the imaginative coding of design in connecting sensual material and conceptual framing; it can also be regarded as a function of design's mediation between the imaginative origin and the material output: Seen not from the perspective of the designer but on the level of design, where something new comes into being, design objects entail an act of schematization in their mediation of imaginative possibility and the process of actualizing.

Thus, design objects can produce a schematization of how possibility is enabled, that is, of the ratio of actuality to possibility in design objects and how the objects render themselves open to possibility. Thus, to refer again to Roger Scruton's (1974) notion of "imaginative perception" in a focusing of the "seeing" of something previously unasserted (see also chapter 7), as a result of entering the field of human endeavors and engaging in mediation, the design object contains a schematizing operation, a new way of seeing, approaching, and experiencing the world in an imaginative fashion. Thus, in a spectrum of figuration and transfiguration, the design object can schematize new modes of experience. As an example, the Toddler Täble baby cutlery, which was designed ergonomically to promote infants' ability to learn how to use cutlery (figure 10.1) and be empowered in the act of eating, not only mirrors a given experience (good design means creating the right tools for the right experience); it also actively frames this experience as something to be promoted and learned. Thus, the cutlery can be seen as a figuration that creates a new frame for experience, schematizes it, and, at its best, by creating a new eating culture for infants, transfigures pregiven contexts of experience.

The schematizing operation can produce meaning with a high degree of detachment from a reference in the given material. On the one hand, the material is the noncircumventable starting point for this process. On the other hand, we can ask how far a rearrangement, a "defiguration" (Iser 2003), of the given can reach in the

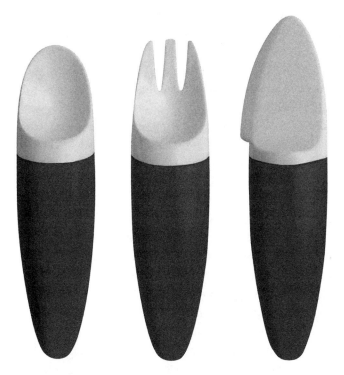

Figure 10.1
Toddler Täble baby cutlery. *Design:* Josefine Bentzen.

direction of a transfiguration. Important for this discussion of schematization on the level of transfiguration, defiguration can be seen as a centrifugal act that lets meaning be dispersed in order to bring something into view that "until this moment was not in view," while at the same time, its virtual character entails a fundamental lack of relation to a reference (Iser 2003, 191). In producing a pure detachment from reference in the materially given, this kind of defiguration enables the possible. This perception may seem problematic in relation to the premise of imagination as having a base in something that it remains in some way attached to and the often concrete, tactile, and materially grounded medium of design. The point is, however, that Iser's approach puts at stake the transcending and, hence, transfiguring potential of defiguration and sees it in a dialectical relationship with the material of the given.

Thus, we can ask three key questions in relation to transfiguring schematization. First, what is the (dialectical) relation between material grounding and defiguring upheaval, and what is the schematizing product of this? Second, we can ask how far reaching the transcending element of meaning construction is, that is, how far the process of defiguration and the act of possibilizing can raise itself from the material basis. Is there a tipping point where defiguration turns into pure transfiguration and maybe into thin air? Third, and in extension of the previous question, we can ask if there is a limit to the possible. Can we speak of a borderline of the impossible? Is there an act of defiguring transfiguration in the aesthetic medium—and in design—that meets a structurally impossible possibility?

In part, these questions will be addressed in the following sections on the direction and scaling of the (trans)figuration of the possible in design, as these issues deal with the scope of the possible. On a structural level of the ontology of the design object, however, some analytical points can be made. First, as aesthetic media that entail a dimension of symbolic meaning, design objects contain the potential to frame and schematize experience in new ways. It may be that their material extension remains the same—as Hammerstrøm's experimental furniture has prerequisites only within the boundaries of furniture design—but they may provoke new constructions of meaning; in the case of Hammerstrøm's *Sofa Set* (see figure 7.7), this is expressed as a very concrete defiguration of furniture elements. On a general level, it is evident in the challenge and often resistance to understanding that many design objects contain, not because they are poorly designed (of course, much design wants to operate seamlessly and thus be "invisible") but because they aim at strategies of engaging, challenging, or including the user. An example is the smoothly designed interfaces of smart phones, which aim for an emotional appeal to the user to encourage playful interaction. As a type of product, smart phones aim not at invisibility but at the user's emotional and reflected commitment to the product. The user is supposed to ascribe meaning to the product and engage in an existential dialogue with it. Thus, smart phones enter a circuit of consumption where they contribute to identity construction on behalf of the user, and at the same time they operate as schematizing devices creating new meaning and frames of experience for the user.

In principle, all design objects contain a potential of evoking—or even provoking—an act of defiguration on the level of experience. Thus, we can state, in accordance with the theoretical statement that design always comprises material as well as immaterial elements, that design has both the character of being a materially grounded presence and of entailing new modes of experience on the level of its schematizing operation. Next, the material anchoring of design imposes certain limits on the possibilities entailed or evoked by design. In essence, it may be difficult to imagine an eschatological reversal of things through the medium of design. Still, it remains a pivotal point for my approach in investigating design as a medium of the possible that it not only has an effect in delivering new products and new visual expressions into a market with ever-changing conditions and logics of consumption, but that design objects and design solutions also have central effects in circumscribing, designating, framing, and schematizing experience. Through design, new modes of experience can be promoted and, in a subsequent step, gain importance in cultural and social contexts. Thus, it may be that defiguration in design can never in principle be converted into a pure reversal of transfiguration, but seen as a latent potential in design, transfiguration renders design open to an act of possibilizing on the level of experience.

In the following, I put the direction and the scaling of the possible on the agenda to raise the question of how we can employ design as a medium that points in the direction of a future still unknown and on which level a possible change in the future could happen.

The Logic of Projection

Seen in a progressive perspective, design can be a means of imagining the future. This is a future that, for example, can be ethically valorized in terms of being desirable or undesirable. An undesirable future in the context of design might be a future where design supports and enhances warfare,[15] and, conversely, a desirable future may be a future of common welfare and an equitable distribution of the goods in the world, or at least the distribution of the necessary tools for obtaining clean water and food and of being able to communicate, as seen in projects like LifeStraw and One Laptop per

Child.[16] In brief, warfare versus welfare might form an ethically informed demarcation line within strivings to project design into the future.

To link this discussion to the element of figuration and transfiguration and the evoking of the possible in design, we may ask not only how design enables possibility (and thus unfolds a wide field of meaning), but also how design can be attributed with a direction, a logic of projection in the balance with the act of making possible, with possibilizing.

The Direction of Transfiguration

Conceiving of the future in an act of projection does, however, imply an inherent paradox. How can we think of the new in the future in radical new terms if our starting point is the prerequisites of the given? That is also the paradox of imagination: How can we imagine something new if the process of imagination is bound to empirical material?[17] And, conversely, if we seek the radically new, as in a transfiguration of the given, how can we then "think of a direction or a trajectory without being able to anticipate a destination?" (Grosz 1999, 19).[18] Design, however, often aims at anticipating a destination (e.g., by offering a solution to a problem), but the problem may be an element of fixation, as pointed out, for example, by Cross (2007), if the goal becomes too deterministic. Thus, we must avoid determinism and can aim at "direction without destination, movement without prediction" (Grosz 1999, 19), but we can also ask how we may keep the mind open to the entirely new, unexpected, and unpredicted without losing our sense of direction. Hence the challenge is to do both: keep the possible open and maintain a direction.

On this point it is vital to differentiate projection from prescription. Whereas prescription is normative in goal and process, projection may contain direction but is open-ended in its search for expression. On this point, Victor Margolin (2007) has made an important distinction between predictive and prescriptive future scenarios where a "predictive scenario is based on what could happen" and involved in "gathering data and organizing it into patterns that make reflection on future possibilities more plausible"; in contrast, "prescriptive scenarios embody strongly articulated visions of what should happen" (5–6). Further, in his discussion of how design may contribute to the construction of its audience, Carl DiSalvo (2009) sets Margolin's concept of prediction in relation to a "tactic of projection" with "proficient use of design to express the range and complexity of possible consequences in an accessible and compelling manner" (53). We can point to two central elements of the tactics of projection. First, it is not marked by closure in trying to predict how things should be in the future. And, second, the open-ended search for the possible in design is led by an "activity of making apparent," plausible, and persuasive (55) by the ability of design to evoke concrete representations and suppositions of the possible.

Still, there is a question of the logic of programming in contrast to the principal contingency of the possible, that is, when we do not know what possibilities will be evoked by the act of possibilizing: How can we program the direction if we do not know even what possibilities will arise and where we should search for them? This is, consequently, a matter of formulating the search for a direction in the realm of the known versus the unknown: The closer the possible gets to the known, the easier it is to program the direction toward it (as when the framework for the design process is clearly stated, for example, as the creation of a new chair), and the more the possible reaches out to something not yet known, the more contingent it becomes (as when, in the case of Hammerstrøm, a development process is experimentally guided by exploring the potential of detailing or specific materials). Of course, the division between known and unknown is never clear-cut, as it also is a matter of defining frameworks for what is known and what is not. In most cases, elements of both the known and the unknown will be present, as will strategies of programming and contingency. Often certain properties will be known, for example, the category of the object or product (e.g., furniture design or a toothbrush), and explorative strategies will be employed in order to find what initially is outside the property of the known, that is, to try to formulate progressive approaches for seeking the contingent and the possible findings it offers. That may occur as a strategy for seeking the new in the experimental exploration of details (as in Hammerstrøm) or in the active reframing of the problem spaces and strategies of defocusing (as in 3PART), where the frame of reference may be displaced. For example, developing a new toothbrush may be not so much about combining different materials in a new way but more about transposing to a framework for posing questions, that is, asking new questions about the culture of mouth hygiene.[19]

In her discussion of how to obtain the new and move beyond the paradox of searching for something not yet known, Elisabeth Grosz, with inspiration from Henri Bergson and Gilles Deleuze, proposes two different models for conceiving the new: that of the "possible" in relation to the real and of the "virtual" in relation to the actual. For Grosz, the possible stands in a position of identity and resemblance to the real, which in its act of realization limits the sphere of the possible. According to this perspective, the possible is bound to the real, and consequently, it cannot not produce anything new that transcends the given.[20] Where the "possible is regarded as a mode of anticipatory resemblance of the real," by contrast, "the virtual never resembles the real that it actualizes" (27). Grosz's statement is clear: "While the concept of the possible doubles that of the real, the virtual is the real of genuine production, innovation, and creativity. It is only actualization that engenders the new" (27).

Likewise, Grosz's aim in differentiating the concepts (possible/virtual; realization/actualization) is clear: she wants to understand "the processes of production and creation in terms of openness to the new instead of preformism of the expected" (28). In my view, however, Grosz does not solve the paradox, which remains noncircumventable; she simply points to two different ways of conceiving the possible in relation to the given. The first is given through the basic structural condition of possibility: that it relates to something, the real, in the same manner that new design is always based on existing material and might perhaps achieve a defiguration of meaning. The second way points to the pure transfiguring potential of the possible in the state of inherent, imaginary unrealization (which I would call her concept of the virtual in this context): It is a pure potential of possibility that differs from the real but in principle can be actualized any time; in this sense it shares the structure of eschatological reversal.

These two models need not be combined in a perfect synthesis, but together they point to the paradox of formulating a logic of projecting: On the one hand, projecting should point in the direction of something in order not to lose its direction, while on the other hand, it should not be limited by the constraints of the existing in its search for the entirely new if the goal is radical innovation. In the following, I will describe a series of approaches to investigating how projecting might operate. I will reach back into design history in order to find paradigmatic models of creating figurations through design and thus of schematizing experience.

Models of Projection

In this section, I describe a series of models of design aimed at creating new paradigms of experience. I move back into design history and point out some exemplary turns and illustrative products that have all attempted to organize and schematize experience in a new way and aimed at offering a projection into a future with a concrete starting point and an abstract intention of carrying out an open exploration of the possible. Here, projection has been engaged in its potential to point in new directions and thus effect shifts of paradigm in experience.

I point to five models: (1) an exploration of design with artistic means, (2) an investigation of the potential of form, (3) the possibilities of experimentation, (4) the role of scenarios, and (5) the challenge of digital technology. The purpose of the following is not to offer an alternative selection of the overwhelming material of design history, even if historical studies will only gain in importance in the future, as historical material can offer a central source of understanding how we arrived at the existing situation and, further, how we project ourselves into the future.[21] Instead, my aim is to employ some of the dichotomies that have hitherto structured my approach to imagination—known versus unknown and closure versus openness—and relate them to questions of linearity of prediction/anticipation on the one hand and the question of disrupting the linearity on the other hand. Thus, my goal is to outline several models of approaches to projection and the conception of experience through design.

The Role of Artistic Means

Even in its early history, design was conceived as a discipline influenced by artistic approaches; a good example of this is the English arts and crafts movement, which reacted to the growing industrialization in the late nineteenth century and claimed the importance of traditional handicraft and the skilled artist. But even more explicitly, the role of the artistic came to expression and debate in the Bauhaus school in Germany (1919–1925 in Weimar, 1925–1932 in Dessau, 1932–1933 in Berlin). Bauhaus initiated a modernist, progressive search for a new order of things with an implicit, linearly conceived anticipation of a new state of being; the means and methods often employed by the staff and students at Bauhaus were frequently characterized by a disruptive and often open exploration of and by artistic means, for example, in the studies of color, forms, and movement conducted by Johannes Itten, Wassily Kandinsky, and László Moholy-Nagy, among others. Hence, Bauhaus was situated in a paradox that was both productive (and influential in terms of artistic exploration) and limiting (as the paradox could not be resolved). Bauhaus, or at least a part of it, aimed at developing a new expression of form that should both reflect contemporary industrial culture and, on a concrete level, be realizable in industrial production, but the artistic base and bias of the exploration of this new language of form was often in contrast and even in contradiction to the requirements of modern industrial production.

One example of this is the lamp *WG24*, which Wilhelm Wagenfeld designed with Karl J. Jucker in 1924. With its clear, geometrical forms, its use of the modern materials of glass and steel, and its transparency of structure and assembly, it was conceived as a direct reflection of industrial aesthetics. And through this tight connection of expression and culture, the lamp was almost deliberately designed to be an iconic reflection of its time. But from the outset, the lamp was impossible to manufacture industrially. It requires handicraft and precision in the glasswork and in the assembly. The lamp reflects industrial culture but does not match its means of production. In this respect, Bauhaus and the *WG24* express a central paradox of design that has been with us ever since: the paradox of artistic ambition of form and expression on the one hand and the requirements of industrial production and mass manufacturing on the other hand.

In relation to the discussion of direction, this represents a complication of means and goal. Apparently the goal is known, although it is vaguely stated—the improvement of contemporary and future culture by means of a new culture of design—while the means, in their artistic constitution as being under constant development, are situated in the realm of the unknown. However, just as the means are blurry, the goal becomes blurry too. There might be a stated formulation of vision and a sense of direction, but the vision may move out of sight if the means are only barely capable of realizing the vision (in focusing the unknown) and actualizing it (in letting the thus obtained focus enter the realm of the known; see figure 7.9). Thus, when the employment of artistic devices entails an open exploration of previous unknown modes of expression, these may not be the obedient servants of the desire to reach a goal; instead, they may lead the process astray or even disrupt the expression of the goal. In this sense, the distance was too distant from the formulation of the first Bauhaus manifesto in 1919 by Walter Gropius with its claim of architecture as the end goal of all creative endeavor, resulting in "the new building of the future" (Gropius 1919), to the disparate workings of the school, until it was closed by the Nazis in 1933.

The Potential of Form

Louis Sullivan's credo of "form following function" has been a central dogma of design, describing form as emerging from function as its pure and logical consequence. The credo has often been understood as the submission of form under function, but in Sullivan's conception, the point was that function and form are organically interconnected and parts of the same unit of expressing the spirit of the modern times. By contrast, matters of form have also been articulated as relatively independent of the question of function. In particular, this is expressed in the tendency toward styling in design, that is, when the inner functional component of the product is considered a premise of the design, whereby the product in question can differentiate itself from other products only by means of "outer" appearance. This is indeed a factor for design objects that strive for visual appeal in a competitive market. An early and essential example of this is the trend of American streamlined design, which was propagated by Raymond Loewy among others. In the design of logos and products for the world of growing consumption, such as toasters, campers, and cars, the claim was the prerogative of sensuous, appealing form in a combination of organic shapes and inspiration from the aesthetics of the industrial world, for example, in the use of the principles of aerodynamics.

As a tendency, the dominance of form contains a clear statement of the means of design, which are to increase their emphasis on parameters of beauty and appearance. Likewise, the goal remains embedded in the same ambition of making things better at the small scale of the product. With a keen awareness of the role of a catchy statement for marketing purposes, Loewy said, for example, "I can claim to have made the daily life of the twentieth century more beautiful"; and further, "Design, vitalized and simplified, will make the comforts of civilized life available to an ever-increasing number of Americans."[22]

Thus, it may be that a design trend such as the streamlined design did not have a far-reaching projection as in a concept of a utopia, but it did provide a clear sense of direction in its exploration of the form language that reflected the modern age. On the level of form and the concrete product, it thus explored the possibilities of experience based on the conditions of modern life. Based on the concrete and properties of the known (e.g., a toaster) and thus not the abstract of a vision residing in the unknown (e.g., a reversal of consumer culture), it sought to employ form as a means of schematizing experience, that is, of enabling new kinds of connection of sensual material (in the expression of form) and conceptual meaning (in improving comfort and furthering the good life). Thus, working with form can be a driver for direction; it takes its starting point in a steady line of anticipation and prediction, as the desired solution is known in advance (e.g., an improved toaster); however, it may suddenly prove to have an additional disruptive effect if the expression of form radically challenges the customary appearance of things and, hence, their ability to fit into the realm of experience. Working with the outer appearance of form can suddenly lead in new directions and evoke new modes of experiencing the surroundings.

Experimentation
Experimental strategies in design play an important role in the development of design. In this context, I mean experimental in the sense of design objects and design solutions that are not primarily aimed at problem solution or seek to apply to a market but investigate their own properties, that is, in what way they constitute design and what design is. Among other examples, this approach is found in the critical design movement and in some of the contemporary designers I have discussed—Louise Campbell, FUCHS+FUNKE, and Ditte Hammerstrøm—whose designs explore the ontology of design more than they aim at problem solving. In design history, however, the employment of means of design in an experimental setting reaches back to movements in the 1960s, such as the Italian antidesign and radical design movements.

Consequently, experimental design is not necessarily in demand in industry, where the focus is often on solving a problem and arriving at a solution that can be converted into a product. Often, then, experiments take place outside industry: in schools or galleries and in the work of independent designers. Reasonably, the question can also be asked why design should be experimental in its setting and questioning of things, and whether it should perhaps just stick to its heritage of being applied art, that is, a way of employing artistic means for a certain purpose. Indeed, should design not just be employed as a means of creating the best possible solutions to the problems we are able to find and state? And, consequently, should we not leave it to art, that is, the "nonapplied" or "beautiful" arts (as in the classical tradition of *les beaux arts*), to pose the essential questions about the being of things? The case is, however, that not only is there an interface between design and art in the multiple phenomena of "designart" or "crossovers," where the zones of the purposeful and the purposeless interact to produce new art objects attributed with a function or new design objects that explore the means and form language of design but which would hardly stand the test of use.[23] Even more important, the self-questioning of design in design experiments is vital for the development of design: Design experiments posit that design is not only a means of reaching a goal, that is, solving the properly stated problem. In fact, on a fundamental level, design is a central interface with reality, which lets design structure experience and provide access to some parts of reality while leaving some elements invisible. To illustrate, Hammerstrøm's experiments question the ontology and cultural properties of furniture, the Placebo project discusses design as a possible medium for visualizing the radiation from electronic products (figure 9.1), and a project like Daniel Rozin's circle mirror project explores the materialization of immaterial technology when a large number of small metal plates respond to the input of a digital camera and image processing, thus producing an analog output with a rough pixelation that marks the transition from one medium and form of technology to another (figures 10.2 and 10.3).

Another example is Thomas Thwaites's design school project of attempting to make a DIY toaster (figure 10.4). Thwaites tried to build a toaster from scratch, including finding the raw material for all the different components. Thus, the process of designing the toaster both investigated and displayed the complexity of production as it became clear that even a seemingly simple product such as a toaster is composed of a large number of complex materials. Thwaites's project shows that even a simple product like a toaster is impossible to design without taking a whole series of cultural prerequisites (e.g., the history of refining materials and technology) into account. In this way, the DIY toaster makes visible that a toaster is not just an object of consumption but also the condensed expression of development in culture and civilization.[24]

Hence, design experimentation reveals and enables reflection on the notion that design, in terms of both the process of designing and the objects of design, is more than a transparent device or medium that improves people's interaction with the world, and that in itself actually produces and reflects meaning. As design experimentation is explicit about the level and production of symbolic meaning and the production of it in design (see chapter 9), it reflects how design can be employed in strategies of

Figures 10.2 and 10.3

Circles Mirror, 2006, by Daniel Rozin. Nine hundred laminated circle prints, motors, video camera, control electronics, custom software, microcontroller. *Photo:* David Plakke. Image courtesy bitforms gallery nyc.

producing culture, creating meaning, and schematizing experience: Design experimentation can visibly display the idea that design objects are media of experience and cultural production. The exploration of design as a medium in its own right may require the projection in design experimentation to stay relatively close to the explored medium itself. The exploratory strategy may point to an environmental or cultural effect (e.g., the electrical radiation or the visualization of electricity in the *Static!* project; see figure 9.4), but the experiments often remain limited in impact and bound to the concrete design object. That is also an advantage of this approach. It begins in the object (and the way in which it is designed and structured by design), not in an abstract vision. In this sense, both the means and the goal of the design are open to an exploration into the realm of the unknown; there is no clear goal setting or any prescribed means. Consequently, design experimentation does not operate with prediction or anticipation but with an open logic of searching, which can often produce disruptive results, as did the DIY toaster. Design experimentation is about investigating the possible of design to the limits of impossibility, challenging design by pushing it to its border, but doing this on the basis of the object—as an emergence of possibilities explored in and through the concrete object.

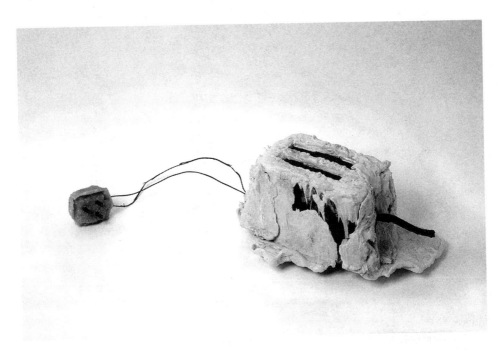

Figure 10.4
DIY Toaster. *Design:* Thomas Thwaites. *Photo:* Daniel Alexander.

The Role of Scenarios

A central means in design methodology is to create concrete visualizations of possible futures. Here, practice-based tools are employed in investigating the emergence of a becoming future, that is, in stating what the goal could be. In this manner, "Rehearsing the Future" is the title of a recent book on the topic (Halse et al. 2010). A range of refined tools has been developed, including "design labs" and "design spaces," as places for a controlled search for the possible[25] or creative techniques for individual and group-based exploration of possibilities. An example is the construction of scenarios for expressing in a concrete form what a given number of possible futures might look like, as Ezio Manzini attempted with his concept of design-oriented scenarios (DOS), in an effort to render visions concrete, probable, and, hence, open to reflection and discussion (Manzini 2003). Thus, the scenario has strength of visualization, employing design as a tool of world construction and a means of social engagement. The scenario is aimed at sparking debate and engaging people when they encounter possible versions of a given condition or place. Scenarios are, in the words of Wolfgang Jonas (2001), "images of possible, probable, or preferable futures or futures to be avoided, and sometimes comprise the steps to achieve them" (76). In Grosz's terms, however, this kind of approach could never foster new knowledge, as it configures, constructs, and stipulates on the basis of known elements. Still, it is an important tool for obtaining new versions of the real[26] and, with Grosz's concepts, being driven further in the direction of achieving something entirely new.

In the historical inventory of approaches to design methods, Otl Aicher has challenged the role and character of projection in trying to make its goal open to possibilities while at the same time keeping the means concrete. In what I will call a progressive phenomenology, Aicher sees design as a means whereby the human subject not only experiences the world (hence, the classic theme of phenomenology) but also seeks to create the world, to project, *zu entwerfen*. By designating a zone that is free from outside influences, the human subject is defined as the starting point for creation through projective cognition. Aicher (1991a) speaks of creative making as an unfolding of the subject and as "the extension of the subject into the self-organized world" (190–191). Aicher explores the potential of the interaction, that is, what happens when designing and projecting are activated. Aicher balances on the cutting edge of accepting the world as it is and assuming, with regard to the artificiality of the modern world, that "the world that we live in is the world as we made it" (185). Projecting means that the world is open to intervention, which means taking responsibility for the way in which things function and evolve. According to Aicher (1991b), design is a cultural and reflective activity that functions as a medium for raising "fundamental questions of human existence" within the modern, "artificial world" (75).

Aicher's projective tool is, as discussed in chapter 9, the model as a way to devise an openness toward the world, as it provides access to reality through its constructive approach. To project is to open up "new spaces of thinking"; to use the model is to focus the openness and give it direction but still keep open the scope of possibility. The model states an open-ended hypothesis, which is the opposite of asserting an idea of finalized truth and of stating scenarios with a determinate extension. Thus, the model differs from the hypothesis based on presumption as in the building of the scenario.[27] Through the model and its projecting, a new space of the possible comes into being; we "transgress the limits of the given world in order to reach new possibilities" (Aicher 1991b, 29). This implies an experimental process, where the feedback mechanism of trial and error is important. He points to design as a process of constant "comparisons and corrections," as projective thinking that "throws itself into the unknown" (28). Aicher prefers the concept of steering over planning as a design methodology. Making plans means deploying an instrumental and abstract logic of principles that misses the dynamics of reality; using a strategy of steering means using "thinking with feedback" based on "observant testing," sticking to the immediate (138), learning from feedback, and constituting a free space in the making. Furthermore, Aicher notes that thinking in the sense of grasping (*be-greifen*) something is always a physical act, where the hands are used as an active medium (24). Aicher thus demonstrates how the classic virtues of design, imagining through visualization, for example, in drawing and shaping mock-ups, can be conceived within a larger framework of a philosophically founded phenomenology of projecting through design. Despite the historical bias of an optimist-modernist tendency, Aicher contributes to the discussion of how to attribute direction to projection when the horizon of possibilities is to be kept open all the way through the act of projecting.

Digital Technology

Modern technology has been a driver of design and, conversely, design has indicated new directions for technology. Design and technology are inextricably interwoven, even to a degree where design can be regarded as a contemporary art of technology (Buchanan 1995), that is, as a mediator and translator between culture and technology and, hence, as a generator of a new culture of technology.

In this context, I focus on the microchip as a paradigmatic example of technology influencing the conception of design, what can be made possible through design, and how design objects act as possibilizing. Microchips are, in the words of Gert Selle (2007), "*the* fundamental design of our age" (215).[28] The radical aspect of the microchip lies primarily in its size. First, its digital technology has revolutionized the handling of information; the limit has not yet been reached in terms of how much information (in the form of bit streams) can be processed by a microchip. Second, the microchip, as reflected in its name, has obtained this in a process of miniaturization; it marks the "cultural fracture of materiality and immateriality" (214). The chip has not yet disappeared, however; it still has a physical extension, and there is of course a physical limit to the smallness of its scale. But it has decreased in size to a point where microchips can be incorporated virtually everywhere. As a result, more and more products employ electronic technology to a degree where we can speak of ubiquitous computing. The microchip has played a leading role in producing a new culture of design that is characterized by anonymous, technical products (and thus producing the direct opposite of a culture of a cult of the designer) and mysterious black box design, where the driver of development is transposed from the outside (of form) to the inside (of capacity of information). Selle claims that the microchip becomes "the new thing of wonder that completely performs its job in hiding. The potency of design that is attributed to it is defined by the changes of the life world that it effectuates" (214). Of course, a microchip will always be only a small component in a larger, more complex entity of design, but by enabling information processing, it carries with it a tendency toward creating new possibilities and organizing knowledge in new ways.

The means of the microchip is known—miniaturization and information processing at an increasingly high speed—but the goal has been more unclear. On the one hand, the development of the microchip has been driven by the ambition of incorporating it in new versions of existing products; on the other hand, the employment of the microchip has often been disruptive in terms of leading to new types of products and to unexpected uses with far-reaching implications. For example, before 2003, it could hardly be imagined how full-tone sound production could be made electronically possible in tiny electronic devices; even the pocket computer in the form of smart phones was hard to imagine before the introduction of the product type in 2007. In the same vein, the radiofrequency ID chip has made possible incorporating information tags in many types of products (and even in animals). As a model of projecting a new mode of experience, the microchip describes the tendency of the seemingly small and insignificant detail with a huge impact.[29]

The microchip is a central device in structuring the interfaces with which we meet the world and which influence the conditions of experience. Thus, interface should be understood not only in terms of designed surfaces (on screens, in computers, in 3D) for our meeting with technology (i.e., the discipline of interface design which has, for example, been described in research into human-compute interaction); *interface* is a much broader term that designates the points of contact between us and our designed environment. What happens is that the increasing use of digital technology in products submits their scope and impact to a process of devisualization (what you get is far more than what you see), which is, paradoxically, mediated by visual means (e.g., in a visual interface).[30] This type of product is in principle limitless in its inner extension.

Furthermore, the digitally operating object can evoke an act of unrealization: it is capable of creating a new, imaginary model of reality at a distance from the world of physical realities. Of course, as a product, the object functions within the world of realities; it can be marketed as a consumer product like any other product. Conversely, however, this kind of object has the potential to create new modes of representing and accessing reality. An example might be the ways in which social relations are established and formulated (and often purposely distorted) through social digital platforms like Facebook and Twitter. Of course, material objects with a limited outer extension may also involve a complex communication of imaginary meaning, but digital objects expand the dimension of imaginary meaning by virtue and means of their inner potential of creating new models or representations of reality. Still, the effects of digital objects are far from William Gibson's dystopian vision of humans with technological implants that generate far-reaching expansions of consciousness in integration with a wider network of consciousness, as described in his 1984 break-through novel *Neuromancer* (where Gibson not only anticipated the Internet but also invented the concept of cyberspace). But on a structural level, the effect is similar: we meet a part of the world through digital technology, and with its expanded internal extension, it has a vast influence on the way we meet the world, that is, how experience is enabled, structured, and staged—in brief, how it is schematized.

Scaling

In concluding the discussion of transfiguration in design, I point to the scope and range of implication in design, that is, the scale of the intended change of not only singular experiences but also on a structural level of the conditions of experience. This relates to ethics in design, as all choices made in designing and using objects have an impact on some level. Even the most "aestheticized" and superficial lifestyle design is embedded in ethical concerns as they affect experience. In this way, the flow of unnecessary products in consumer society also makes an implicit statement about taking a standpoint of, for example, fun and superficial styling and not, for example, environmental sustainability. That would apply to Victor Papanek's position in his 1971 book *Design for the Real World* where he argues that designers should have a moral and social responsibility and a profound consciousness about human beings, and that design should be an innovative, creative, and multidisciplinary tool "responsive to true needs" of people (Papanek 1985, x).

In contrast to this implied moral and ethical condemnation of design that does not serve the right needs (what these are would have to be agreed on in a next step), from a phenomenological point of view, all objects of design have ethical implications in the sense that they make proposals about how to approach the world and experience with and through them. With regard to the structural and, hence, ethically consequential impact of design on human experience, design can be used as a tool for improving things. In this sense, John Thackara (2005) has boldly claimed, "If we can design our way into problems, we can design our way out" (1). Within this framework of all-pervasive ethical implication, aesthetics is not in opposition to ethics. *Aesthetics* has been understood for too long as a term that describes the superficial and the power of beauty and outer appearance, but in the context of conceiving it as an entrance to experience and understanding, it is directly connected to ethics. Aesthetics in design cannot help being anything but ethical.

Having said this, it must also be noted that there are differences in the field of design concerning the level of the proposal. It makes a big difference whether the possible is searched for, and experience is being schematized through a singular, perhaps anonymously operating artifact or the proposal of a system design. Even so, the term *design* is increasingly being used in contexts that reach far beyond the singular artifact. Thus, design has faced the challenge of reaching from small material entities to larger contexts of meaning, from the product to the system and the organization. The different scales of design affect experience differently and engage different dimensions of possibility. One way of entering the different scales of design could be Buchanan's model of the four orders of design: communication (as in graphics), construction (as in physical products), strategic planning (e.g., activities, services, processes), and systemic integration (systems, environments, ideas, values) (Buchanan 1998).

The remainder of this chapter briefly discusses the implication of design on the latter two levels, as much of this book has already dealt with the dimension of products (and perhaps less with images and visual symbols), and the question raised here is focused on the larger scales of design. I will not go deeply into case description but instead point out the challenges posed by these levels of design for the conceptualization of the possible and of transfiguration in design.

Possibility and Transfiguration in Strategic Planning

As Buchanan (1998) states, an emphasis on the order of strategic planning does not mean that the orders of graphics and products are being ousted or replaced; on the contrary. As the different orders of design also represent different ways of approaching design, "characters and disciplines of design thinking" (13), previous orders of design are incorporated in the subsequent order, and here they are conceived of in a new way, for example, as products that gain new meaning when viewed in the context and framework of strategic planning. Thus, in strategic planning, the concrete elements of design are reframed. The reframing produces a new perspective on design, which means that through this reframing, new dimensions of possibilities can potentially be evoked, and the transfiguration of experience may potentially be enabled on a new level and with new means.

An example of this is the design of services. In the book *In the Bubble* (2005), John Thackara has pointed to the role of the social fabric and the transition "from innovation driven by science fiction to innovation inspired by social fiction," which has produced the result that the "design focus is overwhelmingly on services and systems, not on things" (4). Thackara sees this shift in attention as highly ethically motivated: "In a less-stuff-more-people world, we still need systems, platforms, and services that enable people to interact more effectively and enjoyably" (6). This open invitation to create better design for the world on the level of systems, platforms, and services, that is, of approaching design as planning and organizing meaning, is also an invitation to entertain new possibilities. That is, the sense of the possible in this kind of design lies not only in the ways that objects in themselves create possible new meanings and serve as actualizations on the basis of a wider, imaginary meaning. It is also implied in the way that the frame is set for the organization of services. The frame stages the context of meaning that defines the extension and intension of the various types of design employed in the system of the service.

Hence, the defining meaning is stated by the framing, and the act of possibilizing in this kind of design relies very much on the ability to ask the right questions and set the right frame for the design (e.g., by transposing the problem statement from the concrete object of toothbrushes to the frame of mouth hygiene or from cars to transportation systems). The challenge for new design on this level lies in the power and ability to devise a new and innovative setting for the stage of meaning and to connect this with the concrete devices of design so that the visionary impulse of the setting can be realized.[31]

Due to its level of operation, service design produces an effective figuration of experience with a high potential for transfiguration: The best kind of service design is the kind that actively changes people's habits and their modes of engaging with their surroundings. Thus, the core of service design is not only the figuration but also the transfiguration of experience. In the design process, this may lead to a challenge of asking questions about which modes of experience are encouraged, produced, and promoted by the design: how the frame of the service design stages experience at the edge of what is possible and how this can be formulated as a direction for the design.

Possibility and Transfiguration in Systemic Integration

On the level of systemic integration, design is guided by an overall idea or vision. Like the order of strategic planning, it may comprise previous orders and take over when they come to a halt—for example, "Strategic planning breaks down when the larger cultural context is undergoing, or in need of, major transformation" (Buchanan 1998, 16). Instead, the order of systemic integration offers opportunities for rethinking the core values and basing their formulation in learning organizations and knowledge-based organizations, that is, where people are involved:[32] "Transition depends on discovering the core idea, values, and thought which organize a culture or system and propel it forward in a new search for expression in appropriate activities and products" (23). In the context of my discussion of scaling, I will focus on the element of design as driven by values or ideas.

Here, the example may be the prevalent topic of sustainability in design, which I, on this value-driven level of design, believe to be one of the central issues for design in the future. I outline two models of sustainability: one that is based on incremental innovation and one that takes its starting point in radical innovation.

The first model is characterized by optimizing existing products and processes, for example, by making cars more fuel-efficient. In part, Manzini's notion of the scenario can be located here. A key term is durability, where the product lasts longer, for example, when it is attributed with the dimension of emotional meaning that Stuart Walker (2006) suggested. The product, he said, can function as a "more meaningful rendition of materiality that enriches our lives at a deeper, emotional level" (55). Thus, a "sustainable solution can be understood as one that possesses enduring value in terms of its meanings and characteristics" (39).

The second model is the one of interest here, as it radically challenges the conception and values of things. It is represented by Michael Braungart and William McDonough in their environmental manifesto, *Cradle to Cradle: Remaking the Way We Make Things* (2008). It is characterized by rethinking and reframing products and by dealing with the not-yet-existing and not-yet-imagined. Thus in a projective "feedforward" (Braungart and McDonough 2008),[33] new models of design can be invented and employed for reframing things. Thus, the issue here is not to make a product more efficient, for example, the car, but to reconceive its system, for example, by designing a "nutrivehicle," a new transportation infrastructure, or, simply, transportation. Hence,

Walker writes, the designer should not just design "environmentally friendly products" but go further and challenge "our conceptions of products" and thus reassess "our notions of product aesthetics" (3). In this sense, design is not only about solving problems; it is also about creating possibilities, that is, not only creating things as they could be but also how they should be, ethically speaking (37).

In the context of rethinking products, I note two different approaches that may coexist and mutually enrich one another. The first is the engineering approach of Braungart and McDonough (2008). Their starting point is that we have to move away from the idea that we can optimize all products in order to make them "less bad." Instead, we need to rethink the culture of consumption in the light of eco-effectiveness, where we take inspiration from principles in nature to produce things in a radically new way that acknowledges growth, production, and consumption and where waste is not problematic but "equals food" in a new recirculation of materials. Here, their solution is to let form follow evolution to acknowledge the high level of industrial production and to let "the valuable nutrients in the materials shape and determine the design" (104), so that all materials can be recycled and waste eliminated. Here it gets technical, and we can hear the voice of the engineering chemist Michael Braungart speak. He says that we have to differentiate between two metabolisms: one that produces degradable food for a biological cycle and one that produces recyclable materials for a technical cycle. If materials can be either totally degraded or totally reused, which indeed should be the case for very valuable and rare minerals and metals, which are difficult, expensive, and even dangerous to obtain in the first place, then nothing is, in principle, wasted. Concrete proposals for solutions include the production of plastics that are 100 percent degradable and a new model for leasing TV sets, for people who do not own TV sets and lease them. When they want a newer model, they return the old one to the company, which then demolishes it and reuses all the materials.

The basic point is that in the cradle-to-cradle philosophy, sustainability begins in production, and to narrow it down further, in the design of the materials and the design of the combination and use of materials. It works in the real world too. "Cradle to cradle" is not only a statement but also a business, where companies can acquire a cradle-to-cradle certificate if they produce and reuse materials in the right way. An example is Mosa Tegels, a Dutch manufacturer of tiles, which has seized the idea of reusing materials as an opportunity to enhance the product and engage in material innovation and the development of new kinds of tiles.[34] A basic assumption is that creativity is promoted by constraints, that is, that the sense of possibilizing increases within boundaries. The question remains, however, how we can deal with product innovation that transgresses the boundaries of the two metabolisms and produces what Braungart and McDonough (2008) characterize as "Monstrous Hybrids" (98), that is, whether the sense of the possible is too constrained by the limitations of the material.[35] That said, there is no doubt that the potential of being constrained by the materials has not yet been fully explored, and there is still a major potential in rethinking concepts of distributing and owning products.

The second approach is suggested by Stuart Walker (2006) and based on artistic means. He points to the disruptive aesthetic strategies of the artistic avant-garde as an inspiration for obtaining methods for searching for not-yet-existing and the not-yet-conceivable solutions. We must be bold in creating new models of how things can be done. Thus, he points to the importance of experimental, explorative strategies of emerging meaning, even for a field as technical and rational as sustainability, and even when we do not—and cannot—know the result of the search from the outset. Thus, we must maintain an open mind, challenge the given, and formulate the right ideas:

Critical thinking and the challenging of precedents and standards must begin to prefigure the design process and become more commonplace and more substantive than is generally the case today. Designers will still have the important task of translating the ideas into form, but ultimately, it is the strength of the *ideas* that is crucial for the evolution of a lasting, meaningful and, hopefully, more benign material culture. (12–13)

This, in Walker's view, is a matter for design, for designing, and for designers, as designers are used to exploring the unknown: "We do not know what a sustainable approach looks like. This is truly a journey of exploration. . . . To be a designer is to be on uncertain ground. . . . It is the role of designers as well as design educators and researchers, to be in the vanguard of this exploration—to visualize new possibilities and offer new responses" (32). The paradox of projecting the new—that we cannot project the entirely new with the means of the existing—also characterizes Walker's approach, as he constantly points to the need to reach something new but is unable to describe what it is. In summary, we can state Walker's approach as follows: we do not know the precise direction of projection, but we can employ disruptive strategies on an experimental, explorative basis and let these strategies be guided by the formulation of strong ideas.

To employ my vocabulary, the act of possibilizing is both open-ended and attributed with a hint of direction. This idea and hint of direction might then be the overall value of sustainable living. Here, the goal and its scale of implication are set. With a set goal, the challenge is then to keep the space of possibilizing and disruptive innovation open. Furthermore, this explorative approach may engage in a productive dialogue with Braungart and McDonough's idea-driven but more technical and engineering-oriented approach. This lets us propose a design solution on the level of the systemic integration of various design elements that operate together, where Braungart and McDonough's notion of the key role of materials and their notion of a progressive feedforward of new ideas can interact with the notion of the open-ended, disruptive exploration that Walker proposes.

On the level of systemic integration, it is not only a new frame for understanding design that is set. This level also involves formulating open-ended ideas whose extension and implication we do not know yet. The strategic planning of a service design can promote new frameworks for staging design, but normally, it is possible to state these and develop a new design solution (e.g., a new postal service or concepts of mouth hygiene). By contrast, the proposed ideas for large-scale systemic integration need not have an end; they can point to a desired state or situation in some imaginable future, such as new concepts of sustainable living, even before we know how they can be fulfilled or even what they may look like.

The level of systemic integration may be the highest order (Buchanan's term) or scale of design, and consequently, it can employ the widest space of possibilities (what can be made possible) and of possibilizing (the sense and searching for possibilities). Furthermore, it can entail the biggest impact of transfiguration of experience. When the process is open-ended and dynamic, systematic integration can point beyond its existing frame; in the formulation of ideas, it can prefigure both the change of means and understanding of design and the transfiguration of experience that is its ultimate but perhaps never realizable and, in principle, unrealizable, goal.

This pushes design to the borderline of itself: it is a means to achieve experience that is yet to come. And herein resides both the fascination and the frustration of working with imagination in design: it can be employed for setting a framework for understanding the creation of new meaning in design, of dealing with the unknown, but it cannot solve the riddle of how meaning reaches beyond itself in a reversal that would produce an entirely new and, by definition, constitutively never realizable meaning.

Conclusion

A central claim for this book is that design is essentially a matter of framing and structuring human experience or that it has the potential to do so. The world is not all design, but many of its artificial creations, often unnoticed as such, are the result of design choices. However, in structuring a variety of objects and solutions and in providing principles for planning, organization, and systemic integration, design is a pervasive part of contemporary culture, and we need to grasp and comprehend its complex framing of meaning in relation to experience.

In this book, my aim has been to contribute to this discussion by examining how design operates as a medium—or rather a variety of media—of meaning constitution. I have described how design objects can be opened up with regard to their dimension of meaning in relation to creating structures of experience. Design objects are not static, material entities but dynamic containers, reflectors, and creators of meaning. Thus, I have claimed that the possible is of vital importance to design (chapter 2). Design objects are not only the result of possibilities in a design process that eventually narrows down to the resulting solution: the design object. They also operate as stimulators of new possibilities when they engage with and enter culture. However, design objects are not passive vehicles in this process. They carry possibility within as part of their meaning constitution.

I have proposed the framework of an aesthetics of imagination to investigate the possible in design. First, I have proposed a series of entries for investigating the role and becoming of meaning in design: aesthetics, the role of imagination, the imaginary, the symbolic, and the potential for transfigurative effects of experience, that is, of creating new modes of experience. Second, I have sought to connect the concepts in a comprehensive theoretical proposition of the interrelated nature of different dimensions of meaning constitution in design.

The concept of aesthetics in relation to design is a central element in my approach, as it can be employed to differentiate levels of meaning in design. Thus, I have distinguished a sensual-phenomenological, conceptual-hermeneutical, and contex-tual-discursive platform of aesthetics in design (chapter 3).

In describing a sensual, a conceptual, and a contextual paradigm of meaning in design, I have outlined various dimensions of a central possibility-creating force in design, the human imagination. After introducing the historical concept of imagination in a series of structuring dichotomies with relevance for design (internalization-exter-nalization, fullness-emptiness, enthusiasm-reflection, and immanence-transcendence; chapter 4), I have proposed a phenomenology of imagination in design that operates through (sensual) internalization, (conceptual) unrealization, and (contextual) trans-figuration (chapter 5). In combination, these three aspects describe a formation of meaning in design, where meaning enters the imagination (internalization) and, once inside the human mind, is altered and loses its original character (unrealization), only to acquire a new expression (transfiguration). The three aspects can be used as entries for focusing on different phases in the development of design, of meaning in design, and of meaning in design in relation to experience. Thus, the framework of a phenom-enology of imagination in design has provided the structure for the subsequent chapters in the book.

At the level of sensual meaning, imagination relates to the process of designing, that is, when designers internalize and create new meaning by designing. Here, the research frame was a design epistemology, questioning how and by what methods designers enter the design process and, in relation to this, how imagination can be explored as a matter of coding meaning and staging a mental setting in design (chapter 6). In this context, I have proposed schematization as an entry into the operation of imagination in design (chapter 7). As a concept, schematization derives from Kantian epistemology, where it describes a cognitive process of linking sensual matter and conceptual meaning through the imagination. By applying a concept that operates on a structural level, where it creates comprehensive meaning, I have attempted to detach the imaginative operation from its origin in a creative consciousness, thus avoiding the celebration of the creative mind that has been too much a part of the discourse on imagination. I have argued that the open scheme of schematization can be filled out by three metaconceptual settings in the designer's process of externalizing inner imaginings into design objects. The central argument was that these are defined in dichotomies related to knowledge (known versus unknown), perspective (whole versus detail), and focus (focusing versus defocusing). Thus, my argument has been that the designer's imagination process depends on the mental setting and coding of the design process regarding the amount of presupposed knowledge, the imaginative perspective, and the degree of focus. In conclusion, it can be argued that the sense of the possible in the design process, the act of possibilizing, depends on the designer's specific mental setting, for example, in relation to the element of the unknown in the design process.

In relation to unrealization and the creation of new conceptual meaning in the design object, I have pointed to the role of the imaginary for the constitution of meaning in design objects within the research frame of design ontology (chapter 8). When we imagine, we create imaginary constructs of meaning, and as a product of the imagination, the imaginary can be retraced to the act of imagining and be explored as a productive concept for the understanding of meaning constitution in design. Thus, I have sought to bring forward the concept of the imaginary and its roles as presentation, representation, and creator of the possible in relation to design and to explore it as a way of investigating how design objects are not only material entities but are also permeated by layers of meaning in the form of an externalized imaginary. In this sense, a central claim has been that the imaginary is present not only within consciousness but also in its possible materializations. By introducing the concept of the imaginary into the discourse of design, I have attempted to challenge existing conceptions of design as materiality and initiate an open exploration of the implications of this concept for design. I believe that much more can be done to explore and fully understand the imaginary as a productive factor for design.[1]

Relating to the openness of the imaginary, I have furthered the discussion of symbolic coding in design (chapter 9), that is, the capacity of design objects to be attributed a dimension of meaning that exceeds the extension and properties of the design object. Often the discussion about symbolic meaning is attached to value attribution among consumers of design; by contrast, my approach has been to analyze the production of symbolic meaning as a dimension of the design object. By placing and discussing design in spans of extension (products versus systems and organizations), intension (material versus immaterial), and ontology (actual versus possible) and by relating these spans to each other, I have pointed to different models of stating and questioning dimensions of symbolic coding in and through design.

Finally, I have addressed the level of contextual meaning in relation to the ability of design to change the conditions and structure of experience (chapter 10). While the levels of sensual and conceptual meaning in design describe the operation of meaning in and through the (becoming of the) design object, the contextual level deals with the effects of design. Within the research frame of a design phenomenology that looks at the role of design in creating structures of experience, I have proposed a theory of the transfigurative effects of design. In its abstract formulation, this theory addresses how design brings experience to the "other side" of itself, as indicated by the prefix *trans-*, an accomplishment that is made possible by the ability of design to point out new directions of experience and on different scales of implication and thus ultimately create new figurations of experience that surpass given constraints. In designating structures of experience, design is essentially imbued with ethical concerns, for example, in relation to environmental sustainability, an issue that I discuss as an example where design can indicate possible new directions of creating and experiencing the world.

This book contributes to the discourse on design from the domain of the humanities. The questions that it raises about design as an aesthetic medium that is open to the exploration of possibilities—in the creative phase of the design process on the one hand and as the enabling of symbolic meaning and transfigurative strategies on the other—are inherent to the humanities. Taking its methodological starting point in the design object, the book has investigated the constitution of design as a medium—a medium bound in a context of functions, aesthetics, and cultural dynamics and with many different kinds of expression, from graphic design to industrial design and design that is based on wireless digital technology. Together with the phenomenological framework I have applied, this approach is based on humanistic understandings of aesthetic expression, mediation, interpretation, and the role of experience. Fundamentally, my philosophical and theoretical discourse of design (of conceptualizing the possible in general) needs to meet the practical application of design practice (What actual possibilities and potentialities are we dealing with?). Thus, I offer a theoretical framework that can be filled in by design practice and, conversely, offer conceptual tools for nurturing the exploration of the possible in practice. It has been a central element of my work to explore fundamental concepts of design and submit the field of design to the kind of philosophical-theoretical investigation undertaken in other disciplines of human expression, including art and literature. Hence, a key element in my approach is to offer a new framework of understanding, a "detour"[2] of interpretation, where design is seen not only as processes and objects but also as an enabling of the possible and as a creative and dialectical integration of the unknown in the realm of the known. In this sense, there will always be a constitutive difference between theoretical frameworks and the requirements of practical application where the focus is often on direct measurements in relation to design methods.[3]

I briefly point to some aspects of this work that need to be explored further and that I believe can enter into a productive dialogue with elements and processes of design practice as well as the didactics of design education. These aspects may be seen as directions guiding new investigations:

The possible as a driver of design: Design, I claim in this book, is a means of exploring the possible and giving it material expression. Hence, a crucial element of design is its dialectic between the openness of the possible and the closure of form and material, which in turn, and this is a central argument of my approach, does not make the possible disappear but simply alters its means of expression. Design makes the possible tangible; it possibilizes the actual. It investigates the latent opportunities of reality and employs its aesthetic means of sensual expression, creation of meaning, and contextual impact in order to integrate these aspects within the domain of reality. Through the concepts of imagination and the imaginary, I have sought to promote a better understanding of the dynamics of the possible in the phase of designing and, afterward, through the design object. Thus, my approach has aimed at anchoring the discussion of the possible in design and using it as a means of asking open-ended questions in design: How is a field of the possible engaged in design, and what does it mean in relation to the symbolic expression of design? And, further, how do we give the open search for the possible in design clear direction to avoid losing our way in the search process? Here, indeed, more conceptualizations are required.

The role of the unknown: In relation to the search for the possible, a recurring theme is acknowledgment of the importance of the other side of the known: the unknown and its role in the process of dynamic imagining. The different entries into the discussion of the unknown, especially in the context of the related concepts of focusing versus defocusing and whole versus detail, can raise our awareness of the impact of incorporating a borderline to the unknown in design processes. Or rather, as I believe that most designers already work with invisible frontiers of the unknown in their progressive approach to creating the new and not-yet-existing, my work may be seen as a contribution to a reflection on the border of the known and the unknown. Following this line of argument, I believe that it is important to acknowledge and further the element of the unknown as a constitutive, productive factor for design, that is, not as a lack of data but as driver, and to integrate it in the design process.

Impact of design: It is important to discuss and conceptualize further how design conditions experience. Several aspects can be elaborated. First, the framing experience through the symbolic communication in design can be questioned further. Second, the immaterial in design needs to be challenged and explored as in ever more objects, design is present on the inside of objects as part of their operation through digital technology. Today, many objects hide their purpose and vast dimensions of operation; we cannot simply expect to detect the purpose of digitally operating objects by decoding their outer appearance. Much more needs to be done in relation to investigating the consequences of digital technology for the ways we approach and experience the world and for the way we perceive the materiality of objects. Third, we should further question the level of impact of design on experience. On the different levels of scaling, for example, strategic planning and systemic integration, we may ask how design frames experience and how the layers of practical, symbolic, and imaginative framing in design influence our entry into the field of design. As a flexible, dynamic tool of human imagination, design should be laid open to further imaginative intervention.

Notes

Chapter 1

1. Thus, I do not intend to revoke the almost metaphysical belief in the designer's artistic creativity that was characteristic of design history as viewed in the perspective of classic art history and its emphasis on artistic genius. See Pevsner's (1991) focus on the designer's genius.

2. According to the premise of post-Kantian aesthetic theory. See Bubner (1989) and Döring (2010).

3. This is an expression from actor-network theory. See chapter 8.

4. Strictly viewed, Kant's aesthetics in *Kritik der Urtheilskraft* (1790) is only secondarily about art. It deals primarily with the topic of the judgment of taste and the recognition of nature.

5. In this sense, he is an heir of Immanuel Kant, the founder of modern epistemology. In his seminal work *Kritik der reinen Vernunft* (1990), Kant also seeks the ideal conditions for apprehension and comprehension, but in contrast to Husserl, he is not interested in the constitution of phenomena. Kant's aim is not to investigate *das Ding as sich,* the thing in itself, as it is a priori inaccessible for us due to the filters of our perception that structure the appearance of the "thing." There can, according to Kant's epistemology, be only "things for us." See also chapter 7.

6. As a concept, imagination finds its modern manifestation in romanticism, and my understanding of it derives from my previous occupation with poetic imagination in romantic texts. See Folkmann (2006a, 2007a). Throughout this book, I make reference to romantic thinking, partly as a result of my training in romantic aesthetics and partly because the lasting importance of romantic ideas as sources of discourse about imagination and artistic creativity.

Chapter 2

1. The attachment to industrial mass production is often the criterion of demarcation for design historians who typically set the start of the history of modern design at the beginning of the industrial revolution in England (Forty 1986; Raizman 2010, Sparke 2009).

2. In German: "So ließe sich der Möglichkeitssinn geradezu als die Fähigkeit definieren, alles, was ebensogut sein könnte, zu denken und das, was ist, nicht wichtiger nehmen als das, was nicht ist."

3. In German: "Bauwillen und bewußten Utopismus, der die Wirklichkeit nicht scheut, wohl aber als Aufgabe und Erfindung behandelt."

4. Simon has, however, been criticized for employing too broad a concept of "design," involving, for example, "policies, institutions, and behavior" (Schön 1983, 77) and various kinds of human action, along with those not connected with specific means of design (see Galle 2011) with the risk of losing sight of the differences in the "media, contexts, goals, and knowledge contents" of the different kinds of design (Mareis 2010, 130). In essence, both the strength and the weakness of Simon's dictum lie in its all-encompassing claim: it does not take differences in the field of design into consideration, while simultaneously, through its global claim, productively pushing the notion of "design" further.

5. In his bias toward postmodern thinking, Welsch (1996) continues: "Against the modern world of uniforming it will be the role of the postmodern to enable the experience of the unstructured, to provide the unseen, and to create objects in the spirit of the event" (217). Leaving the historical paradigms of modernism and postmodernism behind, I think that in his emphasis on the ephemeral and the event, Welsch points to an important tendency not only in the whole system of design but also in singular objects of design: All objects are not only physical entities and materially present; at the same time, they have effects as nonmaterial events. See chapters 3 and 9 on immateriality in design.

6. This points to the progressive role of practice-based design research. Thus it can be specified how "experimental design research" can offer "concrete images of the *possible* in contrast to the abstract images of the actual in other kinds of research" (Redström 2007, 170).

7. Sloterdijk's point of making the (technical) inside comprehensible is, however, not new to research in human–computer interaction, although his philosophical framing is new.

8. In German: "Ein Designer kann sich nie nur als Kurator des schon Vorhandenen verstehen. Alles Design entspringt einer Anti-Andacht; es beginnt mit der Entscheidung, die Frage nach der Form und Funktion der Dinge neu zu stellen. Souverän ist, wer in Formfragen über den permanenten Ausnahmezustand entscheidet. Und Design ist der permanente Ausnahmezustand in Dingformangelegenheiten."

Chapter 3

1. Portions of this chapter were published as a journal article in *Design Issues*, without any relation to the topic of imagination (Folkmann 2010a). The article deals mainly with the first two of the three platforms of aesthetics described in this chapter.

2. Attempts to establish a scientific discourse for design have instead placed emphasis on other areas of interest: on analyzing and prescribing the methodology in designing, as in the practice-based framework of design methods in the line from John C. Jones and Peter Slann's seminal 1962 conference, Systematic and Intuitive Methods in Engineering, Industrial Design, Architecture and Communications, to, for example, Schön (1983), Lawson (2005), and Cross (2007) or on the impact of culture and social processes on the making and consumption of design (as in

studies of design history and the material culture of design, where matters of aesthetics are often consciously set aside due to an ideological struggle with the pervading notion of "good design" and its prescriptive aesthetics of outer beauty leading to moral improvement; see Forty (1986/2005); Attfield (2000). The connection within the ideology of "good design" between beauty and moral is itself a classical notion that can be traced back to the sentimentalist discourse of the eighteenth century. The issue of meaning in design has also been an object for scientific scrutiny, that is, how form follows meaning and how design makes sense in different contexts (e.g., contexts of use, language, life cycle, and ecology; Krippendorff 1995, 2006). All of these positions have more or less left out any analytical consideration of aesthetics.

3. See http://www.designandemotion.org. In 2012, the eighth conference was held in London.

4. In *Ästhetische Theorie*, Adorno (1970) locates the beginning of the collaboration of art and aesthetics in the philosophy of Schelling: "Ever since Schelling, whose aesthetics is called a philosophy of art, the aesthetic interest has been concentrated on works of art" (97).

5. As clearly stated by Forty (2005), who argues strongly against regarding design as works of art.

6. As early as 1853, the German philosopher Johann Karl Friedrich Rosenkranz wrote on the aesthetic of ugliness, *Aesthetik des Hässlichen*. Thus, to claim certain values as central to aesthetics is problematic and more indicative of an ideological stand (e.g., in claiming morality through beauty, as exemplified by the movement of "good design") than of a neutral assessment of the phenomenon of aesthetics. The point is that parameters of aesthetics can be found anywhere, even in things traditionally perceived as ugly or as kitsch.

7. Just to mention the realm of objects created by human beings. Interestingly, Kant's aesthetic, often praised for initiating the art-oriented aesthetic, focuses primarily on nature as an external ontological entity that transcends human existence and thus challenges human subjectivity. This is also the reason that I mention Schelling to include the first specifically art-focused aesthetic. On nature as an object of aesthetic theory, see Seel (1996).

8. In this context, the vocabulary of the arbitrary and the motivated derives from Saussurian semiotics, where the relationship of the components of sign, signified, and signifier is arbitrary (there is no law of nature specifying what a tree should be called—for example, that a German tree must be called a *Baum*), even though there may be a tendency toward some outside motivation, as in onomatopoeia, that is, words imitating sounds (there is a reason that the cat is said to be "meowing" in English). See Saussure (1972).

9. To quote Genette (1999) in full: "What is uniquely characteristic of works of art is their intentional aesthetic function, that is, their artistic function. To put it in more subjective terms, what endows an object with the status of an artwork in the eyes of its receiver is the impression, warranted or not, that it proceeds from an intention that was at least part aesthetic. Of course, a work that is not received as such can produce the same aesthetic effect as an 'ordinary object'—or none at all, as when, going into a public building to attend to some administrative chore, I give no thought to when it was built or its architectural style" (2). Looking at works of art, Genette focuses on a factor of artistic intention, which is also, counter to Genette's argument about "ordinary objects," evident in relation to design, particularly the artistic moment in the creation and forming of design objects.

10. To models of communication in design, see Crilly et al. (2008) and Barnard (2006).

11. The aim is to wander the road of the aesthetic, as "it is through beauty that one derives at freedom" (Schiller 1910, 162).

12. As Steinbrenner (2010) states, "I stand for the conservative point of view that good design can be seen a successful mixture of functionality and aesthetic or artistic quality" (21).

13. To make explicit what inventory of forms, functions, user appeal, and other aspects design objects have explored and made tangible is in itself, in my view, a good reason for dealing with design history. Without the knowledge of design history, we might fall into the trap of believing that every new invention is something that the world has never seen before, when indeed it might have.

14. Because we encounter many design objects through vision first, for example, when we see mediated images of objects, the discipline of visual culture may have important contributions to make to our understanding of design objects and their sensual appeal in general on visual culture. See Sturken and Cartwright (2009), Rose (2007), and on the connection of visual culture and design, Rampley (2007).

15. Ultimately the harmony of aesthetic experience is bound to destabilize again, as it stands in opposition to the vital forces of life (Shusterman 2000). This is a common philosophical figure of speech. All ambition to stabilize and achieve coherence is inextricably bound to opposite forces. The figure is also found in Coleridge, one of Dewey's sources. See chapter 4 on imagination.

16. Importantly, this does not mean that Dewey's theory applies only to art. In the words of Hans Peter Balmer (2009), works of art in Dewey's conception "should not be idealized; they should not be honored as numinous creations (exhibited in a museum). Simply, they are to be used as clarified and deepened experience" (136). Consequently, art has privilege. Dewey (2005) considers it the "most universal of language" and "the freest form of communication" (282), since it is essentially capable of containing, condensing, and expressing experience.

17. Furthermore, Engholm points to the ability of the subject to create coherent meaning as a hallmark of pragmatist aesthetics: The aesthetic experience occurs when a subject is able to combine the components of an experience into a meaningful whole, the subject's emotions must be activated, and, thus, the aesthetic experience is related to the subject's stance toward objects or situations. This may generate satisfaction and enjoyment, as the subject is able, by virtue of the meaningful whole of the aesthetic experience, to resolve the tension implied in normal experience.

18. The reference is to the second edition of the book; the chapter on somaesthetics was not included in the first edition.

19. Dewey (2005) says that a theory of aesthetics is "a test of the capacity of the system" put forward by the philosopher in order "to grasp the nature of experience itself" (286).

20. In French: "le corps appartient à l'ordre des choses comme le monde est chair universelle."

21. The all-important role of the subject for the operations of experience and cognition stands at the heart of Immanual Kant's influential epistemology in *Kritik der reinen Vernunft* (1781/1987); see also chapter 7. Kant's point is basically that all experience of any "world" is a matter of subjective cognition according to certain unavoidable modes of perception (time, space) and a specific amount of conceptual categories. The weakness of Kant's epistemology is that it does not take into account how the world that we encounter can have different kinds of expression, thus generating a certain feedback on the conditions of experience.

22. The Danish philosopher Carsten Friberg has written widely and comprehensively on these questions; see *Æstetiske erfaringer* (Friberg 2007) and *Det æstetiskes aktualitet* (Friberg and Bisgaard 2006).

23. See especially the essay "Synästhesien" in Böhme (1995, 85–98). Regarding the color blue, Goethe notes, "Rooms with entirely pure blue tapestry may seem spacious but are in reality empty and cold," while Böhme relates this effect to the notion of ambience: "The perception of blue is not about the statement of this color but about a sensation of the ambience, that is, how I feel within" (Böhme 1995, 97; Goethe quoted from 89).

24. Böhme calls it "aesthetic economy," but in my opinion, the concept of experience economy is more powerful, as the aesthetic in this context operates within the framework of experience. See also the seminal work by Pine and Gilmore, *The Experience Economy* (1999), and the sociologically founded work on the experience society by Schulze, *Die Erlebnisgesellschaft: Kultursoziologie der Gegenwart* (2005).

25. I thank Carsten Friberg for pointing this out to me.

26. This point might sound as if Boradkar is dealing with research into human-computer interaction, which is focused on investigating how complicated technology can be made intelligible to users; see also Sloterdijk's concept on the ability of design to translate the content of the hermetic black box of an otherwise incomprehensible product into meaning for users (see chapter 2). Boradkar's goal is not to contribute to the discussion of technological artifacts but instead to focus on the specific dimension in the product where it communicates with the user. This places his ideas within the framework of a phenomenology that is interested in the effects and impacts of design objects.

27. Thus, Boradkar's aim, as I see it, is to combine formalist analysis with culturally informed studies: "Formalist evaluations of aesthetics and meaning, though valuable, are incomplete unless supplemented by other interpretive strategies that include social and cultural concerns" (Boradkar 2010, 158).

28. The central role of the artifact in mediating meaning is also implied in Verbeek's notion of a materialist aesthetic. See Verbeek (2005) below and the discussion of Verbeek's position in chapter 10.

29. This is not quite the same as—but also does not exclude—the dogma in material culture studies of design as a "meaning-making process" that "encompasses the materialization of the physical world as a human project of creation" (Attfield 2000, 20). While Attfield's theory is sociologically founded in its focus on "the way people construct and interact with the modern

material world through the practice of design and its objectification—the products of that process," where design is thus conceived as "a practice of making meaning material" (12, 42), my aim is to emphasize the implications in a phenomenological context of the meeting between subject and object, thus acknowledging the power of the specificity of the object.

30. See my article on ambience and interior design (Folkmann 2013).

31. For the notion of *Gesamtkunstwerk*, the totality of arts in design, see Munch (2001).

32. This was, interestingly, also the ambition of historic functionalism in architecture, for example, in the ideas of Le Corbusier, with the intention of creating new conditions for living through the built environment.

33. See the contemporary commercial movies on YouTube.com. I thank Ida Engholm for making me aware of these.

34. The same critique that can be raised against Böhme for being interested only in how something appears, not what specifically appears, also applies to Seel.

35. Another example of this is a project at the Kolding School of Design in 2008 where design student Signe Fink countered the prevalent Nordic tradition of minimalism with its white, clean interiors (a style that generally goes unnoticed as an aesthetic strategy due to its habitual and ubiquitous presence) and instead aimed for "maximalism" with surfaces in bright colors and the use of textures such as textiles and fur. I thank Helle Graabæk for making me aware of this project.

36. Thus, this way of conceptualizing meaning differs from Krippendorff's semantic theory, which does not explore the actual kind of expression of meaning.

37. For a whole line of aesthetic theory in a German context, see Adorno's seminal and critical *Ästhetische Theorie* (1970); Christoph Menke's *Die Souveränität der Kunst* (1991), and Rüdiger Bubner's *Ästhetische Erfahrung* (1989), both in a critical engagement with Adorno; Karl-Heinz Bohrer's books on the borderlines of the aesthetic (1981, 1994, 1998, 2003, 2004); Wolfgang Welsch's books on new aesthetics in the light of the postmodern (1990, 1996); and the important anthology *Dimensionen ästhetischer Erfahrung* on the variety of aesthetic discourses in the present (but not design!) (Küpper and Menke 2003).

38. Reluctant to speak of aesthetics in design, Attfield instead speaks of "things with attitude" as a category of objects with an inherent self-awareness for envisaging change.

39. Böhme, for instance.

40. Thus, on the one hand Adorno remains pessimistic with regard to change, which is also the conclusion in the 1944 work *Die Dialektik der Aufklärung* (1989, together with Max Horkheimer). Here he argues that the dominance of reason since the Enlightenment in a dialectical movement performs a reversal and leads to barbarism and fascism. His aesthetic in *Ästhetische Theorie* has the same pessimistic tone even if there are glimpses of utopian optimism, as he speaks of an "epoch where the real possibility of utopia—that the Earth, according to the situation of the productive forces, here, now, immediately could be Paradise—on the utmost edge unites itself with the possibility of total catastrophe" (Adorno 1970, 56).

41. In German: "Ist in den Kunstwerken alles und noch das Sublimste an das Daseiende gekettet, dem sie sich entgegenstemmen, so kann Phantasie nicht das billige Vermögen sein, dem Daseienden zu entfliehen, indem sie ein Nichtdaseiendes setzt, als ob es existierte. Vielmehr rückt Phantasie, was immer die Kunstwerke ab Daseiendem absorbieren, in Konstellationen, durch welche sie zum Anderen des Daseins werden, sei es auch allein durch dessen bestimmte Negation."

42. In German: "Arten der menschlichen Involviertheit in reale oder irreale, vergangene, gegenwärtige oder künftige Zustände der Welt. Arten der *Weltbegegnung* werden so zur Darbietung gebracht, wodurch Arten der *Begegnung mit Weltbegegnung* möglich werden."

43. In German: "Objekte der Kunst sind Medien einer Erfahrung, die sich als ein Prozess des Verstehens abspielt, der nicht auf das Resultat eines Verstandenen zielt. . . . Verstehen von Kunst geht es vielmehr um ein andernorts unmögliche Begegnung mit andernorts unmöglichen Möglichkeiten der Wahrnehmung unserer selbst."

44. The full passage in German: "Mit den Rätseln teilen die Kunstwerke die Zwieschlächtigkeit des Bestimmten und Unbestimmten. Sie sind Fragezeichen, eindeutig nicht einmal durch Synthesis. Dennoch ist ihre Figur so genau, daß sie den Übergang dorthin vorschreibt, wo das Kunstwerk abbricht."

45. In the context of romantic thinking and aesthetics, this kind of aesthetic reflection goes under the name of "romantic irony" (see chapter 4).

46. In German: "Das Rätsel lösen ist soviel wie den Grund seiner Unlösbarkeit angeben: der Blick, mit dem die Kunstwerke den Betrachter anschauen."

47. As in James J. Gibson's (1977) concept of affordance, that is, the constrained possibilities for specific actions inherent in an environment or an object. This notion has been especially productive for research on human-computer interaction, and its influence is evident in Donald A. Norman's *The Design of Everyday Things* (2002), where it is used to investigate the "perceived and actual properties" of a thing that "determine just how the thing could possibly be used" (9).

48. For a further description (in Danish), see Folkmann (2007b).

49. Even as functions can be seen under the heading of aesthetics, aesthetics can be seen in the context of the complete sum of functions in design artifacts, that is, as functions accounting for nonfunctional use, as Nathan Crilly (2010) writes as the title of his article: "The Roles That Artefacts Play: Technical, Social, and Aesthetic Functions".

50. See to this concept Donald A. Norman's functionalist credo in *The Design of Everyday Things* (2002): "Natural mapping, by which I mean taking advantage of physical analogies and cultural standards, leads to immediate understanding" (23).

51. This point is indeed a Kantian reflection of aesthetics: When Kant regards aesthetics as a matter of obtaining the right value judgment, he not only considers the dimension of education but also the creation of a foundation for experience that may relate to the metaphysical entities of, say, freedom and immortality, important questions of the eighteenth century.

52. I use the term *aesthetic media* to expand Rancière's reflections from the domain of artworks to other fields, such as design. The feature of Rancière's approach of discussing works of arts and hand-delivering concepts that are relevant beyond this domain is symptomatic of theories of aesthetics.

53. As discussed by Walter Benjamin in his seminal work, *Das Passagen-Werk* (written 1928–1929, 1934–1940: posthumously published), on the Parisian arcades, their cultural impact, and the role of Paris as the capital of the nineteenth century.

54. See also the discussion of Baudrillard in relation to the imaginary in chapter 8.

55. To a Lacanian analysis of the neon sign, see Golec (2010). He points to the dialectic of the materiality of the sign/the aesthetic medium and the sensing subject and focuses on the role of the neon sign for the historical change of notions of subjectivity: "The substance of the subject— or subjectivity—was transformed in the illuminating presence of the neon-sign as electro-graphic architecture, which both stores and transmits data. For that data to be information it must be processed. The act of processing data into information constituted the subject in the neon letters organized by the grid of the Other. . . . Whether transmitter or receiver, the question `What?' is ascribed to the Other—in the Lacanian sense of a desiring, interrupting, traumatizing presence— in the communications circuit" (177). Thus, psychic processes, according to Golec, are external- ized in and through a medium such as the neon sign.

56. Here Verbeek (2005) also precisely points to the fact that it is "the failure to recognize that things have a moral valence that gives rise to technocracy" (216).

57. To borrow an expression from Stuart Walker (2006), who aims to turn away from the obses- sion with styling and beauty in design and instead focus on the more vital issue of sustainability. However, Verbeek's approach to aesthetic—in its mediating, moral role—breaks open the aes- thetic as a cage and positions it as one of the most central concerns regarding the effects and impact of objects.

58. The term *ubiquitous computing* designates the integration of digital technology into everyday objects and activities and was coined by Mark Weiser in 1988 while he was chief technologist of the Xerox Palo Alto Research Center in Palo Alto, California.

59. Of course, the alignment of reflectivity with simulation and nonreflectivity with realism may prove not to be totally watertight. But as an operative tool, it may offer an indication of how design approaches the field of aestheticization.

60. See Barnard (2006) for a discussion of various communicative functions in graphic design, for example its metalinguistic, that is self-reflective, function.

61. On the ontology of the smart phone, see the discussion in chapter 9.

Chapter 4

1. With regard to terminology, I distinguish between fantasy or fancy and imagination. Whereas the former designates a private and psychological matter, the latter not only implies the "image"

or the unreal ontology of the "imaginary"; it also has a history of being conceptualized within contexts of philosophy and *Geistesgeschichte*. *Imagination* is the technical term for the general human ability to create a vision and conceive new meaning. For the older history of the concept, see Klein (1996) and Schulte-Sasse (2001).

2. Conversely, Engell (1980) sees imagination as "the core and *sine qua non* of romanticism and the key to romantic art, literature, and thought"; the "attracting and unifying force of the imagi- nation made romanticism in the first place" (4). This is, however, too strong a claim; romanticism was a more heterogeneous phenomenon, and due to its varying cultural contexts, mainly in Europe, it had a variety of sources and found a variety of expressions (Hofmeister 1990).

3. Then we should perhaps dissect the human brain, but that still does not answer the question of how we grasp the nature of the images and the imaginary produced in the brain. Dissecting Einstein's brain did not, I believe, lead to any conclusion about the nature of his genius. In a similar vein, contemporary neuroaesthetics is trying to access the inside of the mind, albeit through indirect analyses of the response of the brain, for example, to images.

4. John Chris Jones (1980) bases his seminal work on design methods on the assumption that the design process needs to be externalized instead of being intractably bound within the restraint of the individual mind as something designers just intuitively do. Jones further sees a political consequence of this, as the matter is "for the design process to become more public so that everyone who is affected by design decisions can foresee what can be done and influence the choices that are made. Such a change [in approaching the design process] would mean that the public effects of designing become the subjects of political debate" (9).

5. The interdependence of internalization and externalization was often overlooked in the sub- sequent periods, which often criticized romanticism for being the cultural opposite of the Enlightenment, that is, a culture of dark and obscure spiritualism. Nothing could be more wrong. Romanticism shares the aspiration of the Enlightenment of gaining greater knowledge of the world; romanticism then takes the internal turn. As Novalis states, to complete the connection of inside and outside, "Der Sitz der Seele ist da, wo sich Innenwelt und Außenwelt berühren. Wo sie sich durchdringen—ist er in jedem Puncte der Durchdringung" (The seat of the soul is where the inner and outer worlds touch. Where they break through—it exists in every point of the breakthrough) (Novalis 1965, 418). In England, Wordsworth speaks in *The Prelude* (1805) of a "balance, an ennobling interchange / Of action from within and from without: / The excellence, pure spirit, and best power, / Both of the object seen, and the eye that sees" (Wordsworth 1979, 456).

6. This applies especially to most of the phenomenological tradition, which is interested in the image, from Husserl (2006), especially the lectures on "Phantasie und Bildbewusstsein" (1904/05), over Sartre (1940) and Blanchot (1955) to a recent media-oriented adaptation in Wettig (2009).

7. I thank Claudia Mareis for making me aware of Arnheim's work.

8. When one approaches romantic texts with this kind of insight, it becomes evident that they bear the clear marks of this kind of reflection in their own conditions of production. The more abstract the setting, the more clearly the manipulating devices of literary techniques appear, for

example, in Keats's *The Fall of Hyperion: A Dream* (1819). This method—setting the stage that in an abstract way achieves a distance that is deliberately manipulated while leading in new directions (as romantic texts do)—is in good concordance with and can be made productive for the making of settings for design processes: The (idealizing) abstractions enable new ways of framing the problem in a design situation.

9. In the original French edition from 1955: "Ce que nous avons appelé les deux versions de l'imaginaire, ce fait que l'image peut certes nous aider à ressaisir idéalement la chose, qu'elle est alors sa négation vivifiante, mais que, au niveau oú nous entraîne la pesanteur qui lui est propre, elle risque aussi constamment de nous renvoyer, non plus à la chose absente, mais à l'absence comme présence, au double neutre de l'objet en qui l'appartenance au monde s'est dissipée" (Blanchot 1955, 353).

10. "Le *sens* ne s'échappe pas dans un autre sens, mais dans l'*autre* de tout sens" (Blanchot 1955, 354).

11. As an introduction to this line of romanticism, see Behler (1993).

12. On romantic irony, see Strohschneider-Kohrs's classic study, *Die romantische Ironie in Theorie und Darstellung* (1960) as well as Behler, *Irony and the Discourse of Modernity* (1990).

13. This applies not only to the older work of Alexander in *Notes on the Synthesis of Form* (1964) but also to recent theories of design methodology that propose various frameworks of bringing synthesis in connection with analysis and evaluation (Lawson 2005; Cross 2007).

14. The concept of *In-Eins-Bildung* derives from Schelling's *Philosophie der Kunst* (1802/1803). Coleridge labeled the important chapter 13 of *Biographia Literaria,* "On the Imagination, or on Esemplastic Power."

15. Dewey, who follows Coleridge in underlining the unifying force of imagination, even pointing to it as a passage to "underlying ideal truth," states that Coleridge is less interested in imagination as a power "that does certain things" than in the "imaginative experience [which] happens when varied materials of sense quality, emotion, and meaning come together in a union that marks a birth of a new world" (Dewey 2005, 269, 279).

16. Thus, "the products of conceptual blending are always imaginative and creative" (Fauconnier and Turner 2002, 6).

17. James Engell (1980) points out that Coleridge has a tendency to view imagination as a mental activity that is capable of interpreting everything in the framework of its own structure; according to Engell, imagination in Coleridge's conception produces a language that contains "the whole potential of 'potentized' mind" (339). It is important, however, to see Coleridge's project within the context of his own time, where he sees, on the level of cultural politics, an emancipatory potential in imagination as a power of liberation from societal and cultural constraints.

18. In addition, the meaning of implicit references is disputed within research. In this way, the phrase concept "I am" can be seen in relation to God, Fichte's notion of an absolute I, or Schelling's concept of the unconditioned. See Engell and Bate (1984) and Klein (1996).

19. For a rational concept of creativity in romanticism, see the seemingly surprising statement by Novalis: "Ich bin überzeugt, dass man durch kalten, technischen Verstand, und ruhigen, moralischen Sinn eher zu *wahren Offenbarungen* gelangt, als durch Fantasie, die uns bloss ins Gespensterreich, diesem Antipoden des wahren Himmels, zu leiten scheint" (I am convinced that one arrives sooner at *true revelations* through cold, technical reason and a calm, moral mind than one does through fantasy, which only seems to lead us into the world of ghosts, this antipode of true Heaven) (Novalis 1968, 578). Novalis's point is that the road to revelation always has a method, and this method can be analytically described and discursively explored.

20. This is a classical figure in mysticism, leading back to the Confessions of St. Augustine. The subject's reflective subjectivity moves into the background to let something else, which is normally larger than the subject, appear to the subject. In the perspective of theories of creativity, this structure also plays a role in Ainsworth-Land (1982): "If one effects internal change and develops awareness, the world appears changed as well" (20).

21. Thus the subtitle of Scharmer's book: "Leading from the Future as It Emerges."

22. Exceptions do exist in romanticism, however, which equally has a tradition of eschatology in the vision of a becoming utopia. Blake's religious-mythological thinking is situated within a framework of apocalyptic vision, and an example of a eschatological vision in combination with a future-oriented expectation can be found in Friedrich Schlegel's "Über die Unverständlichkeit" (1799, "On Incomprehensibility") where a new era emerges in a process of eschatological-poetical reversal (Schlegel 1988, 2,240). See also chapter 10 on this.

23. Casey (1931, 231) quotes Dewey's *Art as Experience* on this (Dewey 2005, 279).

Chapter 5

1. Sartre is not alone in his interest in negativity. It has been an issue of French thinking since Alexandre Kojève's Hegel lectures in Paris in the 1930s, as demonstrated by Vincent Descombes (1979, English edition 1980).

2. An exchange of different persons' imaginings is impossible, as our personal experience always forms the boundary of our imaginings. In fiction, however, anything is possible. An interesting and provocative example of an otherwise impossible transgression of boundaries can be seen in the 2003 TV series *Angels in America,* where the hallucinations of one character are suddenly invaded by another character, whom the first character has never met. On the level of consciousness, this is an aporia; on the level of fiction, however, it makes sense, as the two characters with their mutual capability for hallucination designate a common layer of meaning.

3. In French: "Ils nous offrent d'échapper à toute contrainte de *monde,* ils semblent se présenter comme une négation de la condition *d'être dans le monde,* comme une anti-monde." Sartre further notes that *d'être dans le monde* (being in the world) is translated from Heidegger's *in-der-Welt-sein.*

4. Accordingly, the philosopher Edward S. Casey (1976) criticizes Sartre's concept of imagination for neither being capable of positing a coherent and consistent domain for experience nor putting

forward a creative and productive power. Casey views this in comparison to what he believes to be an abundance of meaning in the imagination in romanticism: "Beneath their inflated rhetoric Sartre discerns a nihilating mental act which is quite impoverished and threadbare in comparison with the psychic activity rhapsodized by the poets and philosophers of Romanticism" (3). Casey misses the fact that Sartre's point is not to investigate a rich and overflowing imagination but its transformative operation on experience.

5. In French: "Tout imaginaire paraît «sur fond de monde», mais réciproquement toute appréhension du réel comme monde implique un dépassement caché vers l'imaginaire."

6. In French: "Ce visible non-actuellement vu, il n'est pas *imaginaire* sartrien: présence à l'absent ou de l'absent. Il est présence de l'imminent, du latent ou du caché."

7. Together with Michael A. Peters and Simon Marginson, Peter Murphy has coauthored the book *Imagination: Three Models of Imagination in the Age of the Knowledge Economy* (2010). Murphy is the author of the chapters that are relevant for this context: "Imagination," "Creation," and "Discovery."

8. By claiming the harmonizing and coalescing element of imagination and setting it in relation to patterns and "aesthetic principles like proportion, economy, and symmetry" (Murphy, Peters, and Marginson 2010, 82), Murphy brings his concept of imagination in accordance with the part of aesthetic theory that points to principles of equilibrium and order as outstanding aesthetic features (e.g., Dewey and Shusterman). This is, in my view, not unproblematic: the equilibrium and the principle of harmony are implicitly claimed to be a structuring principle of human experience. What about the chaos: we could ask, with support from Nietzsche?

9. Within the field of poetic language, Gaston Bachelard (1957) has made attempts to theorize the imagination as directly "ontologically productive," that is, as something that posits a new unreal reality in poetic language. Thus, Bachelard sees imagination as an image-producing "concentration of the entirety of the psyche" that appears in language and may thus have an immediate effect "on other souls, other hearts" (3). To Bachelard, the imaginary is communicative and may be analyzed in various structures of archetypical provenance: the four elements of fire, water, earth, and air. Bachelard's theoretical approach is problematic: on the one hand, it idealizes the productive powers of consciousness, but on the other hand, it is fixed in and thus limited to poetic language and draws intricate conclusions. On a more problematic note, he does not focus on the actual function of the medium, only on the motifs mediated in the medium. The medium for Bachelard, language, is quite volatile in comparison to the material culture of (most) design, and it may therefore serve as a container for inexhaustible layers of meaning. Bachelard tries to make the dimension of meaning in poetic language physical and almost tangible. Conversely, design is (often) material, which is why I will attempt to enhance the understanding of it by resolving it in an imaginary, nonmaterial meaning.

Chapter 6

1. Not to be confused with the term *mind-set*, which has its origin in decision theory and has made its way into management and design theory. To have a mind-set indicates a global perspective of thinking, whereas a mental setting is local and tactically changeable.

2. Seel (2006) points sharply to the role of human freedom and decision making in relation to mechanisms of causality, as "thorough calculation and prediction" is impossible because the reflectivity and "self-reference of the consideration itself," that is, the fact that we obtain knowledge of determinism and causal relations, allow the consideration to run in different directions, and hence remain undetermined (153).

3. "To properly demystify the art of design we have to recognise that there is no choice but to engage with ideas at every stage of the design process and in order to develop artistic practice we need to express these ideas and feelings in space, words, shadows, light and form to manipulate and shape the quality of experience" (Moore 2010, 9). In her focus on the sensual qualities of design as the texture that circumscribes and creates experience, Moore's approach in many ways resembles Böhme's philosophical-phenomenological investigation of ambience (Böhme 1995, 2001).

4. The notion of being able to generate the right solution through the right analysis (and interpretation) of the problem, which then turns from being open to definition to being fixed and stabilized, has proved an impossible task. This was in fact acknowledged by Alexander in his 1971 foreword to *Notes on the Synthesis of Form*) but is also, and especially, evident in the comprehensive discussion within design theory of the wicked and ill-defined nature of design problems. To do Alexander justice, his ambition is mainly on a metalevel to "invent a conceptual framework" for making "explicit maps of the problem's structure" (Alexander 1964, 132), not to discuss maps of specific problems.

5. An opening point was the conference on "systematic and intuitive methods in engineering, industrial design, architecture and communications" arranged by John Christopher Jones and Peter Slann.

6. The book by Nigel Cross, *Designerly Ways of Knowing* (2007), is a collection of articles published from 1982 onward. In my view, in these articles Cross collects many of the issues from the discussion of methodology in design during the past thirty years. His recent book (2011) mostly summarizes previous findings.

7. Not only the title of the collection of essays, but also the title of the first essay from 1982, first printed in the journal *Design Studies*, which has an editorial focus on design epistemology; its guidelines are: "Original research papers, reporting studies in the process of designing in all its many fields, or furthering the development and application of such new design knowledge" (http://www.elsevier.com/wps/cwsredirect). Nigel Cross is editor in chief.

8. On wicked problems, see Rittel and Webber (1973) and the debate in Buchanan (1995), Lawson (2005), Dorst (2006), and Harfield (2007). Buchanan's comprehensive text synthesizes the concept and is a good entry to the discussion. Buchanan (1995) lists, among others, the following characteristics of wicked problems: "*Wicked problems* have no definitive formulation, but every formulation of a *wicked problem* corresponds to the formulation of a solution" and "Every *wicked problem* is a symptom of another, 'higher level,' problem" (16).

9. See the book by Jens Bernsen on this: *Design: The Problems Comes First* (1982). The argument of the book, stated through a series of industrial design cases, is that once the problem is formulated

properly and precisely, the solution almost emerges by itself. Thus, the problematic premise of the book is that design is a matter of simply finding and articulating the problems.

10. On this point, Lawson's and Cross's approach of circumscribing and refining how designers see the world and approach it by generating proposed solutions to ill-defined problems offers an important contribution to the understanding of the conditions and nature of design processes. The reverse of this clarification of design ability is, however, a (perhaps unintentional) praise of the designer's special skills and uniqueness, as "designing" is regarded as "one of the highest forms of human intelligence" (Cross 2007, 54). Mareis (2010) points out that Cross hereby creates a myth akin to Roland Barthes's (1957) conception of myth by claiming something as natural that is in fact a construct or simply a claim (Mareis 2010, 140). Consequentially, one should be skeptical about any claims of special abilities by any groups in society. Mareis also points out that we cannot see tacit knowledge in design as independent of its social structure and discursive frame (see Mareis 2012). Even if, in my opinion, Cross weakens his argument by claiming superior intelligence for a group with skills that are the result of a social process of professionalization, I think that Cross's and Lawson's approach to design epistemology is important as a way of offering a systematic-structural description of the factors that shape and condition the work of designers instead of viewing their work as the expression of tacit, mysterious knowledge. Their work can also be seen as a response to a need for establishing and legitimizing design as an autonomous discipline in its own right and as a field with professional practitioners and a discursive description of methods. By not devising prescriptive models for design work but instead circumscribing its conditions, they avoid the fallacy of assuming a normative stance in a way that would be in opposition to the real world of design processes.

11. None of the designers that I know see themselves as possessing unique creative capacities (or maybe they are just not willing to admit it!).

12. In particular, sketching has been a topic of research. A seminal contribution is Donald Schön's elaborations on the reflective dialogue with sketching in *The Reflective Practitioner* (1983). See also Goldschmidt (2003) and Tversky and Suwa (2009). To the role of the visual in processes of thinking, see Arnheim (1969) and the brief discussion of his approach in chapter 4.

Chapter 7

1. Thus, in the history of philosophy Kant is the first to separate "reproductive" and "productive" imagination. While the first is a matter of empirical sensation and psychology, the latter plays an active role in the transcendental synthesis of connecting the otherwise disparate matter to coherent meaning (Kant 1990, B151).

2. Kant says that there has to be a "third" mediation between the concepts of reason and the sensual: "which must on the one hand be in concordance with the category, on the other hand with appearance, and which enables the employment of the first on the latter. This mediating conception must be pure (without all empirical material), though on the one hand intellectual and on the other hand sensuous. Such a conception is the transcendental scheme" (Kant 1990, B177). In German, the mediation is something, "Was einerseits mit der Kategorie, andererseits

mit der Erscheinung in Gleichartigkeit stehen muß, und die Anwendung der ersteren auf die letzte möglich macht. Diese vermittelnde Vorstellung muß rein (ohne alles Empirische) und doch einerseits intellektuell, andererseits sinnlich sein. Eine solche ist das transzendentale Schema" (Kant 1990, B177).

3. In his reading of Kant, Martin Heidegger (1991) goes to an extreme in claiming that imagination through schematization not only mediates concepts and sensual appearance but actually precedes them both, as it creates their unity in the same turn. In his critique of abstract metaphysics, Heidegger sees this in connection with founding humanity on genuine human capacities of creating meaning without a foundation outside human beings themselves.

4. In German: "Unter einer ästhetischen Idee aber verstehe ich diejenige Vorstellung der Einbildungskraft, die viel zu denken veranlaßt, ohne daß ihr doch irgendeiner bestimmter Gedanke, d.i. *Begriff*, adäquat sein kann, die folglich keine Sprache völlig erreicht und verständlich machen kann" (Kant 1995, 198).

5. The question of direction will be elaborated on in chapter 10.

6. Within literary studies in particular Gérard Genette (1987) has investigated the taxonomy of narration: how narratives create structures of meaning through order, temporality, voice, focus, and perspective. Likewise, I will look at the enabling of meaning through mental settings in design processes.

7. See the discussion in chapter 4. Sartre (1940) is in line with the impossibility of *creatio ex nihilo*; indeed, he radicalizes it by claiming that the image in consciousness will always be less than worldly perception, as we can learn only from an image that we already know. Thus, Sartre claims an essential poverty and emptiness of the mind, which, in my opinion, pushes the argument of the impossibility of *creatio ex nihilo* too far. The romantic model of the mind is more just to actual mental processes; it may also, on the basis of the given material, give rise to an abundance of imaginings and struggle toward a logic of transformative processes.

8. In German: "Das Unbekannte, Geheimnißvolle ist das Resultat, und der Anfang von Allem. . . . Die Erkenntniß ist ein Mittel um wieder zur Nichterkenntniß zu gelangen."

9. To Novalis's general epistemology and aesthetics, see Folkmann (2006b).

10. I have interviewed 3PART for this book and have followed its work since the beginning of the 2000s (cf. Folkmann 2001).

11. Interview conducted September 10, 2009, in Aarhus, Denmark.

12. Interview conducted December 10, 2009, in Berlin, Germany.

13. Through its work with materiality (in turning the tactility of upholstery inside out), *Bistro Light* is an example of a design that seeks to challenge and question the cultural frames of reference through which we understand design. The design is not primarily aimed at solving a problem but rather constitutes a physical projection of a mental questioning of what design can be seen and formulated as.

14. Again, romanticism may offer concise models for the conceptualization of this. An inherent part of the thinking in early German romanticism (*Frühromantik*) is the concept of the fragment as a means of containing and pointing to an entity that is essentially incomprehensible and inexplicable. The fragment points to something bigger, but by being aware of its own incapability of doing this, it breaks itself off while also indicating that there is always more (see Schlegel 1988; Blanchot 1969).

15. Schelling was, as noted in chapter 3, the first to associate aesthetic theory exclusively with art.

16. Interview conducted December 13, 2009, in Stockholm, Sweden.

17. Interview conducted December 4, 2009, in Copenhagen, Denmark.

18. For a comprehensive unfolding of this argument, see Gumbrecht (2004).

19. Gumbrecht (2003) points to the fact that the experience of presence is "at least in part dependent on the objects of fascination" (207), but he is ultimately more interested in the nature of the experience (i.e., the subject in the aesthetic relationship) than in the properties of the objects that point in the direction of the specific aesthetic experience. Gumbrecht does, however, acknowledge the role of the object and states that due to the rate of historical changes of the aesthetic objects, it is impossible to propose a general theory of the aesthetic object. The rate of change also raises major challenges for a theory of the aesthetically effective design object.

20. As Hammerstrøms sees it, the notion of timelessness in design is a matter of ideology: "There is an ideology about simplicity understood as timelessness that I don't agree with. The point is, however, that most classics are very characteristic—and what we can learn today from the classics is guided by the question of how to create something characteristic, something with strong character."

21. These last factors of design are, of course, not only given by design from within design (as in a fundamental ontology) but are also marked by culturally given and marked expectations. However, because they go to the core of the structure of different kinds of design, I think it is possible to speak of ontology rather than culture.

22. An important proposition regarding the point of being guided by early proposals is Jane Darke's (1979) notion of a "primary generator" that operates as a guiding principle for the design process, as it contains both a delimitation of the problem and a generation of a possible solution. Working with a primary generator as a starting point can often result in strong design solutions that reflect the (often individual) designer's personality, but the basic and early idea can also be maintained for so long, regardless of new input to the design process, that there is a risk of fixation because designers "hang on to their principal solution concept for as long as possible" (Cross 2007, 105). Thus, studies show that "the quality of design solutions produced did appear to be dependent upon a willingness to reconsider early concepts" (106).

23. A classic notion of creativity derives from Henri Poincaré in 1908; it breaks the process of obtaining creativity down to a more or less linear series of stages: preparation where the initial problem is investigated, followed by incubation where the problem is not consciously considered but is nevertheless working within the creative person, and then a more or less sudden illumina-

tion as a breakthrough of an insight of the "new idea" that must subsequently be tested in a stage of verification (Poincaré 1982). An important feature is the dialectical nature of the model and changes in positions and modes, which has also been likened to the dialectic of "Apollonian concentration" and an inwardly processing "Dionysian ecstasy" in the incubation phase where the creative person breaks free from existing ways of thinking (Hammershøj 2009).

24. Traditionally, the metaphor or simile is a linguistic operation of transferring one meaning on another in order to obtain a new meaning ("love [or design?] is a rose") or of describing the hitherto unknown in terms of something known ("this new design is exactly like a Swiss clock"). For design semiotics, the latter may seem especially relevant to design as a device for explaining "the unknown in well-known terms" (Hjelm 2002, 9), that is, as a device for introducing the new. The metaphor, however, can also be used as a strategic device for pushing the framing of the design in new directions as illustrated in the 3PART example.

25. Naturally the implementation of this kind of discourse within design practice will require efforts within education and communication if it is to be successful. This issue may be addressed in the context of upgrading academic knowledge in design practice (Engholm 2008).

Chapter 8

1. Recently Penny Sparke wrote in *The Genius of Design* (2009), "[Design] is, above all else, a reflection of our diverse cultures and a driving force behind their formation" (9).

2. Thus Wunenburger (2003): "Generally speaking, the imaginary makes available a series of techniques of symbolic and analogical thinking (myth, symbol, metaphor, design [*dessin*])" (72).

3. See the recent discussion by Markussen, Özcan, and Cila (2012).

4. Metaphoricity in design is an interesting subject for analysis, but it can be difficult to approach due to aspects of interpretation in considering the tenet and vehicle of the metaphor. Hence, metaphoricity is more a matter of interpretation than something to be calculated as in Wang and Chan (2011).

5. An effective illustration of the limits of mental images is found in Charlie Kaufmann's motion picture *Eternal Sunshine of the Spotless Mind* (2004) where many scenes are generated by the protagonists' minds and there are blank spaces when they have no recollection.

6. In a homology, Wunenburger (2003) points to myth as a comprehensive structure encompassing the real whereby the visible gets diminished as a partially partaking in the invisible: "Thus, myth takes charge of the real by inscribing it in a continuum where the visible only makes sense by relying on the invisible, where the visible is a partial, current, and local manifestation of the invisible" (72).

7. The anxiety of being controlled by a meaning that has turned into something imaginary and threatens to take control and claim itself as reality lies behind Guy Debord's Marxist work, *La société du spectacle* (1967). In this work, Debord sees the "spectacle" as a primary filter of perception whereby all directly lived life (whatever that might be) is inverted and transformed into

illusionary representation. What is interesting about Debord's (2009) approach is not so much its critique of a society that is *"fundamentally spectaclist"* (27) and the implicit claim of an original authenticity to be reached by illuminating and being aware of the illusion. Rather, the interesting part lies in Debord's analysis of the mechanism of transformation when meaning not only becomes imaginary in the sense of negating the "real reality" but also takes on a new expression in spectaclist imaginary: reality is negated, but the negation acquires an outward expression in the spectacle. This spectacle, and Debord's perspective, is illusionary *qua* its origin in negation. What is important, however, is that it acquires an expression: the imaginary is not solely a matter of mental images but even more a matter of influential societal representations.

8. In Saussurean semiotics, the signifier and the signified constitute the entity of the sign that relates to an actual referent outside the sign. In this sense, the sign of representation, that is, the constituent of the act of representation, will always be formed by a relation of signifier and signified, and the referent is the something that is referred to. Semiotics saw the complexities in the sign process of representation (cf. the tradition of analyzing cultural representation from Barthes's *Mythologies*, 1957; see Huppatz 2011). Later poststructuralist and deconstructive endeavors have, however, clearly pointed out the aspect of complex and nondirect representation when the signifier does not function as a transparent vehicle but even more actively contributes to the signifying process, as it is not only posited as different from other signs but also in itself produces difference. To Derrida (1972), it is exactly the production of difference that constitutes the foundation of the production of meaning; he coins the term *différance* (in French pronounced in the same way as *différence* and thus only to be distinguished in writing) as a designation of the two-sided process of difference that both is the origin of meaning and makes impossible any substantial essence or presence of meaning: *"différance* is the non-full, non-simple 'origin'; the origin structured and differentiated of the differences" (12). ("La différance est l'"origine' non-pleine, non-simple, l'origine structurée et différante des différences"). Just as *différance* is based on the blockage of presence, so is the imaginary.

9. The best of the romantic authors investigated the reach and impact of this power, especially to try to see beyond human limitation and to catch a glimpse of an impossible absolute that supersedes reality. In this way, the romantics invented the literary imaginary with a specific, simulated ontology and a force of its own. This claim and the ambition of examining the practice of the imaginary rather than the theory of the imagination are some of the constituent ambitions in my thesis on poetic imagination in European romanticism (Folkmann 2007a). For a condensed version of the argument here, see "The Transfigurative Mode of Romantic Discourse: Poetic Models in Novalis, Keats, and Stagnelius" (Folkmann 2006a) and "Inversive Transfiguration. Imagination und Imaginäres bei Stagnelius" (Folkmann 2010c). Erik Johan Stagnelius (1793–1823) is a Swedish romantic author.

10. In this sense, Baudrillard (2009) differentiates between representation that uses signs in exchange for (real) meaning and simulation that starts "from the Utopia of the sign as value, from the sign as reversion and death sentence of every reference": "simulation envelopes the whole edifice of representation as itself a simulacrum" (170). In other words, representation and simulation connect to two different logics of the sign, where I relate simulation to the imaginary.

11. In French: It is an imaginary that "intégrant en quelque sorte l'activité de l'imagination elle-même, désigne les groupements systématiques d'images en tant qu'ils comportent une sorte de principe d'autoorganisation, d'autopoïétique, permettant d'ouvrir sans cesse l'imaginaire à de l'innovation, à des transformation, à des recréations" (Wunenburger 2003, 12–13).

12. The myth of the origin of a creative intention has been challenged in many contexts, for example, in literary studies where Roland Barthes in 1968 proclaimed the death of the author (Barthes 1977) and in studies in visual culture (Rose 2007).

13. Strictly speaking, the notion of the genius is only marginally a part of romantic discourse itself; rather, it is a formative factor in the different movements of sensitivity in the eighteenthth century, for example, the Goethian Sturm und Drang in Germany. In the age of romanticism, it is mostly conceived by authors and theorists outside the romantic artistic movement (e.g., Jean Paul's 1803 *Vorschule der Ästhetik*). And, of course, the notion of the creative genius has its very own postromantic tradition during the nineteenth century; this tradition may be seen as a kind of constructive reflection of romanticism: it patterned itself on romanticism but created its own value system beyond the actual utterances of romantic authors.

14. This phenomenon can be traced back to the end of the 1990s, when soccer hooligans started to wear the Burberry designs in order not to gain attention from the police. Eventually, this developed into a subculture of its own, where the "chavs" ("chav" meaning "child") wore Burberry-patterned caps. From the perspective of the company, the Burberry designs acquired negative connotations by being used by non-intended groups of consumers; but seen as a cultural phenomenon, it is a clear example of creative consumption: Things are used in new ways beyond the company's intentions: "although the *unintended* costumers incorporated Burberry in their expression and exploited the brand through consumption for their purposes, this did not mean that they changed their behaviour to *fit* the identity that the company and its designers wanted to communicate through the brand" (Hestad and Keitsch 2009, 401).

15. In the manner of Derrida, the ~~origin~~ is thereby crossed out while maintained; we can still read the word *origin* even if it is crossed out.

Chapter 9

1. This, according to Misselhorn (2010), stands in contrast to art that separates the symbolic and the functional (94).

2. The connection of the imaginary and the symbolic, the "imaginative aspect" of meaning and its immaterial, symbolic dimension, is also underpinned by Murphy (Murphy, Peters, and Marginson, 2010, 1).

3. Within the perspective of consumer theory, it is important to develop a grasp of the symbolic function of design and its enclosed meanings in its circulation among people, since design as a "language of products" can offer information about people's styles and conceptions of living (Schneider 2009). Modern consumer theory, for example, consumer culture theory (Arnould and

Thompson 2005), has followed Levy's line of argument in operating within a framework of analyzing the exchange of symbolic meaning through goods within a cultural context that creates self-esteem and social identity for the consumer.

4. In his recent and, in my opinion exemplary, short design history *Design im Alltag. Vom Thonetstuhl zum Mikrochip* (2007), Gert Selle takes the doubling of function and information in design further. He speaks of the visible and invisible design of objects, and whereas in his opinion, visible and tangible are properties rather easy to grasp, the "invisible requires reflection. . . . It stands for a systemic whole, for an interplay of forces that have contributed to the form [of the final product] and in the sense of this form should let the form have effect on the users' self-perception and readiness for identification. Out of objects long only debated within the perspective of art history, comes a problem of perception, research and interpretation in cultural studies. The gaze that is originally focused on the visible will today have to comprehend the complex structure of the invisible conditions, ends and effects of a form" (11). In this way, Selle demonstrates, for example, on the basis of a piece of anonymous design, a white sheet of paper, how it is material but also contains levels of invisible, immaterial design, ranging from its conception to its ways of structuring its own use and of introducing and educating culture.

5. Krippendorff (1995) differentiates four types of context: a context of use dealing with how sense making is enabled by form, a context of language concerned with language-based social practice in relation to the objects, a context of product life cycles (i.e., the creation of meaning within a larger framework of production and consumption), and a context of ecology designating the overall natural and cultural environment of objects. These four types of context may be seen as "constructions for the theory and practice of product semantics" and as "four principal types of cognitive models for designers to create forms that make sense for others" (184).

6. Within studies in design methodology, the focus on the doubling of meaning in design has been vaguer; Bryan Lawson (2006), for example, has pointed to the challenges of "the expressive qualities of design" (105).

7. This is also discussed by Alain Findeli in his important article, "Ethics, Aesthetics, and Design" (1994), which has been republished in the edited volume *The Designed World* (Buchanan, Doordan, and Margolin, 2010). Here, Findeli analyzes all design objects to be situated within the spectrum of the instrumental and the symbolic and conditioned by a threshold of significance (that objects are relevant) and a budget ceiling (what it is economically viable to produce).

8. In German: "daß die Idee im Bild immer unendlich wirksam und unerreichbar bleibt und, selbst in allen Sprachen ausgesprochen, doch unaussprechlich bliebe" (Goethe 1998, 470).

9. Design objects would even, if we were to follow Cassirer, condition our access to the higher principle of the spiritual.

10. As also suggested by Burckhardt (2010) and Selle (2007). Burckhardt's famous phrase was that "design is invisible." One might then claim, as Romero-Tejedor (2007) does, that the designer should always locate a pattern in the totality of object and context of action; however, this runs the risk of overemphasizing the context at the cost of the concrete object. This is one of the problems with Romero-Tejedor's systematic-cognitive approach to design.

11. To quote Stephan (2010): "Thus, Krippendorff's vector of an increasing artificiality is to be supplemented by a feedback loop which also in a descending movement integrates the levels of projects, networks, interfaces, services, and products, as these are not left behind but newly defined in the area of tension between material and cognition" (94).

12. Although singular products may have a wide impact, especially as a richness and high density in a "tight semantic fit" in artistically oriented design (Brix 2009, 6). On the discussion of the semiotic concept connotation in relation to design, see Guldberg (2010).

13. Another example is the *etrans* project, which is under development at the Kolding School of Design, Denmark, together with partners in business and society. The stated aim of the project is "to provide the methodological basis for the development and design work which will help the electric car to become both an environmental and commercial success in Denmark" (http://www.etrans.dk). The project has a specific focus in investigating conditions for establishing electric car transportation on a large scale in Denmark, not only in terms of infrastructure and technology but also in terms of cultural acceptability of the electric cars: how people's habits and cultural perception of electric cars can be changed.

14. See "Better Place Video: The Best Car in the World !!," accessed 2012–June 5, 2012, http://www.youtube.com/watch?v=9Bfz_x9e2Fo.

15. In comparison, the introduction video to *etrans* employs a different strategy: Etrans-Designskolen Kolding, accessed June 5, 2012, http://www.youtube.com/watch?v=l-dXnwpbOkE. The project does not yet have a product but follows a strategy of investigating culturally laden expectations regarding the experience of driving. In the video, three different persons lie on the floor and talk about their relationship with cars. Visually the video is colorful (in contrast to Better Place's plain white), it focuses on people (in contrast to the absence of people in the Better Place video), and with the use of fluctuating graphic elements as pictograms, it is dynamic, organic, and soft in its expression (whereas Better Place may seem hard and cool in its visual style). Thus, comparing Better Place with *etrans*, it is clear that Better Place is indeed cool and technological in its expression and not very explicit about the cultural frame that ultimately constitutes the possibility of its existence: Will people adapt to it or not?

16. Another aspect that is remarkable for such a critical design object is that the cord not only explores design possibilities but is also its own way of being realized as a product for the market.

17. Selle (2007) discusses these examples of anonymous design: how they give structure to experience.

18. In my translation from the German original, I have, for the sake of readability, omitted Aicher's consistent use of *minuscule* in the text. The German text reads: "der zugang zur wirklichkeit, zur welt eröffnet sich durch ein modell, eine konstruktion von aussagen, begriffen und begriffsoperationen. und auch der sprung in die zukunft, in eine neue mögliche welt, bedarf der spekulation, der arbeit am modell. erkenntnis ist übereinstimmung am modell und zukunft ist entwicklung am modell. entwerfen heißt, modelle zu konstruieren." (Aicher 1991a, 195).

19. Indeed, the pictograms have proven to be so effective and groundbreaking in their visual communication that they were used again in the 1976 Olympics in Montreal, and today they are recognized as a seminal piece of graphic design.

20. In this way, Hörisch detects three different Leitmedia that have formed the basis of Western culture: Holy Communion as condensed in the oblate, money as condensed in the plate of the coin, and, finally, the CD-ROM as an example of the concentration and exchange of information in late modernism. Characteristically, all three media are round and flat forms, easy to invest meaning in, and easy to exchange. Ironically, the CD-ROM is now an outdated medium because storing data and communicating through networks have taken over; information has become even more immaterial.

21. The countries are, from 2002, Austria, Belgium, Finland, France, Germany, Greece, Ireland, Italy, Luxembourg, The Netherlands, Portugal, and Spain; from 2007 also Slovenia; from 2008, also Cyprus and Malta; from 2009, also Slovakia; and from 2011, also Estonia.

22. On the design of Web sites and the design history of Web sites, see Engholm (2007); Engholm and Klastrup (2010).

23. The term *ubiquitous computing* was coined by Mark Weiser. For a discussion of the concept, see the anthology *Throughout: Art and Culture Emerging with Ubiquitous Computing* (Ekman 2012).

24. On the impact on design by the invention of microchips, see Selle (2007) and chapter 10.

25. A similar product type is the tablet computer. Although it offers easy interaction on a screen of a considerable size, yet on a portable device, it was long a failure due not to technical problems (which were eventually solved) but to the lack of consumer acceptability (Atkinson 2008). However, since the introduction of the first generation of iPads in 2010, these difficulties appear to have been overcome. A contributing factor to its success is the easy integration of increasingly dynamic Web content, especially images and movies, with the tablet computer, which lets the computer communicate with and unwrap various media formats. In addition, the magic appeal of the smooth surfaces and easy interaction with the Apple products apparently never fails.

26. Vial's reflections are made in relation to the iPhone but apply generally to the smart phone as a type of design. Thus, my focus is on the smart phone as a type of design containing an open internal extension bound within the frame of material intension. Of course, how this task is performed, depends on the actual product design in tactile structures of materials, weight, the feeling of solidity, use of color, and so forth.

27. See also the analysis by Misselhorn (2010).

Chapter 10

1. As mentioned in chapter 2.

2. Hence, the aim is not to not to write sociologically and anthropologically informed "biographies" of singular objects and their embeddedness in culture as in the notion in social anthropology of following the life and changes of objects according to the different contexts of value attribution that they engage in and contribute to. See Kopytoff (1986).

3. On this, see chapter 8.

4. This is not, however, the same as saying that postphenomenology operates with a postmodern notion of a decentered subject; it simply takes its starting point outside the subject.

5. To read about the book in English, consult Stáphane Vial's Web page of the author: http://www.reduplikation.net/en/home.

6. In French: "Le design n'est rien d'autre qu'un générateur d'expérience humaine qui propose aux gens des expérience-de-vivre, que ce soit à travers un produit de grande consommation, une installation urbaine ou un service numérique. Il traite non pas de la *valeur d'usage*, simple condition préalable requise, mais de ce que j'appelle l'*empirie d'usage*, c'est-à-dire la qualité de l'expérience vécue de l'usage" (Vial 2010, 64).

7. In French: "Le design n'est pas un *étant* mais un *événement*, non pas une chose mais une retentissement, non pas une propriété mais une incidence" (Vial 2010, 55–56).

8. Thus, as stated by the design historian Adrian Forty (1986), design "can cast ideas about who we are and how we should behave into permanent and tangible form" (Forty 1986, 6).

9. In his seminal work on European romanticism, Abrams (1973) states that on the background of the French Revolution "faith in an apocalypse by revelation had been replaced by faith in an apocalypse by revolution, and this now gave way to faith in an apocalypse by imagination or cognition," that is, "a total revolution of consciousness." For Abrams, the revolution was internalized; the "external means" is "replaced by an internal means for transforming the world," so that the "design, the ideas, and the imagery" of revolution are translated "into a different dimension of experience" (334–335).

10. In full in the text *Gespräch über die Poesie* (1799), *Dialogue on Poetry*: "For a long time there has been lightning at the horizon of poetry; all the lightning power of the sky was condensed in the one mighty cloud; in one moment it thundered mightily, in another it seemed to pass and flashed only from the distance just to return more horrifying: Soon there cannot be spoken of a single tempest, but the whole sky will burn in one flame. . . . Then the 19th century will really begin."

In German: "Lange has es gewetterleuchtet am Horizont der Poesie; in eine mächtige Wolke war alle Gewitterkraft des Himmels zusammengedrängt; jetzt donnerte sie mächtig, jetzt schien sie sich zu verziehen und blitzte nur aus der Ferne, um bald so schrecklicher wiederzukehren: bald wird nicht mehr von einem einzelnen Gewitter die Rede sein, sondern es wird der ganze Himmel in einer Flamme brennen. . . . Dann nimmt das neunzehnte Jahrhundert in der Tat seinen Anfang" (Schlegel 1988, 2:240).

11. The central points of the work are synthesized in "Radical Imagination and the Social Instituting Imaginary" (Castoridis 1994).

12. The considerations of a past and a tradition are too often forgotten in the primarily future-oriented approach in most design. Of course, we design things for the future, but all future has evolved from the present, which is laden with meaning from the past. Without recognizing the past, in the best case we are designing artifacts that have already been designed (the reinvention of the already existing); in the worst case, we forget that all objects are part of society and that

this society is a product of historically given conditions. A discipline such as design history, which pays attention to the simultaneously mirroring and shaping role of design objects in relation to historical contexts, should play a larger role in informing, for example, disciplines of design methods.

13. Hence, Simon (1996) states in *The Sciences of the Artificial*: "We might look toward a science of the artificial that would depend on the relative simplicity of the interface as its primary source of abstraction and generality" (9).

14. Malcolm Barnard (2006) calls this the magical function of graphic design: it is when graphics clearly transforms "one thing into another thing" (16), that is, almost in the sense of Maurice Blanchot, to make the original object for graphic representation disappear while creating a new presence in the graphic medium.

15. Ever since Hugo Boss designed the uniforms of the Nazis, design has been affiliated with war. A new tendency in the alliance of design and warfare can be seen in a common taxonomy of exploring social interfaces and new "fronts" of meaning (von Busch 2011).

16. See http://www.vestergaard-frandsen.com/lifestraw and http://one.laptop.org, accessed May 6, 2012.

17. This is also the paradox that underlies Scharmer's approach to management in *Theory U* (2007). His solution is to promote a phase of letting go of existing knowledge in order to make room for a "letting come" of a new presence of the future. In my view, Scharmer does not offer a solution to the paradox; he simply claims an answer based on the blurry inspiration of mysticism and anthroposophy.

18. I thank Peter Ullmark for making me aware of this text; see also Ullmark (2011). Grosz (1999) refers to the structure of temporality underlying the progression toward the future: "The ways in which we consider the past to be connected to and thus live on through the present/future have direct implication for whatever concepts of futurity, the new, creativity, production, or emergence we may want to develop" (18). At the same time, she thinks it necessary to propose new models of thinking in order to obtain the ability of being able to envision "the absolutely new" (21).

19. For example as it was done by the Norwegian toothbrush manufacturer Jordan.

20. Grosz (1999) notably says, "The possible is both more and less than the real. It is more, insofar as the real selects from a number of coexisting possibles, limiting their ramifying effects. But it is also less, insofar as the possible is the real minus existence" (26).

21. Far too often, scenario projections of the future do not entail a reflection of the past (see, e.g., Rooden et al. 2011 in a model of time travel), whereby the potential of the past for the future is overlooked: Not only should we acknowledge that the present is made of the past; it might also be that the past contains models that are appropriate to, suitable for, and adaptable to the future (and again: we would prevent the reinvention of the already existing).

22. See http://www.raymondloewy.com/about/quotesby.html, accessed May 6, 2012.

23. Another factor that brings design closer to art is that it is being displayed in art galleries and museums; often it is even created as one-offs that are sold to collectors. In this way, the art market has moved into the domain of design and appropriated part of it; for its part, design has appropriated codes of art in order to communicate on the market of art.

24. To quote the text from the presentation of the TED talk by Thomas Thwaites: "It takes an entire civilization to build a toaster. Designer Thomas Thwaites found out the hard way, by attempting to build one from scratch: mining ore for steel, deriving plastic from oil . . . it's frankly amazing he got as far as he got. A parable of our interconnected society, for designers and consumers alike." http://www.ted.com/talks/thomas_thwaites_how_i_built_a_toaster_from_scratch. html, accessed May 6, 2012.

25. See Binder et al. (2011) on this: "The possible is always contingent and though research may convincingly provide arguments for certain possibilities both search and arguments have to be guided by programs that set a direction" (28).

26. It can also be difficult to create models of the future as we often do not really know our own present. Manzini (2003) says that it is impossible "to foresee how and at what pace this transition will take place, but it is even very difficult simply 'to see the present,' i.e. to recognise how it works today and in which way and where 'the new' is appearing" (2).

27. Even if the scenarios in their concrete expression can serve as a means of articulating some sort of frame for the open-ended hypothesis of the model.

28. In German: "*Das* Fundamentaldesign unserer Zeit." Selle's short text on the microchip (Selle 2007) is, in my view, exemplary in discussing the consequences of the microchip on the level of culture and experience.

29. The opposite of the behavior of microchips as seemingly unnoticeable design objects that achieve a high impact by creating a culture of micro-objects that process information would be (luxury) fashion, which has a high degree of marketing and strives to make itself as noticeable as possible but with an impact on a very different scale. Fashion may be able to set a trend on the level of the culturally important visual coding of objects—how things look—and on the level of the people's identity construction, but it does not have the same impact on the level of structuring experience as the microchip has.

30. Selle (2007) says that miniaturization "eats the body of the things," which are then replaced by a new surface design, *Oberflächendesign*, as an entry to the new "culture-generating 'internal' design of the new immaterial carrier of performance" (216).

31. Thus, the level of strategic planning is connected to the concept of design thinking, if by this we mean a dialectical, oscillating process between the abstract conceptions of service and the concrete means of design: The abstract setting sheds new light on the material objects, and the material object produces new knowledge about what is realizable and prevents the abstract notion from leading the process astray.

32. By this, Buchanan (1998) contrasts his view of systemic integration with the early forms of systems thinking in the first part of the twentieth century where the "wholes were material

wholes—*things*, or information treated as a *thing*" (14). Buchanan stresses the role of people engaged in the culture of collaboration and the "need to integrate many kinds of knowledge in an effective enterprise" (14).

33. To quote Braungart and McDonough (2008) as testimony to their progressive, optimistic approach: "We can consult 'feedforward,' asking ourselves not only what has worked in the past and present, but what will work in the future. What kind of world do we intend, and how might we design things in keeping with that vision?" (145).

34. Further, the emission of carbon dioxide has been reduced by 90 percent. See http://www.mosa.nl/en, accessed May 6, 2012.

35. I love my innovative updated version of the Icelandic sweater, the model *Kaldi* by the manufacturer 66°North, made in 75 percent wool and 25 percent polyester. The sweater is light, warm, has strong fibers and texture—and a nightmare to scrap seen in the context of the cradle-to-cradle ideology.

Conclusion

1. I have tried to explore it in relation to the mediation of design in the context of visual culture; see my article "(In-)Visuality in Design: The Imaginary as Negation and New Creation of Meaning" (Folkmann, forthcoming).

2. In the context of Paul Ricœur's hermeneutic theory, the premise of the concept of *détour* is that it is anchored in the security of turning back to meaning in a process of *retour*: even if we go astray in the hermeneutical process of interpretation, we will always return to the starting point, probably enriched by new understanding. In this way, Ricœur (1975) has stated the productive force of distancing, as it is "also the condition for interpretation": "the alienation is not only something to be overcome by understanding, but also its condition" (210). In the light of the deconstructive notion of *différance*, Jacques Derrida (1972) has questioned this belief in the security of understanding: When difference is at the heart of all meaning, any unity of meaning in the interpretative act is blocked (Derrida 1972; Frank 1993). Derrida, however, draws a strong conclusion from the principal premises that all meaning is generated by *différance*; by contrast, the fact that meaning differs from itself and always will is also an integrated element of the understanding of hermeneutics (cf. Hörisch 1998).

3. Thus, this may also lead to a problem of generating theory out of design practice. As Ken Friedman (2003) states, "One of the deep problems in design research is the failure to develop grounded theory out of practice. . . . Instead of developing theory from practice through articulation and inductive inquiry, some designers simply argue that practice is research and practice-based research is, in itself, a form of theory construction. Design theory is not identical with the tacit knowledge of design practice" (519). Seen in relation to this conception of theory, my aim has not been to "develop grounded theory out of practice" but to develop concepts that can be tested and measured in a dialogue with practice.

References

3PART 2010. Brochure, Århus: 3Part. Accessed August 4, 2010, http://3part.dk/Admin/Public/DWSDownload.aspx?File=%2fFiles%2fFiler%2f3PART+Brochure%2f3PART_UK.pdf.

Abrams, M. H. 1973. *Natural Supernaturalism*. New York: Norton.

Adorno, Theodor W. 1970. *Ästhetische Theorie*. Frankfurt am Main: Suhrkamp.

Adorno, Theodor W., and Max Horkheimer. 1989. *Die Dialektik der Aufklärung*. Frankfurt am Main: Fischer Taschenbuch Verlag.

Agid, Shana. 2012. Worldmaking: Working through Theory/Practice in Design. *Design and Culture* 34 (1): 27–54.

Aicher, Otl. 1991a. *die welt als entwurf*. Berlin: Ernst und Sohn.

Aicher, Otl. 1991b. *analog und digital*. Berlin: Ernst und Sohn.

Ainsworth-Land, Vaune. 1982. Imaging and Creativity: An Integrating Perspective. *Journal of Creative Behavior* 16 (1): 5–28.

Alexander, Christopher. 1964. *Notes on the Synthesis of Form*. Cambridge, MA: Harvard University Press.

Arnheim, Rudolph. 1969. *Visual Thinking*. Berkeley: University of California Press.

Arnould, Eric J., and Craig J. Thompson. 2005. Consumer Culture Theory (CCT): Twenty Years of Research. *Journal of Consumer Research* 31: 868–882.

Atkinson, Paul. 2008. A Bitter Pill to Swallow: The Rise and Fall of the Tablet Computer. *Design Issues* 24 (4): 3–25.

Attfield, Judith. 2000. *Wild Things: The Material Culture of Everyday*. Oxford: Berg.

Bachelard, Gaston. 1957. *La poétique de l'espace*. Paris: Presses Universitaires de France.

Balmer, Hans Peter. 2009. *Philosophische Ästhetik. Eine Einladung*. Tübingen: Francke Verlag.

Barnard, Malcolm. 2006. *Graphic Design as Communication*. Oxon, UK: Routledge.

Barthes, Roland. 1957. *Mythologies*. Paris: Éditions du Seuil.

Barthes, Roland. 1977. The Death of the Author. In *Image Music Text*, edited by Stephen Heath, 142–148. London: Fontana Press.

Baudrillard, Jean. 2009. Simulacra and Simulations. In *Selected Writings*, edited by Mark Poster, 166–184. Cambridge: Polity Press.

Behler, Ernst. 1990. *Irony and the Discourse of Modernity*. Seattle: University of Washington Press.

Behler, Ernst. 1993. *German Romantic Literary Theory*. Cambridge: Cambridge University Press.

Bernsen, Jens. 1982. *Design: The Problems Comes First*. Copenhagen: Danish Design Centre.

Bijker, Wiebe, and John Law, eds. 1992. *Shaping Technology/Building Society: Studies in Sociotechnical Change*. Cambridge, MA: MIT Press.

Binder, Thomas, Eva Brandt, Joachim Halse, Maria Foverskov, Sissel Olander, and Signe Louise Yndigegn. 2011. Living the (Co-Design) Lab. In *Proceedings to Nordes '11: The 4th Nordic Design Research Conference*, May 29–31, School of Art and Design, Aalto University, Helsinki, Finland, 21–30.

Blanchot, Maurice. 1955. *L'Espace littéraire*. Paris: Gallimard.

Blanchot, Maurice. 1969. *L'Entretien infini*. Paris: Gallimard.

Blanchot, Maurice. 1989. *The Space of the Literary*. University of Nebraska Press.

Böhme, Gernot. 1995. *Atmosphäre. Essays zur neuen Ästhetik*. Frankfurt am Main: Suhrkamp.

Böhme, Gernot. 2001. *Aisthetik. Vorlesungen über Ästhetik als allgemeine Wahrnehmungslehre*. Munich: Wilhelm Fink Verlag.

Bohrer, Karl-Heinz. 1981. *Plötzlichkeit*. Frankfurt am Main: Suhrkamp.

Bohrer, Karl-Heinz. 1994. *Das absolute Präsens*. Frankfurt am Main: Suhrkamp.

Bohrer, Karl-Heinz. 1998. *Die Grenzen des Ästhetischen*. Munich: Hanser.

Bohrer, Karl-Heinz. 2003. *Ekstasen der Zeit*. Munich: Hanser.

Bohrer, Karl-Heinz. 2004. *Imaginationen des Bösen*. Munich: Hanser.

Boradkar, Prasad. 2010. *Designing Things: A Critical Introduction to the Culture of Objects*. Oxford: Berg.

Borja de Mozota, Brigitte. 2003. *Design Management*. New York: Allworth Press.

Braungart, Michael, and William McDonough. 2008. *Cradle to Cradle: Re-Making the Way We Make Things*. London: Vintage.

Brix, Anders. 2008. Solid Knowledge: Notes on the Nature of Knowledge Embedded in Designed Artefacts. *Artifact* 2 (1): 36–40.

Brix, Anders. 2009. Does User-Driven Design Drive Design-Driven Users? Reflections on the Conceptual Framing of User Informed Design Processes. Conference, International Association of Design Research.

Brown, Tim. 2008. Design Thinking. *Harvard Business Review* 86(6): 84–92.

Brown, Tim. 2009. *Change by Design: How Design Thinking Transforms Organizations and Inspires Innovation*. New York: Collins Business.

Bubner, Rüdiger. 1989. *Ästhetische Erfahrung*. Frankfurt am Main: Suhrkamp.

Buchanan, Richard. 1995. Wicked Problems in Design Thinking. In *The Idea of Design*, edited by R. Buchanan and V. Margolin, 3–21. Cambridge, MA: MIT Press.

Buchanan, Richard. 1998. Branzi's Dilemma: Design in Contemporary Culture. *Design Issues* 14 (1): 3–20.

Buchanan, Richard, Dennis Doordan, and Victor Margolin, eds. 2010. *The Designed World: Images, Objects, Environments*. Oxford: Berg.

Burckhardt, Lucius. 2010. Design ist unsichtbar. In *Gestaltung denken*, edited by K. T. Edelmann and G. Terstiege, 211–217. Basel: Birkhäuser.

Bürdek, Bernhard E. 2005. *Design: Geschichte, Theorie und Praxis der Produktgestaltung*. Basel: Birkhäuser.

Callon, Michel. 1987. Society in the Making: The Study of Technology as a Tool for Sociological Analysis. In *The Social Construction of Technological Systems: New Directions in the Sociology and History of Technology*, edited by W. Bijker, T. P. Hughes, and T. Pinch, 83–103. Cambridge, MA: MIT Press.

Casey, Edward S. 1976. *Imagining: A Phenomenological Study*. Bloomington: Indiana University Press.

Cassirer, Ernst. 1964. *Philosophie der symbolischen Formen: Dritter Teil*. Darmstadt: Wissenschaftliche Buchgesellschaft.

Cassirer, Ernst. 2009. Der Begriff der symbolischen Form im Aufbau der Geisteswissenschaften. In *Schriften zur Philosophie der symbolischen Formen*, 63–92, edited by Marion Lauschke. Hamburg: Meiner.

Castoriadis, Cornelius. 1975. *L'institution imaginaire de la société*. Paris: Éditions du seuil.

Castoridis, Cornelius. 1994. Radical Imagination and the Social Instituting Imaginary. In *Rethinking Imagination: Culture and Creativity*, edited by G. Robinson and J. Rundell, 136–154. London: Routledge.

Coleridge, Samuel Taylor. 1984. *Biographia Literaria*. Edited by James Engell and W. Jackson Bate. Princeton, NJ: Princeton University Press.

Crilly, Nathan, David Good, Derek Matravers, and P. John Clarkson. 2010. The Roles That Artefacts Play: Technical, Social, and Aesthetic Functions. *Design Studies* 31 (4): 311–344.

Crilly, Nathan, David Good, Derek Matravers, and P. John Clarkson. 2008. Design as Communication: Exploring the Validity and Utility of Relating Intention to Interpretation. *Design Studies* 29 (5): 425–457.

Cross, Nigel. 2007. *Designerly Ways of Knowing*. Basel: Birkhäuser.

Cross, Nigel. 2011. *Design Thinking*. Oxford: Berg.

Csikszentmihalyi, Mihaly. 1995. Design and Order in Everyday Life. In *The Idea of Design*, edited by R. Buchanan and V. Margolin, 118–126. Cambridge, MA: MIT Press.

Darke, Jane. 1979. The Primary Generator and the Design Process. *Design Studies* 1 (1): 36–44.

Debord, Guy. 2009. *Society of the Spectacle*. Sussex: Soul Bay Press.

Derrida, Jacques. 1972. *Marges—de la Philosophie*. Paris: Les éditions de minuit.

Descombes, Vincent. 1979. *Le même et l'autre*. Paris: Les éditions de minuit.

Desmet, Pieter M. A. 2010. Three Levels of Product Emotion. In *Proceedings of KEER 2010, International Conference on Kansei Engeneering and Emotion Research*, Paris, March 2–4.

Desmet, Pieter M. A., and Paul Hekkert. 2007. Framework of Product Experience. *International Journal of Design* 1 (1): 57–66.

Dewey, John. 2005. *Art as Experience*. New York: Penguin.

DiSalvo, Carl. 2009. Design and the Construction of Publics. *Design Issues* 25 (1): 48–63.

Döring, Sabine A. 2010. Ästhetischer Wert und emotionale Erfahrung. In *Ästhetische Werte und Design*, edited by Jakob Steinbrenner and Julian Nida-Rümelin, 53–73. Ostfildern: Hatje Cantz.

Dorschel, Andreas. 2003. *Gestaltung—Zur Ästhetik des Brauchbaren*. Heidelberg: Universitätsverlag Winther.

Dorst, Kees. 2006. Design Problems and Design Paradoxes. *Design Issues* 22 (3): 4–17.

Drügh, Heinz, Christian Metz, and Björn Weyand, eds. 2011. *Warenästhetik. Neue Perspektiven auf Konsum, Kultur und Kunst*. Frankfurt am Main: Suhrkamp.

Duedahl, Marie. 2012. Jeg sigter højere end livsstil. *Politiken* 2012–May 20, 2012, Section 4, 6.

du Gay, Paul, Stuart Hall, Linda Janes, and Hugh Mackay. 1997. *Doing Cultural Studies: The Story of the Sony Walkman*. London: Sage.

Dunne, Anthony. 1999. *Hertzian Tales: Electronic Products, Aesthetic Experience, and Critical Design*. Cambridge, MA: MIT Press.

Dunne, Anthony, and Fiona Raby. 2001. *Design Noir: The Secret Life of Electronic Objects*. London: Birkhäuser.

Ehrenfeld, John R. 2008. *Sustainability by Design: A Subversive Strategy for Transforming Our Consumer Culture*. New Haven, CT: Yale University Press.

Ekman, Ulrik, ed. 2012. *Throughout: Art and Culture Emerging with Ubiquitous Computing*. Cambridge, MA: MIT Press.

Engell, James. 1980. *Creative Imagination*. Cambridge, MA: Harvard University Press.

Engell, James, and W. J. Bate, ed. 1984. Editor's Introduction. In S. T. Coleridge, *Biographia Literaria*. Princeton, NJ: Princeton University Press, xli–cxxxvi.

Engholm, Ida. 2006. *Verner Panton*. Copenhagen: Aschehoug.

Engholm, Ida. 2007. Design History of the WWW: Website Development from the Perspective of Genre and Style Theory. *Artifact* 1 (4): 217–231.

Engholm, Ida. 2008. Master's Degree in Design: Research-Based Master's Programme for Professional Designers. *Nordisk arkitekturforskning* 2: 105–111.

Engholm, Ida. 2010. The Good Enough Revolution: The Role of Aesthetics in User Experiences with Artifacts. *Digital Creativity* 21 (3): 141–154.

Engholm, Ida, and Lisbeth Klastrup. 2010. Websites as Artefacts: A New Model for Website Analysis. Paper presented at the Second International Conference on New Media and Interactivity, Istanbul, Turkey.

Fallan, Kjetil. 2010. *Design History. Understanding Theory and Method*. Oxford: Berg.

Fällman, Daniel. 2008. The Interaction Design Research Triangle of Design Practice, Design Studies, and Design Exploration. *Design Issues* 24 (3): 4–18.

Fauconnier, Gilles, and Mark Turner. 2002. *The Way We Think*. New York: Basic Books.

Featherstone, Mike. 1991. *Consumer Culture and Postmodernism*. London: Sage.

Findeli, Alain. 1994. Ethics, Aesthetics, and Design. *Design Issues* 10 (2): 49–68.

Flusser, Villém. 1993. *Dinge und Undinge*. Munich: Carl Hanser Verlag.

Flusser. Villém. 1999. *The Shape of Things: A Philosophy of Design*. London: Reaktion Book.

Folkmann, Mads Nygaard. 2001. Design as a multiplicity of skills. *Design DK* 3:57–64.

Folkmann, Mads Nygaard. 2006a. The Transfigurative Mode of Romantic Discourse: Poetic Models in Novalis, Keats, and Stagnelius. *Prism(s): Essays in Romanticism* 14:27–56.

Folkmann, Mads Nygaard. 2006b. *Figurationen des Übergangs. Zur literarischen Ästhetik bei Novalis*. Frankfurt am Main: Peter Lang Verlag.

Folkmann, Mads Nygaard. 2007a. Mulighedsrum. Poetisk imagination i den europæiske romantik (Novalis, Keats, Stagnelius). PhD dissertation, University of Copenhagen.

Folkmann, Mads Nygaard. 2007b. *Louise Campbell*. Copenhagen: Aschehoug.

Folkmann, Mads Nygaard. 2010a. Evaluating Aesthetics in Design. A Phenomenological Approach. *Design Issues* 26 (1): 40–53.

Folkmann, Mads Nygaard. 2010b. Umsetzung. Interpretative Herausforderungen praxisferner Designtheorie. In *Entwerfen. Wissen, Produzieren: Designforschung im Anwendungskontext*, edited by Claudia Mareis, Gesche Joost, and Kora Kimpel, 159–176. Bielefeld: transcript Verlag.

Folkmann, Mads Nygaard. 2010c. Inversive Transfiguration. Imagination und Imaginäres bei Stagnelius. In *Romantik im Norden*, edited by Annegret Heitmann and Hanne R. Laursen, 49–72. Würzburg: Königshausen & Neumann.

Folkmann, Mads Nygaard. 2011a. Encoding Symbolism: Immateriality and Possibility in Design. *Design and Culture* 3 (1): 51–74.

Folkmann, Mads Nygaard. 2011b. Spaces of Possibility: The Imaginary in Design. *The Design Journal* 14 (3): 263–282.

Folkmann, Mads Nygaard. 2013. Interior as Place: Aesthetic Coding in Interior Design. In *The Blackwell Book on Interior Design*, edited by Nancy Blossom and J.A.A. Thompson. London: Blackwell.

Folkmann, Mads Nygaard. Forthcoming. (In-)Visuality in Design: The Imaginary as Negation and New Creation of Meaning. In *Trans Visuality: Dimensioning the Visual in a Visual Culture*, edited by Anders Michelsen, Hans Dam Christensen, Tore Kristensen, and Frauke Wiegand. Liverpool: Liverpool University Press.

Forty, Adrian. 2005. *Objects of Desire. Design and Society since 1750*. London: Thames and Hudson.

Foucault, Michel. 1969. *L'Archéologie du savoir*. Paris: Édition du minuit.

Frank, Manfred. 1989. *Einführung in die frühromantische Ästhetik*. Frankfurt am Main: Suhrkamp.

Frank, Manfred. 1993. *Das Sagbare und das Unsagbare*. Frankfurt am Main: Suhrkamp.

Frank, Manfred, and Gerhard Kurz. 1977. Ordo Inversus. In *Geist und Zeichen*, edited by H. Anton, 75–92. Heidelberg: Festschrift Arthur Henkel.

Friberg, Carsten. 2007. *Æstetiske erfaringer*. Copenhagen: Multivers.

Friberg, Carsten, and Ulrik Bisgaard, eds. 2006. *Det æstetiskes aktualitet*. Copenhagen: Multivers.

Friedman, Ken. 2003. Theory Construction in Design Research: Criteria, Approaches and Methods. *Design Studies* 24 (6): 507–522.

Fry, Tony. 1988. *Design History Australia*. Sydney: Hale & Iremonger.

Gabriel, Yiannis, and Tim Lang. 1995. *The Unmanageable Consumer: Contemporary Consumption and Its Fragmentation*. Thousand Oaks, CA: Sage.

Gadamer, Hans-Georg. 1960. *Wahrheit und Methode*. Tübingen: Mohr.

Galle, Per. 2008. Candidate Worldviews for Design Theory. *Design Studies* 29 (3): 267–303.

Galle, Per. 2011. Foundational and Instrumental Design Theory. *Design Issues* 27 (4): 81–94.

Gedenryd, Henrik. 1998. *How Designers Work: Making Sense of Authentic Cognitive Activities*. Lund: Lund University Cognitive Studies.

Genette, Gerard. 1987. *Narrative Discourse: An Essay in Method*. Ithaca, NY: Cornell University Press.

Genette, Gerard. 1999. *The Aesthetic Relation*. Ithaca, NY: Cornell University Press.

Gibson, James J. 1977. The Theory of Affordances. In *Perceiving, Acting, and Knowing*, edited by Robert Shaw and John Bransford, 67–82. Mahwah NJ: Erlbaum.

Goethe, Johann Wolfgang von. 1998. *Maximen und Reflexionen*. Edited by Erich Trunz, 12:365–547.Munich: DTV.

Goldschmidt, Gabriela. 2003. The Backtalk of Self-Generated Sketches. *Design Issues* 19 (1): 72–88.

Golec, Michael J. 2010. Logo/Local Intensities: Lacan, the Discourse of the Other, and the Solicitation to "Enjoy." *Design and Culture* 2 (2): 167–181.

Gropius, Walter. 1919. Bauhaus Manifest, accessed August 15, 2011, http://www.kunstzitate.de/bildendekunst/manifeste/bauhaus_1919.htm.

Grosz, Elisabeth. 1999. Thinking the New: Futures Yet Unthought. In *Becomings: Explorations in Time, Memory and Futures*, edited by E. Grosz, 15–28. Ithaca, NY: Cornell University Press.

Guldberg, Jørn. 2010. Singular or Multiple Meanings: A Critique of the Index/Anzeichen Approach to Design Semiotics/Semantics. In *Proceedings of DeSForM 2010, Design and Semantics of Form and Movement*, 71–84.

Gumbrecht, Hans Ulrich. 2003. Epiphanien. In *Dimensionen ästhetischer Erfarung*, edited by Joachim Küpper and Christoph Menke, 203–222. Frankfurt am Main: Suhrkamp.

Gumbrecht, Hans Ulrich. 2004. *The Production of Presence*. Stanford: Stanford University Press.

Hagan, Susan M. 2007. The Imagined and the Concrete: What Is an Artifact? *Artifact* 1 (1): 23–25.

Hall, Stuart. 1980. Encoding/Decoding. In *Culture, Media, Language*, edited by Stuart Hall, Dorothy Hobson, Andrew Lowe, and Paul Willis, 128–138. London: Hutchinson.

Halse, Joachim, Eva Brandt, Clark Brendon, and Thomas Binder, eds. 2010. *Rehearsing the Future*. Copenhagen: Danish School of Design.

Hammershøj, Lars Geers. 2009. Creativity as a Question of Bildung. *Journal of Philosophy of Education* 43 (4): 545–558.

Hampe, Beate, and Joseph E. Grady. 2005. *From Perception to Meaning: Image Schemas in Cognitive Linguistics*. Berlin: De Gruyter Mouton.

Harfield, Steven. 2007. On Design "Problematization": Theorising Differences in Designed Outcomes. *Design Studies* 28 (2): 159–173.

Haug, Wolfgang Fritz. 1986. *Critique of Commodity Aesthetics: Appearance, Sexuality and Advertising in Capitalist Society*. Cambridge: Polity Press.

Heidegger, Martin. 1991. *Kant und das Problem der Metaphysik*. Frankfurt am Main: Vittori Klostermann.

Heilig, Sebastian. 2008. Der Sportler-Strich von Munich. Spiegel Online, accessed August 24, 2011, http://einestages.spiegel.de/static/topicalbumbackground/1515/der_sportler_strich_von_muenchen.html.

Heskett, John. 1980. *Industrial Design*. London: Thames and Hudson.

Heskett, John. 2002. *Toothpicks and Logos*. Oxford: Oxford University Press.

Hestad, Monika, and Martina Keitsch. 2009. Not Always a Victim! On Seeing Users as Active Consumers. *International Journal of Product Development* 9 (4): 396–405.

Hjelm, Sara Ilstedt. 2002. *Semiotics in Product Design*. Stockholm: CID, Centre for User Oriented IT Design, accessed April 16, 2010, http://citeseerx.ist.psu.edu/viewdoc/download?doi=10.1.1.130.1873&rep=rep1&type=pdf.

Hjelm, Sara Ilstedt. 2007. Energi som syns. In *Under ytan: En antologi om designforskning*, edited by Sara Ilstedt Hjelm, Åsa Harvard, Ulla Johansson, Arantza Elisabeth Niño, Lisbeth Svengren Holm, Peter Ullmark, and Bo Westerlund, 118–131. Stockholm: Raster Förlag and SVID.

Hobbes, Thomas. 1998. *Leviathan*. Oxford: Oxford University Press.

Hofmeister, Gerhart. 1990. *Deutsche und europäische Romantik*. Stuttgart: Metzler.

Hörisch, Jochen. 1998. *Die Wut des Verstehens*. Frankfurt am Main: Suhrkamp.

Hörisch, Jochen. 2009. *Bedeutsamkeit*. Munich: Hanser.

Howard, Thomas J., Stephen J. Culley, and Elies Dekoninck. 2008. Describing the Creative Design Process by the Integration of Engineering Design and Cognitive Psychology Literature. *Design Studies* 29 (2): 160–180.

Huppatz, D. J. 2011. Roland Barthes, *Mythologies*. *Design and Culture* 3 (1): 85–100.

Husserl, Edmund. 2006. *Phantasie und Bildbewusstsein*. Hamburg: Felix Meiner.

Iser, Wolfgang. 1991. *Das Fiktive und das Imaginäre*. Frankfurt am Main: Suhrkamp.

Iser, Wolfgang. 2003. Von der Gegenwart des Ästhetischen. In *Dimensionen ästhetischer Erfahrung*, edited by J. Küpper and C. Menke, 176–202. Frankfurt am Main: Suhrkamp.

Jakobson, Roman. 1960. Closing Statement: Linguistics and Poetics. In *Style in Language*, edited by Thomas A. Sebeok, 350–377. Cambridge, MA: MIT Press.

Jonas, Wolfgang. 2001. A Scenario for Design. *Design Issues* 17 (2): 64–80.

Jones, John Christopher. 1980. *Design Methods: Seeds of Human Futures*. New York: John Wiley.

Jordan, Patrick. 2000. *Designing Pleasurable Products*. London: Taylor & Francis.

Julier, Guy. 2008. *The Culture of Design*. London: Sage.

Julier, Guy. 2009. Value, Relationality and Unfinished Objects: Guy Julier Interview with Scott Lash and Celia Lury. *Design and Culture* 1 (1): 93–103.

Kant, Immanuel. 1990. *Kritik der reinen Vernunft*. Hamburg: Felix Meiner.

Kant, Immanuel. 1995. *Kritik der Urtheilskraft*. Köln: Könemann.

Kātz, Barry M. 2011. Introduction: Some Nonobject(ive) Reflections on the Nonobject. In *Nonobject*, edited by B. Lukić, xxi–xxix Cambridge, MA: MIT Press.

Kavakli, Manolya, and John S. Gero. 2001. Sketching as Mental Imagery Processing. *Design Studies* 22 (4): 347–364.

Kearney, Richard. 1994. *Wake of the Imagination*. London: Routledge.

Kearney, Richard. 1998. *Poetics of Imagining: Modern to Postmodern*. New York: Fordham University Press.

Kimbell, Lucy. 2011. Rethinking Design Thinking: Part I. *Design and Culture* 3 (3): 285–306.

Klein, Jürgen. 1996. Genius, Ingenium, Imagination: Aesthetic Theories of Production from the Renaissance to Romanticism. In *The Romantic Imagination*, edited by Frederick Burwick and Jürgen Klein, 19–62. Amsterdam: Editions Rodopi.

Kopytoff, Igor. 1986. The Cultural Biography of Things: Commoditization as Process. In *The Social Life of Things: Commodities in Cultural Perspective*, edited by A. Appadurai, 64–94. Cambridge: Cambridge University Press.

Knorr-Cetina, Karin. 1997. Sociality with Objects: Social Relations in Postsocial Knowledge Societies. *Theory, Culture and Society* 14:1–30.

Knorr-Cetina, Karin. 2001. Objectual Practice. In *The Practice Term in Contemporary Theory*, edited by T. R. Schatzki, K. Knorr-Cetina, and E. von Savigny, 175–188. London: Routledge.

Krämer, Sybille. 2008. *Medium, Bote, Übertragung. Kleine Metaphysik der Medialität*. Frankfurt am Main: Suhrkamp.

Krippendorff, Klaus. 1995. On the Essential Contexts of Artifacts or on the Proposition That "Design Is Making Sense (of Things)." In *The Idea of Design*, edited by R. Buchanan and V. Margolin, 156–184. Cambridge, MA: MIT Press.

Krippendorff, Klaus. 2006. *The Semantic Turn: A New Foundation for Design*. New York: Taylor & Francis.

Küpper, Joachim, and Christoph Menke, eds. 2003. *Dimensionen ästhetischer Erfahrung*. Frankfurt am Main: Suhrkamp.

Kyndrup, Morten. 2008a. Aesthetics and Border Lines: "Design" as a Liminal Case. *Nordic Journal of Aesthetics* 35:24–31.

Kyndrup, Morten. 2008b. *Den æstetiske relation*. Copenhagen: Gyldendal.

Lash, Scott, and Celia Lury. 2007. *Global Culture Industry: The Mediation of Things*. Cambridge: Polity Press.

Latour, Bruno. 2005. *Reassembling the Social*. Oxford: Oxford University Press.

Latour, Bruno. 2008. A Cautious Promethea? A Few Steps towards a Philosophy of Design (with Special Attention to Peter Sloterdijk). Keynote lecture for the Networks of Design meeting of the Design History Society, Falmouth, Cornwall, September 3. http://urbanstudiesprogram.files .wordpress.com/2011/07/latour-20081.pdf.

Law, John. 2004. *After Method: Mess in Social Science Research*. London: Routledge.

Lawson, Bryan. 2004a. Schemata, Gambits and Precedent: Some Factors in Design Expertise. *Design Studies* 25 (5): 443–457.

Lawson, Bryan. 2004b. *What Designers Know*. Oxford: Architectural Press.

Lawson, Bryan. 2005. *How Designers Think*. Oxford: Architectural Press.

Lawson, Bryan, and Kees Dorst. 2009. *Design Expertise*. Oxford: Architectural Press.

Levy, Sydney J. 1959. Symbols for Sale. *Harvard Business Review* 37:117–124.

Liddament, Terry. 2000. The Myths of Imagery. *Design Studies* 21 (6): 589–606.

Liessmann, Konrad Paul. 2010. *Das Universum der Dinge. Zur Ästhetik des Alltäglichen*. Vienna: Zsolnay.

Lukić, Branko. 2011. *Nonobject*. Cambridge, MA: MIT Press.

Manovich, Lev. 2001. *The Language of New Media*. Cambridge, MA: MIT Press.

Manzini, Ezio. 2003. Scenarios of Sustainable Wellbeing. *Design Philosophy Papers* 1. http://www .changedesign.org/Resources/Manzini/Manuscripts/Manziniscenarios.doc.

Mareis, Claudia. 2010. Visual Productivity: Reflections on the Foundations and Correlations of Design Thinking. In *Proceedings of the Twenty-First Congress of the International Association of Empirical Aesthetics,* Dresden, 25–28.

Mareis, Claudia. 2012. *Design als Wissenskultur: Interferenzen zwischen Design- und Wissensdiskursen seit 1960*. Bielefeld: transcript Verlag.

Mareis, Claudia, Gesche Joost, and Kora Kimpel, eds. 2010. *Entwerfen, Wissen, Produzieren: Designforschung im Anwendungskontext*. Bielefeld: transcript Verlag.

Margolin, Victor. 1989. Introduction. In *Design Discourse: History, Theory, Criticism*, edited by V. Margolin, 3–30. Chicago: University of Chicago Press.

Markussen, Thomas. 2010. Conceptual Blends in Interaction Design: Toward a Cognitive Semiotic Framework for Online Meaning Construction and Embodied Interaction. PhD dissertation, Kolding: Kolding Design School.

Markussen, Thomas, Elif Özcan, and Nazli Cila. 2012. Beyond Metaphor in Product Use and Interaction. In *Proceedings of DeSForM 2012: Meaning.Matter.Making,* 110–119, Wellington, New Zealand.

McCracken, Grant. 1986. Culture and Consumption: A Theoretical Account of the Structure and Movement of Cultural Meaning of Consumer Goods. *Journal of Consumer Research* 13 (June): 71–84.

McCracken, Grant. 2005. *Culture and Consumption II: Markets, Meaning, and Brand Management*, vol. 2. Bloomington: Indiana University Press.

Menke, Christoph. 1991. *Die Souveränität der Kunst*. Frankfurt am Main: Suhrkamp.

Merleau-Ponty, Maurice. 1945. *Phénonénologie de la perception*. Paris: Gallimard.

Merleau-Ponty, Maurice. 1960. Le langage indirect et les voix du silence. In *Signes*, 49–104. Paris: Gallimard.

Merleau-Ponty, Maurice. 1964. *Le visible et l'invisible*. Paris: Gallimard.

Michel, Ralf, ed. 2007. *Design Research Now*. Basel: Birkhäuser.

Miller, Daniel. 1987. *Material Culture and Mass Consumption*. Oxford: Blackwell.

Miller, Daniel. 2010. *Stuff*. Cambridge: Polity Press.

Misselhorn, Catrin. 2010. Die symbolische Dimension der ästhetischen Erfahrung von Kunst und Design. In *Ästhetische Werte und Design*, edited by Jakob Steinbrenner and Julian Nida-Rümelin, 75–96. Ostfildern: Hatje Cantz.

Moles, Abraham. 1972. *Théorie de l'information et perception esthétique*. Paris: Denoël/Gonthier.

Moles, Abraham. 1995. Design and Immateriality: What of It in a Post Industrial Society? In *The Idea of Design*, edited by R. Buchanan and V. Margolin, 268–274. Cambridge, MA: MIT Press.

Moore, Kathryn. 2010. *Overlooking the Visual: Demystifying the Art of Design*. Oxon: Routledge.

Munch, Anders V. 2001. Design as Gesamtkunstwerk. Historical Transformations of a Vision from Wagner to Morris and Verner Panton. *Scandinavian Journal of Design History* 11:32–59.

Murphy, Peter, Michael A. Peters, and Simon Marginson. 2010. *Imagination: Three Models of Imagination in the Age of the Knowledge Economy*. New York: Peter Lang.

Musil, Robert. 1978. *Der Mann ohne Eigenschaften*. Hamburg: Rowohlt.

Norman, Donald A. 2002. *The Design of Everyday Things*. New York: Basic Books.

Norman, Donald A. 2004. *Emotional Design*. New York: Basic Books.

Novalis (Friedrich von Hardenberg). 1965. *Schriften 2. Das philosophische Werk I*. Edited by Richard Samuel, Hans-Joachim Mähl, and Gerhard Schulz. Stuttgart: Verlag Kohlhammer.

Novalis (Friedrich von Hardenberg). 1968. *Schriften 3. Das philosophische Werk II*. Edited by Richard Samuel, Hans-Joachim Mähl, and Gerhard Schulz. Stuttgart: Verlag Kohlhammer.

Oldemeyer, Ernst. 2008. *Alltagsästhetisierung: Vom Wandel ästhetischer Erfahrung*. Würzburg: Königshausen & Neumann.

Olins, Wally. 1989. *Corporate Identity*. London: Thames and Hudson.

Oncotype. 2006. *Thorvaldsens Museum*. http://tilbygningen.dk/.

Papanek, Victor. 1985. *Design for the Real World*. London: Thames and Hudson.

Petersen, Trine B. 2010. Design, adfærd og magt—En diskussion af design som adfærdsregulerende praksis med udgangspunkt i Statsfængslet Østjylland. PhD dissertation, Kolding School of Design.

Pevsner, Nicolaus. 1991. *Pioneers of Modern Design*. Harmondsworth: Penguin.

Pine, B. Joseph, and James H. Gilmore. 1999. *The Experience Economy*. Boston: Harvard Business School Press.

Poincaré, Henri. 1982. *The Foundations of Science*. Washington, DC: University Press of America.

Preston, Beth. 2012. *A Philosophy of Material Culture: Action, Function, and Mind*. New York: Routledge.

Raizman, David. 2010. *History of Modern Design*. London: Laurence King.

Rampley, Matthew, ed. 2007. *Exploring Visual Culture. Definitions, Concepts, Contexts*. Edinburgh: Edinburgh University Press.

Rancière, Jacques. 2004. *The Politics of Aesthetics*. London: Continuum.

Rathgeb, Markus. 2007. *Otl Aicher*. London: Phaidon Books.

Redström, Johan. 2007. En experimenterande designforskning. In *Under ytan: En antologi om designforskning*, edited by Sara Ilstedt Hjelm, Åsa Harvard, Ulla Johansson, Arantza Elisabeth Niño, Lisbeth Svengren Holm, Peter Ullmark, and Bo Westerlund, 164–176. Stockholm: Raster Förlag and SVID.

Ricœur, Paul. 1975. La fonction herméneutique de la distanciation. In *Exegesis*, edited by F. Bovon and G. Rouiller, 201–215. Paris: Delachaux & Niestlé.

Rith, Chanpory, and Hugh Dubberly. 2007. Why Horst W. J. Rittel Matters. *Design Issues* 23 (1): 72–91.

Rittel, Horst, and Melvin Webber. 1973. Dilemmas in a General Theory of Planning. *Policy Sciences* 4:155–169.

Romero-Tejedor, Felicidad. 2007. *Der denkende Designer*. Hildesheim: Georg Olms Verlag.

Rooden, Theo, Paul Eg, and Rianne Valkenburg. 2011. Time Travel: A Method for Playful Futureoriented User Research. In *Proceedings of Nordes '11: Fourth Nordic Design Research Conference*, May 29–31, School of Art and Design, Aalto University, Helsinki, Finland, 288–292.

Rose, Gillian. 2007. *Visual Methodologies*. London: Sage.

Rylander, Anna. 2009. Bortom hajpen—designtänkande som epistemologiskt perspektiv. *Research Design Journal* 1:20–27.

Sartre, Jean-Paul. 1940. *L'imaginaire*. Paris: Gallimard.

de Saussure, Ferdinand. 1972. *Cours de linguistigue générale*. Paris: Editions Payot.

Schäffner, Wolfgang. 2010. The Design Turn: Eine wissenschaftliche Revolution im Geiste der Gestaltung. In *Entwerfen, Wissen, Produzieren: Designforschung im Anwendungskontext*, edited by Claudia Mareis, Gesche Joost, and Kora Kimpel, 33–46. Bielefeld: transcript Verlag.

Scharmer, C. Otto. 2001. Self-Transcending Knowledge: Sensing and Organizing around Emerging Opportunities. *Journal of Knowledge Management* 5 (2): 137–150.

Scharmer, C. Otto. 2007. *Theory U: Leading from the Future as It Emerges*. Cambridge, MA: Society for Organizational Learning.

Schelling, F.W.J. 1991. *Philosphie der Kunst*. Edited by Werner Beierwaltes. Stuttgart: Reclam.

Schiller, Friedrich. 1910. *Über die ästhetische Erziehung des Menschen*. Edited by E. Kühnemann. Leipzig: Verlag der Dürr'schen Buchhandlung.

Schlegel, Friedrich. 1988. *Kritische Schriften und Fragmente 1–6*. Edited by Ernst Behler and Hans Eichner. Paderborn: Ferdinand Schöningh.

Schneider, Beat. 2009. *Design—eine Einführung. Entwurf im sozialen, kulturellen und wirtschaftlichen Kontext*. Basel: Birkhäuser.

Schön, Donald A. 1983. *The Reflective Practitioner: How Professionals Think in Action*. New York: Basic Books.

Schulte-Sasse, Jochen. 2000. Einbildungskraft/Imagination. In *Ästhetische Grundbegriffe*, edited by Karlheinz Barck, Martin Fontius, Dieter Schlenstedt, Burkhart Steinwachs, and Friedrich Wolfzettel, 88–120. Stuttgart: Metzler.

Schulze, Gerhard. 2005. *Die Erlebnisgesellschaft: Kultursoziologie der Gegenwart*. Frankfurt am Main: Campus.

Scruton, Roger. 1974. *Art and Imagination: A Study of the Philosophy of Mind*. London: Methuen.

Seel, Martin. 1996. *Eine Ästhetik der Natur*. Frankfurt am Main: Suhrkamp.

Seel, Martin. 2000. *Ästhetik des Erscheinens*. Munich: Hanser.

Seel, Martin. 2006. *Paradoxien der Erfüllung*. Frankfurt am Main: Fischer Verlag.

Seel, Martin. 2007. *Die Macht der Erscheinung*. Frankfurt am Main: Suhrkamp.

Selle, Gert. 1997. *Ideologie und Utopie des Design. Zur gesellschaftlichen Theorie der industriellen Formgebung*. Vienna: Pumhösl.

Selle, Gert. 2007. *Design im Alltag. Vom Thonetstuhl zum Mikrochip*. Frankfurt am Main: Campus.

Shelley, P. B. 2002. A Defence of Poetry. In *Poetry and Prose*, edited by Donald H. Reiman and Neil Fraistat, 510–535. New York: Norton.

Shklovsky, Viktor. 1993. *Theory of Prose*. Normal, IL: Dalkey Archive Press.

Shusterman, Richard. 2000. *Pragmatist Aesthetics: Living Beauty, Rethinking Art*. Lanham, MD: Rowman & Littlefield.

Simon, Herbert. 1996. *The Sciences of the Artificial*. Cambridge, MA: MIT Press.

Skov, Martin, and Oshin Vartanian, eds. 2009. *Neuroaesthetics: Foundations and Frontiers of Aesthetics*. Amityville, NY: Baywood Publishing Company.

Sloterdijk, Peter. 2010. *Der Welt über die Straße helfen: Designstudien im Anschluss an eine philosophische Überlegung*. Munich: Fink.

Sørensen, Bengt Algot. 1963. *Symbol und Symbolismus in den ästhetischen Theorien des 18. Jahrhunderts und der deutschen Romantik*. Copenhagen: Munksgaard.

Sparke, Penny. 2009. *The Genius of Design*. London: Quadrille Publishing.

Steffen, Dagmar. 2000. *Design als Produktsprache*. Frankfurt am Main: Verlag form.

Steinbrenner, Jakob. 2010. Wann ist Design? Design zwischen Funktion und Kunst. In *Ästhetische Werte und Design*, edited by Jakob Steinbrenner and Julian Nida-Rümelin, 11–29. Ostfildern: Hatje Cantz.

Stephan, Peter Friedrich. 2010. Wissen und Nicht-Wissen im Entwurf. In *Entwerfen. Wissen, Produzieren: Designforschung im Anwendungskontext*, edited by Claudia Mareis, Gesche Joost, and Kora Kimpel, 81–100. Bielefeld: transcript Verlag.

Stolterman, Erik. 2007. Designtänkande. In *Under Ytan: En Antologi om Designforskning*, edited by Sara Ilstedt Hjelm, Åsa Harvard, Ulla Johansson, Arantza Elisabeth Niño, Lisbeth Svengren Holm, Peter Ullmark, and Bo Westerlund, 12–19. Stockholm: Raster Förlag/ SVID, Stiftelsen Svensk Industridesign.

Stolterman, Erik, and Harold G. Nelson. 2003. *The Design Way*. Englewood Cliffs, NJ: Educational Technology Publications.

Strohschneider-Kohrs, Ingrid. 1960. *Die romantische Ironie in Theorie und Darstellung*. Tübingen: Max Niemeyer Verlag.

Sturken, Marita, and Lisa Cartwright. 2009. *Practices of Looking: An Introduction to Visual Culture*. Oxford: Oxford University Press.

Thackara, John. 2005. *In the Bubble*. Cambridge, MA: MIT Press.

Troika (C. Freyer, S. Noel, and E. Rucki). 2008. *Digital by Design*. London: Thames & Hudson.

Tversky, Barbara, and Masaki Suwa. 2009. Thinking with Sketches. In *Tools for Innovation*, ed. A. Markman, 75–84. Oxford: Oxford University Press.

Ullmark, Peter. 2011. Research and Design Practice: An Exploratory Update of Donald Schön. In *Proceedings to Nordes '11: Fourth Nordic Design Research Conference,* May 29–31, School of Art and Design, Aalto University, Helsinki, Finland, 171–177.

Verbeek, Peter-Paul. 2005. *What Things Do: Philosophical Reflections on Technology, Agency, and Design*. University Park: Pennsylvania State University Press.

Vermaas, Pieter E., Peter Kroes, Andrew Light, and Steven Moore, eds. 2009. *Philosophy and Design: From Engineering to Architecture*. London: Springer.

Vial, Stéphane. 2010. *Court traité du design*. Paris: Presses Universitaires de France.

Vihma, Susann. 1995. *Products as Representation*. Helsinki: University of Art and Design.

von Busch, Otto. 2011. Design at the Front. In *Proceedings to Nordes '11: The Fourth Nordic Design Research Conference,* May 29–31, School of Art and Design, Aalto University, Helsinki, Finland, 21–29.

Walker, Stuart. 2006. *Sustainable by Design: Explorations in Theory and Practice*. London: Earthscan.

Wang, David, and Ali O. Ilhan. 2009. Holding Creativity Together: A Sociological Theory of the Design Professions. *Design Issues* 25 (1): 5–21.

Wang, H.-H., and J. H. Chan. 2011. An Approach to Measuring Metaphoricity of Creative Design. In *Design Creativity 2010*, edited by N. Yukari and T. Taura, 89–96. London: Springer.

Welsch, Wolfgang. 1990. *Ästhetisches Denken*. Stuttgart: Reclam.

Welsch, Wolfgang. 1996. *Grenzgänge der Ästhetik*. Stuttgart: Reclam.

Wershler, Darren. 2010. The Locative, the Ambient, and the Hallucinatory in the Internet of Things. *Design and Culture* 2 (2): 199–216.

Wettig, Sabine. 2009. *Imagination im Erkenntnisprozess. Chancen und Herausforderungen im Zeitalter der Bildmedien*. Bielefeld: transcript Verlag.

Wordsworth, William. 1979. *The Prelude*. London: Norton.

Wunenburger, Jean-Jacques. 2003. *L'imaginaire*. Paris: Presses Universitaires des France.

Yaneva, Albena. 2009. Making the Social Hold: Towards an Actor-Network Theory of Design. *Design and Culture* 1 (3): 273–288.

Yukari, Nagai, and Toshiharu Taura, eds. 2011. *Design Creativity 2010*. London: Springer.

Zahavi, Dan. 2007. Fænomenologi. In *Humanistisk videnskabsteori*, edited by F. Collin and S. Køppe, 121–138. Copenhagen: DR Multimedie.

Zamenopoulos, Theodore, and Katerina Alexiou. 2007. Towards an Anticipatory View of Design. *Design Studies* 28 (4): 411–436.

Index

3PART Design consultancy, 9, 105, 111, 116–118, 121–122, 132–134, 137, 199

Absence, 74, 89, 143
Abstraction, 4, 114
Actor-network theory (ANT), 8, 61, 142, 187
Added quality, 44–48, 108
Adorno, Theodor W., 6, 28, 45–47, 109–110, 114, 130, 148
Aesthetic appreciation, 30, 44
Aesthetic coding, 26, 30, 42, 44, 53, 151
Aesthetic experience, 123
Aesthetic function, 48, 52–53, 157
Aesthetic ideas, 107–108, 151, 181–182
Aestheticization, 26, 28–29, 44, 57–66, 185
Aesthetic perception, 41–42, 127
Aesthetics, 6–7, 25–66, 123, 188, 211
   conceptual-hermeneutical paradigm of, 6, 9, 42–54, 180, 217
   discursive-contextual paradigm of, 7, 9, 54–66, 129, 181, 218
   and emotions, 27–28
   as epistemology, 6
   and imagination, 6–7, 25–26, 43, 189, 218
   pragmatist approach of, 33
   as a relation, 29–32, 44
   self-reflective, 48–54, 63
   sensual-phenomenological paradigm of, 6, 9, 32–42, 121, 180, 218
Aesthetic schematization, 81, 119
Aesthetic theory, 32–34, 44

Affordance, 20, 163, 183, 229n47
   symbolic-connotative, 163
Aicher, Otl, 168–172, 194, 207–208
Alexander, Christopher, 99, 108, 114–115, 235n4
Ambience, 6, 35–36, 38–42, 48–49, 56, 147
An-aesthetics, 55, 59–60
Anonymous design, 52, 59, 65, 168, 209, 211, 242n4
Anticipation, 108, 198, 201, 203, 206. *See also* Prediction
Antidesign movement, 65, 180, 203
Appearance, 6, 8, 11, 15, 25–26, 32, 36–42, 127
Apple Inc., 37, 59, 90, 177, 244n25
Apps, 66, 178, 180
Arnheim, Rudolf, 72–73
Art, 6–7, 25, 28–30, 33, 44–46, 108
Art design, 5
Artistic means, 201–202
Arts and crafts, 201

Baudrillard, Jean, 57–58, 147, 175, 240n10
Bauhaus, 31, 185, 201–202
Baumgarten, Alexander, 28, 33
Better Place, 162–164
Black box design, 21, 60, 209, 227n26
Blake, William, 78, 233n22
Blanchot, Maurice, 73–74, 175
Böhme, Gernot, 8, 33, 35–36
Boradkar, Prasad, 37–38, 187–188
Buchanan, Richard, 160, 166–168, 211–213, 216
Burberry, 149–150, 241n15

Campbell, Louise, 49–53, 65, 71, 87–88, 151, 203

Casey, Edward, 79, 191, 233n4

Cassirer, Ernst, 157–158, 168

Castoriadis, Cornelius, 90–91, 192–193

Chairs, 1–2, 16, 43–53, 56, 65, 80, 82, 87–88, 90, 99–100, 119–122, 124, 126, 135, 142, 145, 151, 155–156, 173, 190, 199

Cognition, 6, 44, 95, 97–98, 103, 106, 118, 137

Coleridge, Samuel Taylor, 69, 71, 77–78, 91, 147–148, 192

Concept design, 140, 190

Connotation, 161, 171

Consciousness, 6, 8, 35, 89, 98, 210

Consumption, 141, 149–150, 162, 197, 214

Cradle-to-cradle, 213–216

Creatio ex nihilo, 71, 114, 192, 237n7

Creative leap, 19, 109, 116

Creativity, 4, 19, 111, 133, 135. See also Imagination, and creativity

Critical design movement, 21, 65, 121, 155, 166, 203–204

Cross, Nigel, 101, 123–124, 131–132, 198, 236n10

Cultural analysis, 29

Cultural construction, 176

Cultural context, 86, 88–89, 93, 110, 126, 128–129, 140, 154, 157, 161–162

Culture, 20

Danish modern, 128–129

Decoration, 126, 128

Defocusing
and focusing, 131–135, 145–146, 148, 151, 199, 221

Design
close-structure, 173–176
connecting the sensual and the conceptual, 25 (see also Meaning, sensual and conceptual)
as a discipline, 13–15
and experiential knowledge, 95
as an exploratory, emergent activity, 116
as framing of experience, 8, 188
ideational conception of, 120
imaginative coding of, 194
and intention, 22
as an interface with the modern world, 15
as Leitmedium of modernity, 15, 159
as a medium, 15–18, 21, 47, 92, 105, 110, 135, 191, 220
and the not-yet-existing, 17–18, 117–118, 166, 182, 191, 213, 215, 221
open-structure, 176–182
orders of, 160, 211
from a phenomenological perspective, 7 (see also Phenomenological approach; Phenomenology)
philosophy of, 7
as schematizing of experience, 185, 200
in strategic planning, 211–213
systemic integration, 213–216
and technology, 13–14
as a term, 211

Design epistemology, 9–11, 19, 100–104, 150, 218

Design history, 140, 200, 203, 223n1, 225n2, 226n13, 242n4

Design methodology, 5, 13, 28, 105, 113, 130–131

Design methods movement, 100, 224n2, 231n4

Design objects, 3–5, 139–142, 196. See also Product, and system

Design ontology, 9, 11, 20, 121, 140–142, 150, 152, 164, 219

Design phenomenology, 9, 11, 20, 186–190, 219. See also Phenomenological approach; Phenomenology

Design problems, 95, 101–102, 113–114, 131, 137
and solution generation, 102, 131

Design process, 3–5, 20, 101, 110, 113, 114–115, 126, 134, 148, 218

Design semantic, 143–144, 154–155

Design semiotics, 144, 239n24

Design theory, 19–20

Design thinking, 14
Detailing, 128–129, 199
Dewey, John, 33–34, 42, 67, 70, 91–92,
    216n16, 232n15, 234n8
Digital technology, 1, 176–180, 208–210,
    220–222

Electric cars, 162–163, 194, 243n13
English empiricism, 68, 96, 106
Enthusiasm, and reflection, 75–76
Ethics
    in design, 11, 54–55, 188, 197–198
    and aesthetics, 32, 210–211
Evaluation, 101–102, 113
Everyday aestheticization. *See* Aestheticization
Experience, 7–8, 168
Experimental design, 5, 20, 53, 121, 155, 196,
    204
Experimental strategy, 118, 120, 203–206, 215
Exploration, of details and materials, 120–121,
    126, 199

Fantasy, 68. *See also* Imagination
Featherstone, Mike, 57–58
Findeli, Alain, 32, 101, 242n7
Ford Model T, 161–164
Form, 32, 50, 119, 124, 202–203
    and material, 105
Foucault, Michel, 55–56
Framing, 62, 79, 101, 105–106, 117, 131–132,
    137, 166, 168, 170, 176, 180–181, 194, 197,
    199, 212–213, 217, 221–222
    and unframing, 118, 131–134
FUCHS+FUNKE, 99, 111, 116, 118–120, 203
Furniture design, 105, 121–130
Future-orientation, 19, 21. *See also* Prediction

Genius, 4, 149, 223n1, 241n13
German classicism, 6
Goethe, Johann Wolfgang von, 36, 157–158,
    171
Graphic design, 65, 169–176, 194
Grosz, Elisabeth, 199–200, 207
Gumbrecht, Hans Ulrich, 128

Hammerstrøm, Ditte, 9, 82, 111, 121–122,
    124, 126–130, 137, 196, 199, 203–204
Hermeneutics, 42–43
Humanities, 220
Husserl, Edmund, 7

Idea generation, 105, 131–132
Idealization, 73–74, 77
Ideas, as drivers for design, 213–216
Ideology, 48, 189
Image
    in imagination, 67, 72–75, 99–100, 144
    potential virtuality of, 75
Imaginary, 7, 22, 86, 139–152, 164, 185, 210,
    219. *See also* Social imaginary
    control of, 146
    in design, 11
    and materiality, 92–93, 151
    and the possible, 150–152
    as presence, 144–146
    and the real, 89, 145–147, 194
    as representation, 146–150
    as simulation, 147
    and symbolic meaning, 153
Imagination, 3–6, 11, 67–80, 105–138, 216
    and creativity, 67–68, 72, 110
    and design epistemology, 95–104
    and empirical foundation, 78–79, 114
    as a faculty, 4, 70, 84
    intersubjective, 90
    and material output, 194
    and perception, 72–73
    and phenomenology, 23, 81–93, 218 (*see also*
        Phenomenology)
    prism of, 111–113, 135–136
    productive, 67, 106
    romantic concept of, 10, 67–80
    and schematization, 104
    structural coding of, 95, 97–100, 110–112,
        135–136
    and transformation, 77
    visionary, 78
Imagining, 4, 75, 95, 150
    through visualization, 208

Immaterial aesthetics, 151. *See also* Aesthetics
Immateriality, 43–44, 182, 185. *See also* Materiality, and immateriality
Immaterialization of design, 142
Impossibility, 18–19, 196, 206. *See also* Possibility
Incomprehensibility, 46–47
Industrial design, 105, 132, 220
Innovation, 14, 22, 29, 101, 103, 149–150, 161, 163, 200
  incremental, 213–215
  radical, 66, 213–215
Intentionality, 8, 96
Interface, 209–210
Interior design, 38–42
Internalization, 10, 81–82, 86, 89
  and externalization, 69–71, 84–85, 90, 97–99, 103, 105, 137
Internet, 176–177, 210
Interpretation, 117. *See also* Hermeneutics
Invisibility. *See* Visibility, and invisibility

Jones, John Chris, 108–109, 113
Julier, Guy, 140, 159, 161

Kaldi sweater, 248n35
Kant, Immanuel, 28–29, 42, 44, 68, 72, 96, 106–109, 118–119, 126, 129, 157, 181, 190, 218
Kolding School of Design, 228n35, 243n13

Latour, Bruno, 18, 142
Lawson, Bryan, 102, 113, 132, 236n10
Lifestyle design, 52, 65, 210
Loewy, Raymond, 202–203
Luxor hotel, 147

Material aesthetics, 61–62, 151, 187. *See also* Aesthetics
Material culture, 140–141, 225n2, 227n29
Materiality
  and immateriality, 3, 11, 13, 61, 64, 153, 160–164, 189 (*see also* Immateriality)
  of objects, 139

Mathsson, Bruno, 90
Meaning
  construction, 6–7, 15, 22, 48, 104, 113, 129, 135, 139, 196
  imaginary, 4, 143–152, 212 (*see also* Imaginary)
  sensual and conceptual, 2, 25
Mental setting, 17, 69, 95, 99, 103–106, 110–113, 115–117, 120–121, 126, 130, 132–133, 135–136, 145, 148, 150, 218–219, 234n1
  of focus: defocusing versus focusing, 130–135
  of knowledge: unknown versus known, 113–120
  of perspective: whole versus detail, 120–130
  stages of, 135–138
  taxonomy of, 111 (*see also* Schematization)
Merleau-Ponty, Maurice, 8, 34–36, 42–43, 47, 53–54, 85–86, 89, 96, 145, 186–187, 189–190
Metadesign, 123
Metaphors, 134–136, 143, 239n24, 239n4
Microchips, 14, 177, 208–210
Miniaturization, 209
Model, 168–169, 208
Money, 173–176
Moore, Kathryn, 72–73, 98
Multiperspectivism, 105, 132, 135
Murphy, Peter, 67, 90–91, 99, 194, 234n8
Musil, Robert, 16–17

Naming, 131
Negation, 4, 11, 82–83, 89, 143, 151
  of inner visualization, 73
Neon sign, 60, 62
Neuroaesthetics, 96
Novalis, 69, 109, 115–116, 143, 231n5

Object turn, 140
Organization design, 162, 168

Panton, Verner, 1–2, 15–16, 38–42, 48–49, 52, 56, 62, 65

Pervasive computing. *See* Ubiquitous
    computing
Phenomenological approach, 7–8, 26
Phenomenology, 7–8, 34–36, 54, 71, 186–187,
    190
  and imagination, 81–93 (*see also*
    Imagination)
  progressive, 168, 207
Philosophical aesthetics, 43
Pictograms, 169–172
Placement, 166–169
Poincaré, Henri, 75, 238n23
Possibility, 3–4, 9, 16–23, 165, 217. *See also*
    Impossibility
  and actuality, 3, 84, 89, 191
  as a driver for design, 221
  extension and limitation of, 17–19
  as an inherent structure in design objects,
    22, 150–152
  phases of, 19–23
  and potentials, 18
  searching for, 67, 135–138
  sense of (Möglichkeitssinn), 16–17, 80
  space of, 5, 18, 22, 55, 60, 83, 85, 87, 153,
    155, 168–169, 178, 180, 183, 186, 216
Possibilizing, 79–80, 90, 103, 135–138, 191,
    194, 196–199, 208, 212, 214–216, 219
  and actualizing, 79, 136, 194
Postal service, 3, 65, 133, 176, 216
Postphenomenology, 8, 54, 81, 142, 187, 189
Prediction, 20, 108, 116, 201
Prescription, 198–199
Product, and system, 11, 153, 160–164
Projection, 108, 117, 198–200, 207
  and direction, 186, 197–198
  models of, 200–210
  of the new, 215
Prototypes, 71, 102–103, 118, 145

QR codes, 62–63, 177

Radiofrequency ID chips, 209
Rancière, Jacques, 55–56, 59, 62

Representation, 61, 66, 154
  simulated, 146
  of the unrepresentable, 45
Rittel, Horst, 101, 113
Romanticism, 4, 68, 75, 77–79, 95–96, 115–
    116, 147–148, 191. *See also* Imagination,
    romantic concept of

Sartre, Jean-Paul, 8, 67, 71, 83–86, 89, 95–96,
    144–145, 149, 152, 183
Scaling, 210–216
Scenarios, 198–199, 207–208, 213
Scharmer, C. Otto, 78–79, 115–116, 137,
    246n17
Schelling, Friedrich Wilhelm Joseph, 28, 45,
    123, 225n4
Schemata, 26
  aesthetic media as, 46, 65
Schematization, 105–138, 194, 218
  without concept, 107, 109, 126, 129–130,
    151
  as connection of sensual and conceptual
    meaning, 43, 113–114, 145
  of experience, 186
  Kantian, 106–108, 119, 218
  at the interface of consciousness and mate-
    rial world, 104
  of known and unknown, 113–120, 147–148
  as meaning construction, 132
  as a product of imagination, 107, 145
Schewen, Anna von, 111, 124–125, 128,
    143–144
Schiller, Friedrich, 6, 31
Schlegel, Friedrich, 76, 191, 233n22
Scruton, Roger, 46–47, 109, 114, 194
Seel, Martin, 33–34, 41, 46
Selle, Gert, 154, 159, 208–209, 242n4
Sensuous appeal, 13, 32–36
Service design, 3, 65, 105, 116, 134, 160, 165,
    168, 174, 176, 190, 212–213, 216
Shusterman, Richard, 33–34
Simon, Herbert, 17, 101–102, 121, 158, 185,
    193, 224n4

Simulation, 58, 61, 64, 75, 147–149, 175–176,
    181, 240n10
Sloterdijk, Peter, 21–22
Smart phones, 2, 58, 62, 66, 152, 174, 177–
    180, 196–197, 209
Social imaginary, 7, 192–193. *See also*
    Imaginary
Social platforms, 210
Sociology, 141
Streamlined design, 202–203
Subject
    creative, 8
    and object, dichotomy of, 4, 6, 8, 35
    and team, 117, 135
Surface qualities, 27, 32
Surplus of meaning, 45–52, 108–109, 148
Sustainability, 163, 210, 213–215, 220
Symbol
    epistemological model of, 157–158
    ontological model of, 157–158
Symbolic coding, 11, 86, 93, 153–157, 159–
    161, 172, 219
    dimensions of, 182–183
Symbolic meaning, 4, 9, 153, 157–159, 168
Synaesthesia, 36
Synthesizing, 77–79, 107, 113
System design, 162, 170, 173, 175, 211

Tablet computers, 58–59, 66, 152, 244n25
Theme parks, 58–59
Tilbygningen.dk, 87–88, 151, 177
Toasters, 2, 202–204, 206
Tooth brushes, 173, 199, 212
Transcendence
    and immanence, 77–80
Transfiguration, 4, 10–11, 89–93, 180, 185–
    216, 219
    and defiguration, 195–197
    of experience, 190–194, 212, 216
    and figuration, 190–195, 212
Transportation, 162–164, 212–214, 243n14

Ubiquitous computing, 1, 62, 177, 209,
    230n58

Unknown, 108, 112–113, 136, 151, 164, 173,
    199, 201, 216, 220
    as a constitutive, productive factor for de-
    sign, 221
    exploration of, 215
    interface of known and, 115–116, 147
Unrealization, 10–11, 84–88, 143, 146, 153
Users, 117, 135, 149, 177
Utopia in design, 48, 180, 191

Verbeek, Peter-Paul, 54, 61–62, 187
Vial, Stéphane, 15, 188–189
Visibility, 144
    and invisibility, 43, 54–56, 85–86, 145–146,
    166, 189

Walker, Stuart, 213–216
Web design, 83, 87, 140, 176–177
WG24 lamp (Bauhaus lamp), 201–202
Wheelchair, 134–135
Wunenburger, Jean-Jacques, 92, 143, 149–150

DATE DUE

MAY 2 8 2017			
NOV 2 ? 2021			

Demco